MYTHOMANIA

First published in the United Kingdom in 2016 by Thames & Hudson Ltd,
181A High Holborn, London WC1V 7QX

First paperback edition 2017

British Library Cataloguing-in-Publication Data
A catalogue record for this book is available from the British Library

ISBN 978-0-500-29354-6

Printed and bound in India by Replika Press Pvt. Ltd.

PETER CONRAD

MYTHOMANIA

TALES OF OUR TIMES, FROM APPLE TO ISIS

Thames & Hudson

Contents

Acknowledgments

This book had its origins in a request from David Stenhouse, who in the summer of 2014 asked me to write and present on BBC Radio 4 a series of talks entitled *21st Century Mythologies*. David's idea was to find contemporary equivalents of the subjects whose mystique Roland Barthes examined in his book *Mythologies*. After some friendly haggling we settled on fifteen topics; I can now hardly remember who suggested what, although it was certainly David who ensured that Nando's remained on the list (and, despite my initial reluctance, I am glad that he did). David's enthusiasm and his generosity with his own ideas made this one of my happiest and most invigorating collaborative experiences.

'Radio 4 has all sorts of people talking all day long,' David said at the start. 'These programmes have to be different: they have to be Barthesian.' I secretly quailed at the thought of having to match Barthes' exalted intellectual manner, and I was relieved that David allowed me to go my own way. I tried to devise a personal version of Barthes' method, but despite my admiration I became increasingly aware of the distance between his times and our own, which made me question some of his attitudes and assumptions. His prejudice against the bourgeoisie now seems quaint, as does his mockery of America; it also worried me that his semiotic theory defined myth too narrowly and ignored its cultural history. My talks developed into a good-humoured argument with Barthes, not an act of mimicry.

They may not have been Barthesian, but they were certainly different, and that seemed to appeal to listeners. After the broadcasts, which were spread over three weeks in late September and early October 2014, David sent me an anthology of comments circulated on social media by members of our invisible audience. Among them was one from a man who called me his 'mindgasm'; more touchingly – if a little more tamely – a woman told her Facebook friends that one of the talks had cheered her up while she was waiting in the rain for a bus that never arrived. To my delight, a series of monologues had opened out into a conversation.

Unable to leave the subject alone, I decided to make the programmes the basis of a book. Revised, expanded and rearranged into a cumulative story, the radio scripts reappear here. I have added essays on neon, Dubai, Michael Jackson, and the Incredibles, which derive from articles commissioned by *The Observer*. The remaining chapters – on Banksy, Stephen Hawking, Judge Judy, Air Force One, dinosaurs, vampires, technosex, the Pacific garbage patch, and apocalyptic science fiction – are new, as are the opening and closing sections, which reflect more generally on the place of myth in our society, our economy, and the political and religious disputes that currently agitate our lives.

Sadly, this is the last book of mine to have been commissioned by Jamie Camplin, who has left Thames & Hudson to resume his own writing career. I look back on our long friendship with gratitude, though that meagre sentence hardly conveys what Jamie's support has meant to me: a hug in a Covent Garden street after our most recent lunch said it better. Sophy Thompson, the firm's new Publishing Director, has my thanks for taking over the project, and for some astute advice that enabled me, I hope, to improve the text.

1 *Sky Signs*

Before geography positioned us in space and history kept track of time, myths gave us our bearings, and made us feel at home in the world.

Existence is random, chancy and perilous; we need a sense of purpose, a destiny and a destination. Myths are the stories we tell ourselves to resolve contradictions that we find intolerable. We dislike the idea that we happened into being accidentally in a universe that is the product of a random explosion. We therefore invent a creator who designed nature to serve us and allotted us a privileged place in it. Surely we are not just blundering between one oblivion and another? No, we would rather see life as a journey, perhaps even a pilgrimage or a quest. The necessity of dying predictably outrages us. It's a simple matter to overleap that obstacle by imagining an afterlife.

We protect these deluding, comforting tales from scrutiny by treating them as wisdom handed down from on high. At best, however, they are supreme fictions, exercises in rationalizing a world that remains unreasonable.

The first myths were symptoms of fear. Our remotest ancestors kept watch on the sky and guessed at its moods. Weather issued verdicts that were usually critical: a lashing downpour, dyspeptic thunder, angry lightning bolts. Disasters had to be astrological, the result – as the word itself proclaims – of a disagreeable or ill-disposed star. Only if some higher power were appeased would the winter end.

Eventually human beings crept out of the woods and looked around with clearer eyes. Now, after uncountable millennia, we live in culture not nature, in an environment we have fabricated. We may have outgrown our cowering reverence for the gods who determined nature's unforgiving rules, but we are more than ever at the mercy of myths, which tug at us subliminally. We are no longer so alert for signs from above, but signals at ground level still do their elementary job of telling us to stop or go, to turn this way or that, and we follow their orders because they trigger ancient, ingrained connections. Green equals bucolic calm, red warns of danger; perhaps when the colours change at the street corner we dimly recall a paradise garden and an inferno. Science, technology and contemporary atheism have not yet entirely enlightened our fantastical, traumatized minds.

Biblical fables cast a lingering shadow. The first myth revived and reinterpreted in this book is that of Eden, although the garden now sprouts inside a slim silver case. The last is Armageddon, which for many people today has become a longed-for consummation, not a terrifying last judgement. In between comes a man who saw himself as a Messiah from another planet and explained that he had descended to earth as a healer. Somewhere else in the book, *Messiah* is the name given to a spacecraft that carries a team of human beings in the opposite direction: they are sent into deep space to dispose of a comet that threatens our earth. Do we still need a saviour, now that we have astronauts to perform such tasks?

Science at its most advanced continues to operate under the aegis of myth (and that aegis is itself mythological, because the word refers to the protective shield held up by Zeus or Athena). One cosmologist hopes to understand what God was thinking as the universe was combustibly created; another worries about the wisdom of experimentally re-enacting the moment when subatomic particles first exploded into life. Luckily a so-called symbologist, who has revised the Bible's account of Christ's sex life and located the whereabouts of the Holy Grail, is on hand to prevent a nuclear disaster. This book contains a glimpse of heaven, located on the upper floors of a high-rise building, and a brief descent into a foul, grease-choked hell beneath city streets.

At the same time, in their own mythological realm, the Olympian deities here enjoy the latest of many revivals. Aphrodite squirms into a gladiatrix costume, flaunts a feather boa, and struts in kinky high heels; the Adonis with whom she copulates is all the more attractive because he happens to be a corporate tycoon. A more matronly Roman goddess dispenses justice with a fly swatter. Two putative presidents of the United States behave like elected gods, in one case single-handedly routing a gang of terrorists, in the other vanquishing a horde of alien invaders. The residents of Mount Olympus were adept at metamorphosis: to prove the point, a paterfamilias who was once an Olympic athlete shows off a new female physique in the kind of slinky dress that is known as a goddess gown.

At the edges of this playground will be found a glamorous clan of blood-drinkers, a litter of pampered pet dogs with the egos of operatic divas, and some saurians cloned from the DNA of transgendered bullfrogs. Neo-pagans invent new vices, which can be indulged without Christian guilt. One is the auto-erotic addiction to snapping photographic self-portraits, and another goes by the name of 'autophilia', which is not a kind of self-love but a lust for fast, expensive cars. Commodities offer magical transmutations to those who use or consume them. People who once smoked cigarettes vaporize or atomize instead; people who once ate stodgy donuts now bite into laminated pastries that dissolve into metaphors on the tongue.

This collection of myths advances with scary speed from Genesis to Revelation, from prehistoric carnivores to post-biological robots. We have accelerated evolution, which leaves us wondering whether our species can develop any further. And where else can we go, now that we have almost used up our fragile planetary habitat? The earliest myths guessed at what had happened before human history began; contemporary myths make urgent efforts to imagine what will happen when human history ends, as it soon may do.

*

What we look for in moments of doubt is a sign – some indication of where we are, and an explanation of how we got there. With luck there might be an arrow, like an index finger directing us higher or at least pointing us ahead.

Testing the principle on the roof of my house in London, I see a jagged frieze of peaks that send out mixed signals. Half a dozen churches poke their spires upwards from streets nearby, and I can glimpse the pseudo-medieval pinnacles of the Palace of Westminster; these look stunted when compared with the chimneys of the gutted power station at Battersea, which might be the stiff legs of a gigantic quadruped lying dead on its back. Nearby, a plantation of construction cranes hauls new skyscrapers out of the earth, and beside the river stands a pipe-shaped residential tower into which a helicopter crashed one foggy morning a while ago. To the east, the tallest building in the city, with planes of sharp glass not quite joining at its summit, grazes the clouds. On a rooftop ledge across the way, a neighbour has arranged a palisade of plastic cones, scavenged from the streets where they direct traffic around roadworks: they resemble missiles, ready to be launched – at what? Not, I hope, at the queue of planes that screech overhead as they turn west towards the airport; perhaps at the colony of squawking crows that leave their perches in a churchyard at the end of the street to rip open garbage bags and sort through the contents. Sooty chicken bones occasionally tumble down my chimney, souvenirs of the scavenged meals the crows enjoy up above. In the world we have only too successfully remade, creatures forget their natural appetites and turn into consumers of culture, or of what it leaves behind. I once surprised a fox daintily snacking on a chocolate bar in my back garden.

In a poem about the correspondences between earth and sky, Baudelaire called nature a temple, supported by 'living pillars' that babble enigmatic words and cluster into 'forests of symbols'. Culture, as the view from my roof suggests, is unconsecrated, a mess of lowly urges and loftier strivings, with primitive monsters – those meat-eating crows, Jurassic predators on a mercifully smaller scale – and engineered marvels side by side. Baudelaire refers to green prairies, a heady pharmacopoeia of amber, musk and incense, and 'the expansion of infinite things' in an obligingly empty personal universe. By the time he wrote the poem in 1857, industrialism had altered that pristine, fragrant scenery, cutting people off from the land and the solar or seasonal routines that were tracked by the first myths. Most of us now live in cities, which are mazes of manufactured stage sets. Subtle, sneaky messages are addressed to us on all sides, as if by Baudelaire's vocal pillars, but with no religious authority to lend them credence. How can we interpret this artificial wilderness?

In 1853 Dickens began his novel *Bleak House* with an act of dislocation – the opposite of myth's initial promise to orientate us. The setting is at once up-to-date and primeval, recognizable but alarmingly strange. The streets around the Law Courts in central London are bogged down in squelching mud on a foggy November day, so it looks 'as if the waters had but newly retired from the face of the earth, and it would not be wonderful to meet a Megalosaurus, forty feet long or so, waddling like an elephantine lizard up Holborn Hill'. The wonder-working agency is metaphor, which alters what it describes and either exceeds or supersedes nature by crossbreeding an elephant with a lizard. As Dickens' allusion to Genesis hints, God's creation is here revised. People on bridges across the Thames peep 'over the parapets into a nether sky of fog … as if they were up in a balloon and hanging in the misty clouds': a second metaphor has made the sky collapse into that trough of murk. The unsettling jokes compress time and invert space, and in doing so suggest that myth can estrange us from the world as well as rooting us in it.

G. K. Chesterton gave a similarly mystified account of Times Square on his first visit to New York in 1921. 'What a glorious garden of wonders this would be,' he remarked, 'to anyone who was lucky enough to be unable to read.' Illiterate Adam would not have known that the galaxy of signs recommended commodities that ranged from pork to pianos and remedies for gout; he could imagine that he was staring at 'the flaming sword or the purple and peacock plumage of the seraphim'. Dickens used myth to confound history, undoing God's separation of land and water and returning nature to its chaotic, inchoate state. Chesterton, soon to be converted to Catholicism, relied on myth to chastize history. He regretted that Times Square vulgarized 'the two most vivid and mystical gifts of God, colour and fire'; he wanted to resurrect Eden, the original garden of wonders, but he recognized that its modern equivalent was an emporium stuffed with charismatic merchandise, and he said he would not have been surprised to see insignia for Paradise Tooth Paste and Seventh Heaven Cigars shining in the night sky above Broadway.

A few years later, dismayed by contemporary scepticism, Chesterton decided that 'Mythology is a lost art', and added 'What are called the Gods might almost alternatively be called the Day-Dreams.' He was wrong: the modern world whose disbelief he deplored retrieved those atavistic, amoral stories, and rather than dwindling into daydreams, the gods who rampaged through them became nightmares. In *The Golden Bough*, a study of fertility and sacrifice in ancient religions published between 1890 and 1915,

J. G. Frazer described the succession of ceremonial murders that regulated nature and ensured its annual reincarnation. In *The Waste Land*, T. S. Eliot adapted Frazer's anthropology to his own rootless society with its sexual desiccation. At once savage and sophisticated, Lulu in Frank Wedekind's play – the source for Alban Berg's opera and G. W. Pabst's film – is an 'Erdgeist', an earth spirit whose feckless promiscuity mimes the way that nature springs back to life after its demise in winter. Stravinsky invented a pagan vegetation rite that is danced to the death in his ballet *Le Sacre du printemps*, then had second thoughts about this violence and pleaded that the revels of Dionysus must 'submit to the law – Apollo demands it'. It was a vain hope: the deity responsible for our desires and appetites has never deferred to his luminous colleague. Myth, whenever it reappears, is evidence of compulsions that remain incurable.

*

In the affluent, contentedly secular society of the mid-twentieth century, the meaning of myth underwent a change. The word once referred to stories that told hallowed truths, which as believers we took on trust. Now, in common usage, it refers to a tissue of more or less amusing lies, like the urban legends about albino alligators splashing in the Manhattan sewers or the pirate's treasure buried somewhere on the little island that is the Statue of Liberty's podium. The lost art was recovered by the writers of advertising copy, who had a sly awareness of its fictionality. Ancient myths were theological; although their contemporary equivalents are commercial, the products they tout still pretend to purvey spiritual benefits.

Irritated by this symbolic imposture, Roland Barthes in 1954 began a series of essays analysing popular fads and newsy novelties, which were published in a French magazine under the heading 'Mythology of the Month' – a profane equivalent of the sententious editorials that newspapers used to call 'Thought for the Day'. The column's title was a deliberate tease. Traditionally, myths are eternal, as far as can be from the topicality of journalism. In Barthes' essays, collected in his book *Mythologies*, first published in 1957, there were no freakish mutants like

Dickens' waddling lizard, no flaming omens like those at which Chesterton blinked. Instead, combining impish humour and high-minded gravity, Barthes examined ephemera such as children's toys, travel brochures, restaurant menus, and the sage advice dispensed by agony aunts, our modern seers or Norns.

Among his subjects was the sighting of flying saucers, a hallucination provoked by a genuine dread: those hurtling discs deputized for the atomic bombs that might soon be bandied back and forth between America and Russia. 'It is in the sky that the Terror exists,' said Barthes, implicitly contrasting this with the Terror of the French revolutionaries, which raged at ground level. He called off our quest for supernatural correspondences by declaring that 'the sky is henceforth without metaphor'. It had become the source of death, as nuclear suns exploded.

During the Cold War, Barthes' warning was timely, and the beings who once lived above the clouds decamped in a hurry. He reported on this undignified descent in an essay about a select group of pretenders to European thrones who had made common cause for a summer cruise around the Greek islands. Slumming while on holiday, the would-be kings shaved themselves without being lathered by flunkeys, and their consorts strolled the decks wearing cotton-print dresses bought at a chain store. A 'mythological heaven', Barthes said, had crash-landed, depositing its occupants in 'ordinary life'.

In passing, Barthes noticed that the classical gods had modern imitators. He mistrusted 'the Olympus of elevated feelings' at which idealistic politicians directed their 'ascensional' gaze in flattering campaign portraits, though he was impressed by the 'Olympian snaps of the fingers' with which gangsters in Hollywood films cued bursts of gunfire, like Zeus whipping up storms. As well as noting pagan prototypes, Barthes glanced sideways at Christianity when he described a streamlined car as the modern equivalent of a Gothic cathedral. He joked that the new Citroën – called the D. S., a designation that identified it as a 'Déesse' – had apparently 'fallen from the sky', like those monarchs in mufti on the Greek yacht. Yet in being made available to potential buyers, the automotive goddess was desanctified. Barthes observed customers stroking her doors, palpating her upholstery, fondling her leather cushions, in effect ravishing her. The result, he said, was a new kind of 'exorcism' – a reversal of the Church's procedure, because instead of expelling an evil spirit it degraded a deity. In popular culture, myths are trampled, soiled, despoiled.

But the demotic revels on board the Greek yacht demonstrated that ordinary life also had its rites, ceremonies and associated dress codes; the topics Barthes dealt with uncovered the hidden mythical content of daily reality. In the 1950s, for the first time in human history, a modicum or even surfeit of comfort seemed to be within reach of everyone – or at least of those who lived on the right side of the Iron Curtain. Air travel was propelling middle-class travellers into the arena of the gods. On the ground, newfangled detergents promised not only to cleanse but to purge and purify kitchens and bathrooms, fighting a holy war against germs. Plastic, another of Barthes' subjects, had begun its lightweight, flexible refabrication of the world: polypropylene and polystyrene were both invented in 1954, and given Greek names that might have belonged, Barthes joked, to shepherds in a classical pastoral. The synthetic protoplasm suggested to Barthes that 'the whole world *can* be plasticized', which implies it was being reshaped along American lines; myth, which submits the stories it tells to 'infinite transformation', was just such an experiment in plasticity.

The mundane nature of Barthes' subjects – including a drearily utilitarian display of office furniture, designed to exemplify the sacred idea of organization – did not bother him. Content mattered less than form, which endowed material objects with significance and thereby sustained 'social appearances'. 'Every object in the world,' Barthes insisted, 'can pass from a closed, silent existence to an oral state', like detergents that sing their own praises in cheery jingles. Of course, that passage from silence to speech depended on the ventriloquism of Barthes himself, who gave dictation to the loquacious household products rather than transcribing their confidences, and he acknowledged that he might have been stretching a point. Taking the part of a dubious reader, he asked 'Everything, then, can be a myth?' 'Yes,' he replied, 'I believe this.'

Perhaps he did, although he did not believe in the myths themselves. He shared the equivocal attitude of Claude Lévi-Strauss, who introduced his account of Amazonian folklore in *The Raw and the Cooked* by advising that 'it would not be wrong to consider this book itself as a myth: it is, as it were, about the myth of mythology'. Lévi-Strauss added that 'the mythologist ... cannot believe in myths because it is his task to take them to pieces'. Dealing with mass-produced articles that were closer to home than Lévi-Strauss's exotic legends, Barthes set himself the same task. The bourgeoisie, he argued, had 'elaborated a universalist religion guaranteed by God, or by nature, or last of all by science'. The universality was that of capitalism's global market, the religion was a new cult that replaced spiritual aspiration with aspirational spending, and the God supplying the guarantee was the same cosmic treasurer whose name appears on every American dollar bill and makes it trustworthy. Nature lent credence to this faith because the consumerist economy claimed to set free our inborn instincts. The relevant science was the new discipline of semiotics, which decoded the cryptic signs that made the merchandise on offer irresistible.

For Barthes, the advertisements or magazine articles that promoted this trade were acts of 'mystification' that turned a car into a goddess and a soap powder into a puritanical crusader. The anthropologist Bronisław Malinowski, writing in 1926 about what he called 'primitive psychology', argued that myth devised tales to make men obey the gods, and in doing so 'gave rituals a hoary past and thereby sanctioned them'. Nowadays we do not expect the past to be particularly hoary: any sanction or whiff of sanctity will do, so long as it sustains our most compulsory ritual, which is shopping. As consumers, we are overfed yet perpetually hungry, naive and cynical at the same time; case-hardened after so many bogus promises, we are instinctive ironists. But have we really cast off the credulity of our forebears?

*

Mistrusting myths, Barthes called them alibis or disguises, 'masks covering up signs', and he set out to uncover the 'ideological abuse' they conceal as they whisper in our ears, play on our fears and pander to our desires.

Hence his frequent references to exorcism, or to vaccination – on the one hand an old priestly ritual for casting out demons, on the other a new medical technique for implanting a demon's seed in the body to stimulate its resistance to infection.

'One inoculates the public with a contingent evil,' Barthes remarked, 'to prevent or cure an essential one.' Advertisements recommending margarine to French consumers typically began with a housewife expressing disgust at the nasty oily stuff. Then, after a taste test, the unbeliever was converted. Barthes found the same sanctimonious 'truth-vaccine' in Elia Kazan's *On the Waterfront*. Although Marlon Brando is coerced by his labour union into betraying a fellow worker, a woman's love and a priest's counsel save him from despair. He takes a beating to vouch for his integrity; sympathizing with his cosmetically applied welts and bruises, we blame the thugs who batter him and forget that by their corruption and criminality they are enriching an unseen, unseeing class of bosses, who ought to be the targets of our disapproval. Capitalism remains intact, unctuously blessed by religion. According to Barthes, the bloodied, defaced Brando who staggers back to work at the end of the film is a 'new Christ', whose Calvary is on the Brooklyn docks – or he would be, if we did not question Kazan's logic by applying 'the method of demystification Brecht proposes'.

Barthes relied on an 'ideological critique' like Brecht's to challenge what he called 'the bourgeois norm', which was displayed in magazines that showed off a world of glut and smugness, 'well-fed, sleek, expansive, garrulous'. *Paris Match* attracted advertisers by bragging that half its readers had bathrooms in their houses and cars parked on the street outside, whereas in France in 1955 only thirteen per cent of the population had a bathroom and twenty-two per cent a car. For Barthes, there were more important things in life than sanitary plumbing and private transport, those extraneous American benefits; the majority, denied conveniences we take for granted, might not have agreed. Jean-Luc Godard remarked during the 1960s that his young contemporaries were 'the children of Marx and Coca-Cola', paradoxically combining radical politics with avid enjoyment of a newly affluent society. Barthes too felt these opposing pressures, which is why he said that in *Mythologies* he was 'living to the full the contradiction of my times'.

Our times, however, are different. Marx has lost most of his advocates, while Coca-Cola goes on reinventing itself as a fizzily inexhaustible fountain of life. As well as offering a choice between Classic Coke, Diet Coke and Coca-Cola Zero, it has even individualized its mass-produced wares by conducting a universal census. In a recent promotional ploy, containers were labelled with the names of likely customers – alphabetically extending from Aaran, Aaron and Aarron to Zac, Zachary, Zack, Zahra, Zainab and so on – together with endearing titles like Mom, Dad, Sis and Bestie. Customers were invited to tweet selfies with their personalized cans and bottles to @cokezone for display in a digital gallery. What unites the workers of the world, apparently, is a taste for American soft drinks.

In his essay on the royal cruise, Barthes joked about the evacuation of Olympus. But his mythological heaven has not remained empty; gods of a kind have since reoccupied the sky. Every November on Thanksgiving Day, a procession of inflated balloons wends down the avenues of midtown Manhattan. Bloated figures bob between the skyscrapers, buffeted by crosswinds but tethered from below by squads of handlers. Thomas the Tank Engine bumbles past, along with Papa Smurf, the Kool-Aid Man, SpongeBob SquarePants and the Pillsbury Doughboy (always described by the commentators as 'lovable'). Spiderman unfurls his web, and a Skylander, who personifies a video game, occupies a floating island high above the street. Inflated by helium and hype, they are advertisements for seasonal toys on sale at Macy's. The parade is a version of the march-past of armaments that rumbled through Red Square on May Day in Soviet Russia – equally ideological, though these soft giants are surely preferable to the trundling weapons that threatened to puncture the sky or set it alight. During breaks in the television relay, commercials reiterate the abiding American myth of eternal youth: there are ads for Olay Regenerist skin lotion and Neutrogena Rapid Wrinkle Repair Serum. A feast at home is meant to follow the parade, so another myth reconvenes the happy family. In 2014 the chef Marcel Cocit whipped up a Thanksgiving dessert for the television audience and smarmed 'To me, chocolate is love.'

That week, what Americans ecumenically call the holiday season starts with a shopping binge: bargain hunting in department stores on Black Friday, repentant visits to modest local establishments on Small Business Saturday, a stampede online on Cyber Monday. Commerce has co-opted Christian observances, just as Christianity once took over the seasonal rites of pagan religions by aligning Christ's birth and death with festivals that marked nature's demise in winter and its resurrection in spring. Caritas, the selfless love exemplified by sacrifice, has come to mean generous gift-giving at Christmas, and faith is replaced by a credit rating that tallies our promptness in paying our bills.

These rites are as compulsory as church attendance used to be. We are warned that unless we heed the ads and go shopping we will drag the economy into recession. Following the terrorist attacks in Paris in January 2015 – one at the offices of the satirical magazine *Charlie Hebdo*, where eleven staff members were killed, another at a Jewish supermarket – turnover at department stores faltered, either because people were afraid to go out or because anxiety made them question their need to renew their wardrobes. Philippe Guilbert, the manager of the Toluna polling institute, concluded that his compatriots were 'behaving more like citizens than consumers'. The remark signalled an epochal change. Citizenship, an idea glorified by the French Revolution, has given way to consumerism, which sees the public space we share as a retail outlet, not a forum opened up for communal action and engagement. Citizenship is in retreat, identified by Guilbert with stay-at-home timidity; the streets rightly belong to those with disposable incomes.

In America, the disparity that troubled Guilbert no longer exists. The websites of presidential candidates double as shops where supporters can buy T-shirts, coffee mugs, baseball caps, even headphone skins: the elector is a customer, and a vote cast is a purchase made. In 2015 Hillary Clinton's website neatly sorted its wares into three sections – Apparel, Accessories and Signage. The third category included stickers to be worn on coat lapels or attached to bumpers, a fridge magnet labelled

Cars & Stripes, outsize metal banners with grommets to be fastened onto the sides of buildings, and yard signs to be propped up in front gardens. Ensigns used to be the pennants, streamers or banderoles carried by armies or navies to trumpet an allegiance and uphold a national identity. Now they identify the brands to which we are invited to pledge our loyalty.

Aristotle defined man as a political animal, by which he meant that people were designed to live together in a polis. We define ourselves differently, omitting Aristotle's concern with interdependence and the common good: for us, men and women are animals who shop. After consorting with vampires in Stephenie Meyer's novel *Twilight*, the heroine Bella reacclimatizes herself to the human condition by making a trip to her local Thriftway. 'It was nice to be inside the supermarket,' she reports; 'it felt normal.' There is no alternative to this norm, since revolution today means acquisition on the fast track, bypassing the checkout counter. The London rioters in 2011 had grievances about racial inequality and social exclusion, but instead of torching the Houses of Parliament or climbing the walls of Buckingham Palace, they smashed shop windows and made off with Nike trainers or Apple electronics, enticed by the flashy sign that recalls the winged Victory from Greek myth and defying the Old Testament tale that identifies the half-eaten apple as evidence of our original sin. Lurking below the level of consciousness, the old stories still send out wordless signals, confident that their commands will be obeyed.

2 A Newer Testament

APPLE'S APPLE

Every morning when we press a button to wake up our computers, we re-enact the most primal of myths. As the machine recovers from its sleep, we experience the creation of the world – at least we do if we are using a Mac, supposedly the choice of creative spirits.

First comes that musical tone, a chime in F-sharp major, not far from the reiterated E-flat with which Wagner described the welling up of the primordial river at the start of his opera *Das Rheingold*. Ever since Pythagoras, mystics have claimed that the universe is held together by harmony, and the sound of the Mac's reveille, actually produced by a synthesizer, could be one of the tones that vouch for planetary unison in the Pythagorean system.

With luck the screen glows into life, as if in response to the command 'Let there be light', after which a second myth comes into play. The first week in Genesis now begins all over again, although on the laptop's lid a back-lit icon advances rapidly from creation to the fall of man and his ejection from the happy garden: it shows a white apple from which the first fatal bite has already been taken. According to the biblical myth, the fruit Adam and Eve were warned not to eat grew from the tree of knowledge. Computers contain knowledge, or at least information, so does the logo warn us that the contents of the sleek machine may be deadly? Perhaps Steve Jobs, who co-founded Apple Computer Inc., should have named his company Pandora, after the Greek version of Eve – the inquisitive woman who was told not to open a box that held every conceivable evil, and who of course instinctively did so.

When Rimsky-Korsakov heard an F-sharp major chord he thought of the colour green, perhaps imagining an unripe apple; analysts of the affinities between pitch and emotion say that the key emits a wordless sigh that signifies relief. Despite that reassurance, Apple's apple has a snarled and litigious history, whose ins and outs reveal the mutability of myths, their liability to be mistranslated or their promiscuous willingness to mean whatever we fancy. The icon picked out by Jobs in 1976 had previous owners. In 1968, when the Beatles set up Apple Corps Ltd to manage their business activities, they chose as their branding image a green Granny Smith, still unbitten. Despite this visual literalism, the word concealed a pun: the Beatles, whimsical anarchists, were signalling that the corporation was not their core business, because an apple core is casually thrown away after you have finished eating it. In the era of flower power, they hankered after an Eden not yet invaded by the serpent, a paradise of common property and communal togetherness. Among their other holdings was the Apple Boutique, which sold trendy clothes and fashionable accessories on Baker Street in London. Paul McCartney called it 'a beautiful place where you [could] buy beautiful things – a controlled weirdness – a kind of Western communism'. The paradox was unsustainable, and the boutique closed after a few months because of unstoppable shoplifting by staff as well as customers. In 1978, Apple Corps Ltd sued Apple Computer Inc. for infringing its trademark. The case lasted until 2006, with courts ordering Jobs' company to pay hefty damages. Eventually Apple Computer acquired Apple Corp's rights to the symbol, allegedly for the sum of $500 million: in the orchards of corporate capitalism, what grows on trees is money not apples.

To begin with, Jobs' apple was not a sign of anything else, and possessed no particular significance. It may have had a personal resonance: Jobs, a hippie as well as a geek, spent time during the 1970s at a commune in Oregon, where one of his hobbies was pruning the apple trees. When he and Steve Wozniak discussed names for their company, Jobs suggested calling it Apple Computer, which fondly recalled bucolic Oregon while elbowing a competitor out of the way as it queue-jumped Atari in the phone directory. A colleague worried that the two words clashed oxymoronically: apples were organic, computers electronic. But that, Jobs and Wozniak decided, would serve as a teaser to stimulate 'brand awareness'. Perhaps their later strategy also imitated the orchard. Whereas Bill Gates confined Microsoft to computers, Apple has progressively enlarged its range of products, just as fruit-growers have grafted and hybridized apples to produce everything from Adams's Pearmain to Zabergau Reinette, with McIntosh somewhere in between – as many varieties as there are breeds of dog.

At its simplest, the apple evoked nature, suggesting a vegetarian version of pastoral: back then, the faddish Jobs was on a fruitarian diet. The apple also vouched for patriotic pride, as in the old-fashioned declaration that something, or anything, was 'as American as apple pie'. For technocrats, the inevitable association of ideas was with Isaac Newton, who formulated the theory of gravity after watching an apple drop from a tree. Apple's first logo depicted this scene, with Newton sitting directly beneath a pendulous apple that glowed as if radioactive and seemed about to deliver an inspiring knock to his bewigged head.

No one in the company considered the malediction attached to the apple in Eden, which in fact was probably not an apple at all. Other versions of the story nominate a pomegranate or even a mushroom, though if the aim was to associate fruit with sin and prohibited delight I would have chosen a plump, suckable fig, or maybe a papaya with its uterine cavity of black seeds. The ban imposed by God had nothing to do with the wickedly tasty properties of the fruit: it was an arbitrary demonstration of divine power, like an order not to walk on the grass or feed the pigeons. Anything else would have served the purpose, but an apple got the blame, and its incrimination was the result of verbal mischief. Translators confused the Latin word for apple, 'malum', with the same word that, differently accented, means evil. Conveniently, the error could be passed off as a pun, superimposing a fruit and an idea that had nothing in common.

By chance, the apple did qualify for the new symbolic status wished on it in Genesis. Its taste has a slightly alarming acidity, and an aggressive action, tantamount to a moral decision, is necessary when biting into it. Under attack, the first fatal apple even bit back. The male larynx is known as our Adam's apple because it recalls the imagined moment when Adam gulped while attempting to swallow the chunk of the apple that Eve offered him. It was too late for him to cough it up, so – in an outcome that the Bible takes to be perfectly just – all of us in succeeding generations are condemned to die, as if we were victims of choking.

Jobs ignored this grim iconographic heritage. When the designers presented him with two emblematic apples – one still whole, the other already sampled by some invisible Adam or Eve – he chose the bitten one. The reason, as his biographer Walter Isaacson reports, had nothing to do with the desire of our progenitors to share divine knowledge. Jobs was concerned that the whole apple might be mistaken for a cherry, whereas the bite mark was a measure of the apple's superior size. As the popular idiom implies, a bite of the cherry is a meagre share, and Jobs' ambitions went well beyond that modest apportioning of benefits.

Appropriately enough, his bitten apple has become the symbol of consumerism, the cult that has taken over from the traditional religions. Now there is no need to pray or do penance; thanks to the ready availability of credit, all wishes can instantly be gratified. This may be what the Apple apple signified when it went iridescent. Until 1990 it was layered with a rainbow of stripes, which were not applied in the order of their appearance on the spectrum (except for the band of green, which had to be at the top because that's where the stalk attaches the apple to the tree). The rainbow was the sign of God's covenant with Noah, a partial remission of the penalty for eating the apple; Jobs liked it because a polychrome apple promised pleasure, not a savourless diet of data. He spurned the grey sobriety of IBM, with its dour output of 'international business machines'. Jobs may have had a workaholic's surname, but the computers he designed were also playthings.

Gradually the icon cast off all traces of the censorious biblical myth. In the current monochrome version, the hole on the apple's right side no longer looks like a cavity. When Eve sinks her teeth into the forbidden fruit in Milton's *Paradise Lost*, she metaphorically chomps God's green earth:

> she plucked, she eat:
> Earth felt the wound, and Nature from her seat
> Sighing through all her works gave signs of woe,
> That all was lost.

To erase any suggestion of this ravenous violence, the bite in Apple's apple has no teethmarks; the edges of the indentation are smooth. Looked at abstractly, the bite could be the open mouth of the apple itself, the aperture through which it utters that F-sharp major tone and lets light into the world. Nor is there any recollection of the forcible plucking mentioned by Milton, which is Eve's assault on nature. Apple's apple has a leaf but no stalk and therefore no attachment to a tree. Like a cratered moon, it bobs unsupported in space, not even subject to gravity like Newton's apple. Here is the ultimate floating signifier.

Is the missing mouthful a pun, like the two overlaid meanings of 'malum', which sneakily equates apple and evil? 'Bite' spelled with an 'i' means a dental incision; 'byte' with a 'y' refers to a measure of digital memory, the basis of computing. Yet 'byte' with a 'y' is an arbitrary formation – a merger of 'bit', meaning a unit of information, and the kind of bite only teeth can make – and even 'bit' with its three simple letters is a compression of the technical term 'binary digit'. As soon as we examine myths, we are befuddled by words. Language is a series of signs that do not necessarily refer to things; generating synonyms, it may just be showing off its own versatility and virtuosity.

A rumour used to circulate that Jobs' apple was a coded reference to the death of Alan Turing, now recognized as the forefather of computing. In 1936 Turing dreamed up a hypothetical machine with an unlimited memory and a capacity to scan symbols. Then in 1952, after wartime service as a code-breaker, he was prosecuted for being homosexual and sentenced to a humiliating course of estrogen injections, known as chemical castration. When he died of cyanide poisoning in 1954, a half-eaten apple was found beside his bed, and an inquest concluded that he had committed suicide by infusing a bedtime snack with the deadly chemical. He may have got the idea from one of his favourite films, Walt Disney's *Snow White and the Seven Dwarfs*, in which the malevolent hag entices Snow White to eat a red apple she has dipped in a foul brew to 'let the sleeping Death seep through'.

Snow White is a good Christian, less wayward than Eve, and she kneels to say her evening prayers in the cottage she shares with the dwarfs. The crone undermines this piety, but not by offering knowledge: she tempts Snow White with 'a wishing apple' and invites her to fantasize as she eats it. Succumbing, Snow White takes the opportunity to dream about her idealized prince. A prayer is an abject appeal, or perhaps a manipulative negotiation with some higher power. A wish is a different matter, because imagination, if sufficiently intense, can make dreams come true. In a culture where the gods are not vindictive moralists, the story need not end badly. The apples that grew in the garden of Hesperides conferred immortality on those who consumed them; Snow White's apple renders her comatose, but she is kissed back to life by the prince. Jobs, asked whether he had Turing and Disney in mind when he chose his icon, said he wished he had made the connection but admitted he had not.

Did Turing misinterpret the myth he was re-enacting? He had designed a machine that could think, helping us to acquire the 'capacious mind' that Milton's Satan boasts about when he beguiles Eve and defies God's decree that human beings should 'know to know no more' – but that is no reason to accept the penalty imposed in Eden. In any case, the police never conducted forensic tests on the apple they found beside Turing's body. Myths imprint or implant significance from the outside, as if injecting poison into a harmless piece of fruit. The joy of Jobs' logo is that it rejects all moral aspersions, and reminds us that the apple is innocent until proven guilty.

DEVILLED CHICKEN

In a consumer economy, everything is theoretically edible. Shopping makes money circulate like blood, which means that whatever we buy is supposedly essential to life, refreshing, nourishing and invigorating us. In 2015 the co-founder of Reddit even explained the site's decision to keep its obscene or offensive content available to users who logged in with a password, saying that they should retain their 'freedom to consume it' – as if they were eating the distasteful images of corpses they had chosen to look at or the racist rants they had elected to listen to.

When the act of consuming becomes metaphorical, food, which actually does travel through our bodies, has to be sold for non-alimentary reasons. In the 1950s advertisers recognized that they were selling the sizzle not the steak: the product's aura – what Barthes mock-sanctimoniously called its 'halo of virtualities' – mattered more than its taste or its capacity to fill our stomachs. Today, competition makes the seller's task harder. Food may be essential, but restaurants are optional. Before we pay someone else to cook a meal and serve it, we need to be persuaded that we will be having an experience, not merely eating dinner. It takes a myth to lure us through a restaurant door, even if we are only passing beneath a golden triumphal arch. Sitting down to eat, we are not customers but, as Barthes put it, 'myth-consumers'.

This is certainly true of Nando's, a chain of restaurants that specializes in grilled chicken marinated in chili sauce. It caters to people who can afford fancier places but still hanker after more elementary food, though they may not be prepared to go slumming with takeaways; it is casual, but smartly so – the gastronomic equivalent of dress-down Fridays at the office. Its website calls Nando's 'legendary', and it has indeed devised a proprietary myth that serves to spice up its fare. What could be duller than grilled chicken? Only boiled chicken, the insipid diet of invalids. But Nando's purports to be 'the arch-enemy of bland', and its chickens are the protagonists of a fraught metaphysical drama. Your plate turns into a battleground where religious dramas, legal disputes and imperial wars are fought all over again as your knife and fork tear the meat apart.

The name above Nando's front door is a half-word, a bite-sized abbreviation, which vouches for the casual Latin populism of the place. Perhaps less importantly, since mythic words don't need to have a meaning, it commemorates Fernando Duarte, an engineer whose family migrated from Portugal to South Africa when he was four. In 1987 Fernando acquired a chicken shack in a mining settlement outside Johannesburg and changed its name to Nando's. A few branches opened elsewhere in South Africa; now there are over a thousand, in thirty countries on all five continents.

Next to the name you find the establishment's icon, a rooster rearing on its legs to crow, with a flame-red comb, flapping wings of the same colour, and a heart that it wears outside the body, emblazoned on the black feathers of its breast as if it is suffering from heartburn. The dyspeptic bird derives from Barcelos, a town in northern Portugal. Here, in the seventeenth century, a pilgrim on his way to Santiago de Compostela was accused of stealing some silver and sentenced to hang. He appealed to the local judge, who interrupted his dinner to hear him. The condemned man swore that he was innocent, and in desperation pointed to the chicken on the judge's plate and predicted it would rise up and crow to vindicate him as he swung on the gallows. The judge ignored his entreaties but pushed his meal aside, having lost his appetite. The sentence was carried out, and on cue the dead bird, still uneaten, got to its feet and let out a screeching cry. The judge hurried to the place of execution and found that fortuitously the accused had been spared because the hangman's rope was badly knotted; he was released and resumed his journey to the shrine in Santiago.

The menus at Nando's retell this story, an odd foundational myth for a restaurant. It makes sense as a Christian miracle, a rustic mimicry of Christ's resurrection, with the crowing of the cock as a spiritual wake-up call and also a pagan reminder that the dying and reborn gods of myth represent the indestructibility of nature. But in a place where everyone is eating chickens that are supposed to be well and truly dead, the religious meaning is hardly appropriate. To reverse the transition from raw to cooked – which for anthropologists marks the change from nature to culture – is hardly sanitary, given our concerns about salmonella. Nando's therefore does some quick-footed arguing to avoid embarrassment. As far as the restaurant is concerned, the rooster's return to life signifies something less than outright immortality; at best we are assured that it has only recently been killed. The menu testifies that the birds served at Nando's are fresh not frozen – though that too contradicts the binary logic of anthropology: as Lévi-Strauss points out when discussing these categorical pairs, the opposite of fresh should be rotten, which is not a word that restaurants like to hear used.

Nando's additionally claims that its avian corpses conform to standards so strict that 'you could take 'em home to meet your mother!' But why would you want to? We are back in the realm of blandness, where chickens can usually be found. Boyfriends or girlfriends who get taken home to meet the family are probably innocuous, well-behaved, and not much fun when you're alone with them. In an essay on steak and chips, Barthes drew attention to the sanguinary mythology of meat: its visible bleeding honours the slaughtered beast and at the same time fortifies the eater, who becomes a blood-drinking participant in a primitive rite. Roast beef, especially if rare, was the food of England when it was fighting and winning wars all over the world. But chicken has to be well cooked, with no blood to give it a heroic swagger. To make matters worse, its meat is naturally white, lily-livered, the colour of cowardice. When one of the gay men in the HBO series *Looking* opens a Portuguese peri-peri chicken restaurant in San Francisco, a scurrilous friend comments that it's bound to succeed with its intended clientele, because 'chicken is the queen of meats'. Beef may be virile, but chicken – which has white, yielding flesh, at least until a hot garnish is slathered on – sends out more androgynous signals.

Nando's has devised a bold and brazen solution to this deficiency. The emblematic chicken, thanks to the miracle in Barcelos, has God as its protector; Nando's recruits the devil to baste it. What saves the white meat from being as tasteless as tofu is a coating of red sauce, made from a variety of chili that flourishes across the South African border in the former Portuguese colony of Mozambique. By adding peri-peri, Nando's demonizes its menu. This is an establishment that understands our inclination to eat on the wild side: when the witch offers Snow White a choice between sour-looking green apples and an apple with scorching red peel, she instinctively chooses the blush-coloured option. At your table in Nando's you therefore ride a perilous moral roller coaster, which plunges into hellish torments and then shoots skywards to a divine rescue.

Sometimes the heights and depths overlap: the chicken is 'flame-grilled', like a heretic barbecued by the Portuguese Inquisition. The menu's description of the hottest peri-peri recalls a biblical martyrdom. Customers are warned that the taste will be equivalent to 'tackling a dragon in a fiery furnace'. Nebuchadnezzar thrust Shadrach, Meshach and Abednego into that oven to be burned alive as punishment for their devotion to the wrong God; intervention from above reprieved them, but Nando's offers no such assurance. The menu conjures up the dragon, a mutation of the serpent that coaxed Eve to eat the apple, and leaves us to tackle it with no help from St George.

Is this over-heated rhetoric about a condiment excessive? Actually it isn't, because there is a precedent for such fanaticism: in an early speech, Osama bin Laden railed against Tabasco sauce as a symbol of the West's spiced-up depravity, perhaps because it had corrupted his playboy brother Salem, who once ordered five thousand cases of the stuff – enough to last many lifetimes, with leftovers for the afterlife – to be flown to him in Saudi Arabia.

At its most existential, the bill of fare at Nando's proposes a shared platter of thirty chicken wings, basted with sauces that vary from mild to searing. 'Who'll trigger the extra hot?' it asks as a challenge; the dish is called Wings Roulette, on an analogy with Russian roulette. It takes a certain mythopoeic daring to sell a meal as a means of committing suicide. Even the drinks at Nando's are lashed into a froth of hysteria. The sangria, for instance, contains a 'frenzy of fruit'. Try imagining a frenetic apple, very different from the one that Steve Jobs chose as his symbol of knowledge. In a calmer mood, the vegetarian menu pays punning homage to Eden: it groups its soya bean and chickpea burgers under the heading 'Vegetarian Peridise'.

Rhetorically at least, Nando's serves up risk, temptation, perdition, seething intensity, erotic anguish – anything but the happy meals on sale at McDonald's. The Nando's nearest me in south London, under the railway arches in Vauxhall, makes good this diabolical bravado by its choice of location. A street away is an all-night dance club called Fire, and even nearer are a dark catacomb whose customers are men in black leather and a pub with a drag cabaret. Wise to this carnality, Nando's has published a book about peri-peri called *Pain and Pleasure*, which treats eating spicy food as an experiment in sado-masochism.

After this titillation, the company collapses at the foot of the Cross: it saves its clientele from scorched palates and pitchforks in the entrails by borrowing a sacred religious talisman and making a joke about its fictionality. The ultimate Nando's myth is its notional High Five Card, equivalent to the Golden Tickets hidden in Willy Wonka's chocolate bars. This prize is rumoured to be a year's worth of free meals, but there is a catch: since no one has ever seen the elusive card, 'can you be sure,' the restaurant's website asks, 'it really exists?' The promotional spiel goes on to whisper that perhaps it's 'just a legend', like the unicorn. Then comes an audacious admission. The High Five Card, we are warned, may have been 'created by Nando's to give fans a holy grail to yearn for'. The Grail was the chalice from which Christ drank at the Last Supper, and – according to medieval developments of the myth – it was retrieved from the infidels during the Crusades and safeguarded by the Knights of the Round Table. There is no such Communion vessel, but in its absence we make do with pitchers of demented sangria; the menu sides with peppery-breathed dragons, not the saints on horseback who set out to kill them.

As well as extending vertically from heaven to hell, Nando's stretches horizontally around the world. This is a multinational business, an empire that is commercial not political. Its official history inserts Fernando Duarte into a grand tradition of scientific discovery and political conquest that goes back to the Renaissance: 'the Nando's story started centuries ago, when the Portuguese explorers set sail for the East in search of adventure and the legendary spice route'. Voyages like Vasco da Gama's enriched

Portugal by bringing back camphor from Borneo, sandalwood from Timor, coconuts from the Maldives, nutmeg and cloves from the Moluccas, and cinnamon from Ceylon; the inventory of colonial tribute makes no mention of peri-peri. Duarte's excursion to the rough Johannesburg suburbs hardly matched da Gama's intrepidity in rounding the Cape of Good Hope, and by the time the first Nando's opened, Mozambique and Portugal's other African colonies had fought their way to freedom from the regime in Lisbon. The soundtrack at Nando's obliterates the memory of Portugal's protracted wars of national liberation in a fusion of beats defined as 'Afro-Luso'. Can a common liking for peri-peri chicken make all men brothers?

To establish Nando's liberal credentials, one of Africa's remaining political ogres has been barred from its premises. A recent South African commercial showed the Zimbabwean despot Robert Mugabe dining alone at Christmas as he pined for happier times when he could frolic and feast with toppled colleagues like Muammar Gaddafi, Saddam Hussein and Idi Amin. The advertisement was suppressed after a juvenile militia of Mugabe loyalists threatened armed reprisals. Perhaps Nando's flatters itself about Mugabe's craving for its chicken: having bankrupted Zimbabwe for his personal benefit, he can afford to eat more expensively.

Nowadays wealth is not as aromatic as it once was when it wafted down the spice route along with camphor, cloves and cinnamon. It consists of numbers and electronic ciphers and, because it can travel instantly across oceans from one computer to another, it has no national loyalties. Duarte long ago sold Nando's to a South African family that, according to a *Guardian* investigation, keeps its profits in a trust based in the Channel Islands. The restaurant's Portuguese pedigree is a sign that points in the wrong direction, away from the slippery twists and turns of corporate finance. The food at Nando's is not bad; it is the mythology of the place that may cause indigestion.

A NEON COVENANT

Every night, on the corner beneath the windows of my apartment in Greenwich Village, two words inflame and intoxicate the sky. One is red, the other green, imitating the universal code for Stop and Go, prohibition and permission. Spelled out in thin letters arranged vertically, the green word is WINES, though its acid colour suggests unripe grapes. The red word, marching along horizontally in letters that are thicker and therefore seem louder, is LIQUORS; inside these blockish capitals, smaller yellow lines crackle like sparks. The two words flare from a neon sign that advertises an establishment known as Imperial Vintners, an off-licence squeezed into a corridor so cramped that it might be the entry to some underground lair, accessible only to those possessing a password. I have never been inside the shop, but I regard the sign as my beacon. Whenever I arrive from London, it is thrillingly raffish to tell a taxi driver 'Pull up by the liquor store.' Neon, writing its brazen enticements across the darkness and contributing its simmering hum to the uproar of the street, for me sums up the nocturnal romance of the American city.

What makes WINES and LIQUORS glow is a gas – air chilled until it liquefies, then slowly reheated – that is trapped in tubes and excited by electrodes. The tubes are heated in advance, and can be blown or twisted into any shape you please; a phosphorescent coating gives them an eerie, spectral glare. The technology has something magical and deviant about it, because gas is another name for chaos. The etymology is the same: gas hints at the turbulence and instability of nature, with contending forces engaged in perpetual combat – the elemental mess that preceded creation, tidied up when God separated earth and sky, the waters and the dry land. The Belgian chemist Jan Baptista van Helmont, who coined the word in the early 1640s, regarded gas as an immaterial spirit, perhaps a demon. Afloat in an intermediate zone between solid and liquid, it has uncanny powers: it can make you laugh or lift you off the ground, concuss or kill you, even though you may not be able to see it. Studying carbon dioxide, van Helmont found that it was emitted by belches: like a neon sign, our digestive system is a long, curvaceous tube full of gases that breathe fire.

Along with helium, xenon and krypton, neon was first extracted from the air in 1898. Sir William Ramsay and Morris Travers discovered a category of gases missing from the periodic table, and the Greek names they assigned to them paid tribute to their occult source. Helium refers to the sun, in whose chromosphere it was traced, while xenon means strange – as in xenophobia, which warns against foreigners – and krypton implies that the gas is cryptic, in need of decoding. The word neon succinctly identifies something new, enigmatic and unclassifiable.

Unlike hydrogen and oxygen, neon, krypton and the others do not enter into combinations with other elements, which is why they were called noble gases: chemistry has its small snobberies, and this low reactivity was taken to be a sign of aristocratic exclusiveness. Despite that pedigree, neon has happily lent itself to the most ignoble uses. Throughout America, it announces LIQUORS or EATS. When the stretch of Eighth Avenue above 42nd Street in New York was a raunchy red-light district, neon yelled XXXX!!! in the flushed red windows of adult video stores, and usually added that there were PREVIEW BOOTHS inside for furtive patrons. It is seldom used to mark a museum or a library – although it is capable of deploying its lurid palette to reprimand the vices that it otherwise encourages. In the Manhattan neighbourhood of Hell's Kitchen, not far from the galactic glare of Times Square, a homeless shelter that was once a church has a cruciform neon sign which terrorizes those who take refuge in the place by declaring SIN WILL FIND YOU OUT. The paint on the metal cross has turned leprous with age, and the creaking threat hangs above the street like a multicoloured cadaver rotting on the gallows.

Neon enjoys sending such mixed messages: in one part of the city it goads us to misbehave, in another it utters a thunderous reproach. Uptown in Harlem, the New Covenant Holiness Church betrays its compact with believers whenever it switches on its sign. HOLINESS is surely not a red word, and on the sign's vertical axis the letters of NEW COVENANT, also infernally tinted, are intertwined by serpentine tubes that have not been blacked out to render them invisible. The theological message is respelled by those links: COV looks like OOY, and NANT could be WANT. Neon often makes such mischief. The developers who bought the Chelsea Hotel on West 23rd Street have now turned off the vertical sign clamped to the front of the Queen Anne pile. It was a wise move, because for years the tubes had been fitfully burning out. During the 1980s the sign sometimes spluttered HO and got no further: not the chuckling glee of Santa Claus, more like the abusive monosyllable that is street slang for whore. On other nights it managed to say HO EL HEL, as if advertising a hellhole.

Neon lends itself to such omens or maledictions; it tends to be wasted when used to advertise humdrum domestic amenities. On 14th Street between Sixth and Seventh Avenues the outline of a vacuum cleaner glimmers in pale blue neon in the window of a repair shop – beautiful but somehow incompatible with tidy household chores. Pest control, which does away with infestations of cockroaches, is another matter: the baleful word EXTERMINATOR cries out for neon, preferably red.

The French inventor Georges Claude first put luminous tubes of gas to commercial use early in the twentieth century, when electricity made it possible for cities to rout the darkness that slowed them down. Claude patented his system after showing off the results at the Paris Motor Show in December 1910. He chose the occasion well. The new form of lighting, made possible by electrodes that worked like an ignition switch turning on an engine, suited the cult of speedy modernity; when neon was first introduced to America in 1923, it marked the site of a Packard car dealership in automobile-addicted Los Angeles. Although Claude was celebrated as 'the French Edison', Edison's bulbs were meant for indoor use – they were praised for their domestic mellowness, an improvement on sinister, wispy gas lamps – whereas Claude's tubes carried the illumination across longer distances; bending glass into all the letters of the alphabet, they made light verbal or vocal. Electricity had turned Broadway into 'the Great White Way'. Neon made that description seem anaemic, so the journalist Meyer Berger renamed it 'the Rainbow Ravine'.

Darkness became a screen for the projection of slogans. G. K. Chesterton worried that the kaleidoscope above Broadway debased the divine mystery of incandescence. In fact, in photographs of Times Square in the heyday of neon, the vista seems tame, laughably wholesome. Gillette touted its razor blades in ruby and turquoise, Pepsodent blazed as whitely as freshly polished dentures, Planters Peanuts promised that 'A Bag A Day Gives You More Pep', and the collars of Arrow Shirts sang the praises of the buttoned-down life. What now look mildly sleazy are the neon signs that advertised cigarettes: back then, a penguin on an ice floe smoked a mentholated Kool, and a man who testified to the virtues of Camel – SLOWER BURNING, as the torrid letters said – puffed out smoke rings with the help of giant bellows that stood in for his charred, poisoned lungs.

Today LED panels on the sides of the new skyscrapers have transformed Times Square into a cataract of harder-edged, more agitated images. Light-emitting diodes, which are semiconductors triggered by computers, enable entire buildings to act as signs; outdazzling the daylight, they have no need to wait for sunset. With streets closed to cars and café tables set out for rubber-neckers, Times Square has become an alfresco, interactive television studio. Passing through on a recent afternoon, I saw a gaggle of tourists on what used to be a traffic island, waving at a display in mid-air: they were saluting a gigantic replica of themselves on a screen a dozen storeys above the street.

These brasher light sources have driven neon into retreat in dimmer, quieter corners of New York. But an antiquated technology is likely to become an object of sentimental regret, protected by those who baulk at the pace of change. There is already a Museum of Neon Art in Los Angeles, with the acronym MONA: at its original location, the figurehead was a neon Mona Lisa, her smile reduced to two labial squiggles, her hair pyrotechnically exploding in an outburst of yellow, blue and hot pink strands. Lacking any such institution, neon in New York has a champion in Kirsten Hively, an architect whose hobby is photographing the signs that still iridescently fizz and sizzle in Manhattan and the outer boroughs. Her slogan, an invitation to fellow travellers, is 'Follow a girl as she follows the glow'.

Hively – whom I met one summer evening at a bar near Union Square, chosen because she loves the fuzzy conviviality of its neon sign – is a flâneur whose wanderings began as a course of self-administered therapy. Her architectural career stalled after the financial collapse in 2008. She compromised by taking an office job that supplied her with health benefits and enabled her to keep her apartment, but, as she told me, 'I needed to find a reason to go on loving the city. And I was looking for something to get me through the winter, during all those blizzards.' Hively grew up in Alaska, which taught her to regard the months of depressive darkness as a psychological ordeal. Now she responded to the gloom by picking up her camera after work and tramping through New York's snowdrifts and slushy bogs or slithering on its glassy, ice-sheeted sidewalks to track down obscure neon signs. 'My friends used to say "You're going out tonight? It's sub-zero!" I was always glad when I saw the sign for a pharmacy, because I could stock up on cough syrup. In Alaska we don't stand around in the street with our feet in puddles; we go everywhere in heated cars.'

Like every self-respecting New Yorker, Hively is a tireless, fearless pedestrian. 'I'm motivated,' she told me: that's as good as being motorized. 'I started just following a random trail; after a while it got more systematic. If I saw some beautiful colours a block away, I'd head for whatever it was, then notice another sign a block further off. Before long I was in neighbourhoods I would never go into on my own, even during the day – but if you have a purpose, you don't think about being safe. A lot of the little stores that still have neon signs close early, so many times I'd see something wonderful up ahead and then by the time I'd trudged through the snow they'd have turned the sign off. Now it's August, it's sunny until late, and I'm impatient because I want to see the neon. I must be the only person from Alaska who's real keen for the days to get shorter!' We waited until the arrival of what Hively calls 'the gloaming', then set off on a ramble through SoHo, the Bowery and Alphabet City, the dodgy precinct east of First Avenue where the thoroughfares are identified by letters not numbers. After a day of stifling humidity, it began to rain: imagine a sticky, unrefreshing shower of sweat. But the oppressive atmosphere flattered the neon signs, which blurred in the pearly air and leaked reflections onto the slick streets, as if the gas inside them were turning moist all over again.

Hively is a connoisseur with an acute eye, eclectic sympathies and a few strict prejudices. 'Yellow neon is kinda weird,' she said with a sniff as we passed an Italian cake shop. 'I don't like pink generally in life – I mean, for clothes and stuff. But I love pink neon, especially when it's combined with lime green. And the way they paint some of the tubes black so you don't see the connections between the letters reminds me of Kabuki, where you have actors pretending not to be there.'

With Hively striding on ahead, I found a succession of treasures, all of them invisible during the daytime. The Heartbreak Bar on East 2nd Street is a shadowy den in which you can doctor your misery with a drink: HEART and BREAK, both in bleeding red neon, are split apart at right angles on the street corner. Hively then led me to Katz's Deli, which advertises its salami and frankfurters inside a blue neon map of the United States. 'Beautiful apostrophe,' I said, admiring the curly punctuation mark in Katz's name. 'Just wait,' said Hively. 'There's a great ampersand just up ahead.' The logogram appears in the neon sign in the window of RUSS & DAUGHTERS, a catering firm whose shop is known, because of its cured salmon, as 'the Louvre of lox'. Russ's '&' resembles a mermaid with a slippery green fin, and on either side of the salmon-pink subheading APPETIZERS two aquamarine neon fish frolic, diving towards the door as if in haste to be killed, sold and eaten. A nearby restaurant called Lobster House gives one of its neon crustaceans an animated right claw, which ghoulishly scratches the surrounding murk.

Our tour concluded outside a Ukrainian church, the Orthodox Cathedral of the Holy Virgin Protection, also on East 2nd Street in an area once crowded with immigrants from Eastern Europe. A patriarchal cross juts out from its facade, fastened by a rusty chain. The crucifix is outlined in white neon, as cold as a corpse and as thin as a skeleton. No words are necessary, and it's impossible to look at the outstretched horizontal arms of the crucifix and the short, slanting lower crossbar without imagining a tormented and emaciated body pinned there, with nails through the hands and feet.

Neon specializes in spectral apparitions like this. Alfred Hitchcock read the messages it writes on the sky as prophecies of doom. A neon sign, smeared by rain as if seen through tears, beckons Janet Leigh to her doom at the motel in *Psycho*. Anthony Perkins, not long before he kills her, confides that business is so slow that sometimes he doesn't bother to turn the sign on; on this particular night he evidently needed company. In *Rope* two young men murder a friend and stow his body in a chest in a corner of the room where they then serve cocktails to the victim's family and friends. Outside their New York apartment, the separate letters of a neon sign for a warehouse, at first seen only partially and at odd, unintelligible angles, finally come together to utter a secret that none of the characters has guessed: the unheeded clue to the whereabouts of the corpse – a hint placed on view by some retributive heavenly power – is STORAGE. In *Vertigo*, in a cheap San Francisco hotel room, James Stewart makes love to a woman whom he thinks has arisen from the dead. They embrace in a luminous fog exhaled by the neon sign clamped to the wall outside the window; the green miasma it exudes is the colour of decay, the sickly exhalation from a tomb.

Morbidity is not essential. In Francis Ford Coppola's *One from the Heart*, neon saturates the air of Las Vegas with sensation. Colours pulse and throb, like blood beneath the skin. In a lingerie shop, a titillating pink sign promises INTIMATE MOMENTS. Nastassja Kinski, a trapeze artist, visits the boneyard in the desert where neon signs junked by the casinos are sent to die; gas canisters abandoned in the sand are a rueful reminder of the chemistry on which the illusion depends. The signs all stir back to life when she appears, glowing as they sketch silhouetted palm trees and fan-dancers with feathered headdresses. 'This is the garden of the Taj Mahal!' says Kinski, who climbs up a pylon, dodges high-tension wires, and performs a tightrope walk with sparklers in her hands like an electrified fairy.

Neon always was an incitement to this kind of hedonism, which is perhaps why Tracey Emin, in her show at White Cube in London in 2009, thought of using it to confide the sodden regrets of the morning after. Across the clinical walls of the gallery, Emin scribbled a maudlin love note in pink neon tubes that looked like extracts from her tangled intestines: 'Oh Christ I just wanted you/To fuck me/And then/I Became Greedy, I Wanted/You To Love Me'. She was more discreet when, in response to a request from David Cameron, she created a neon missive for 10 Downing Street. Her sign, installed above the door of the Terracotta Room in the prime minister's residence, says MORE PASSION – unwise advice for politicians, but neon is incorrigibly excitable.

The flaring tubes usually utter public pronouncements; Emin the exhibitionist makes them broadcast private confessions. Jenny Holzer has done something braver and more altruistic, employing neon to denounce the excesses of Times Square: her installation there during the 1980s re-educated the resident signs, rebuking their consumerism. PROTECT ME, said a devout revolutionary prayer that blazed on the side of a skyscraper, FROM WHAT I WANT. Bruce Nauman's neon slogans manage to have it both ways. One of them advises us to RUN FROM FEAR, while a variant underneath proposes the opposite by the simple expedient of blacking out sections of the first letter: now it tells us to derive FUN FROM FEAR. Three capitals light up one by one and raunchily semaphore RAW. Then they switch on again in reverse order to bellow WAR.

Nauman also makes mysteries materialize in neon. Coiled inside a red snailshell, blue letters testify that THE TRUE ARTIST HELPS THE WORLD BY REVEALING MYSTIC TRUTHS. Or are those truths inflammatory lies? A blitz of words arranged like an asterisk or a hurtling asteroid flashes on and off, naming the impulses that drive us to heed the commands of the signs: HOPE DREAM DESIRE NEED. Nauman's small glossary sums up the reasons why, like Kirsten Hively, we follow the glow. God, creating nature, said 'Let there be light'. But when darkness arrives in the city, the world belongs to the devil, and he spells out his inducements – whether they are alcoholic, erotic or merely commercial – in neon.

ON SACRED GROUND

Uniquely, the United States is a nation founded on myth not history, on futuristic dreams – an open frontier, illimitable aspiration, stardom for all – rather than a lovingly tended heritage.

Since this is God's country, the place where invidious European history was cancelled out as if the world were being recreated, it contains reminders or relics of the original connection between the level earth and the domed sky, ladders that lead straight up to heaven – on the West Coast the redwood trees or the Olympic mountain range in Washington State; on the East Coast the New York skyscrapers, which prompted Le Corbusier to say that the men who built them, rode in hydraulic boxes inside them, and occupied corner offices with supercilious views must be superhuman.

Barthes had his doubts about the American myth, but he called New York 'the most stupendous city in the world'. In one of his essays he defended it against the painter Bernard Buffet, who had emptied its streets and replanted its buildings in a geometrical waste: Barthes accused him of delivering a 'coup de grâce' to New York by turning the skyscrapers into tombstones. Such violent metaphors came easily to Barthes, who, as he admitted in 1971, equated signs with weapons, argued that 'every meaning is warlike', and called war 'the very structure of meaning'. The rhetoric was excessive. All Buffet did was to depopulate the city so that he could emphasize the angular rigour of its buildings; he made it look stark and harsh, but left it undamaged. He was not capable of finishing off New York, as Barthes claimed, and neither were the terrorists who on 11 September 2001 reduced the World Trade Center to smoking debris, killing three thousand people.

The myth of unchecked growth and rowdy, go-getting liberty took a hit on that day, but almost immediately America set about refurbishing its natal myth of recovery and resurrection. Oprah Winfrey, the country's matriarchal therapist, told a prayer meeting at Yankee Stadium soon after the attacks, 'I believe that when you lose a loved one you gain an angel whose name you know.' In retrospect, victims were reclassified as victors: advertising vacancies in 2002, the New York Fire Department used 'Heroes Wanted' as its recruitment slogan. The heroic easily slithered into the erotic, and on the cover of the FDNY's calendar for that year a muscular fireman, his uniform peeling from an oiled torso, preened beside the Empire State Building, now reinstated as Manhattan's perkiest phallic symbol. On later anniversaries, vertical beams from searchlights were aimed at the sky from the spot where the Trade Center once stood, as if the twin towers had returned as sentinels. In Oliver Stone's film *World Trade Center* a police sergeant played by Nicolas Cage, pinioned under rubble in a lift shaft after the collapse of the first tower, appeals to a colleague who is trapped nearby. 'Can you still see the light?' he asks. He is referring to a crevice far above, visible before a convulsion dumped more concrete on them. His buddy replies that yes, the light is still there. Hope is inextinguishable, and also justifiable: the men are soon hauled back from underground. Their saviour is a former Marine who confers with his pastor in a Connecticut church where the Bible on the lectern is open to the Book of Revelation, then gets himself ritually buzzcut, changes back into his uniform, travels to New York, sneaks into the cordoned-off site, and makes it his task to recover or resurrect the dead.

Now, at Ground Zero and beneath it, a nation unaccustomed to defeat and unfamiliar with tragedy has devised memorials that try hard not to be mournful. During operations to clear the site in the months after 9/11, a pear tree with a scorched trunk and severed roots was discovered in the rubble; nursed back to life, it has been replanted and is referred to as 'the Survivor Tree'. It blossoms again every spring: a sign of hope, though also a cruel reminder that human beings, unlike trees, are not annually reincarnated. On the ground occupied by the original towers – called their 'footprints', since a tender elegiac sentiment has anthropomorphized the two blockish, boxy piles designed by Minoru Yamasaki – are a pair of gaping black sluices, plugholes down which a gushing cascade of water endlessly pours. As with the tree, the symbolism is tricky. Do those cataracts represent tears shed for the dead, whose names are spelled out around the rim, or does the void into which they gush suggest the forgetful fluency of time and the slipperiness of memory? The tanks are best understood as twin Niagaras, installed to show how the sublimity of open space can relieve us of quaking personal fears and give us a sense that the universe – as American kids like to say – is 'awesome'.

Between the pools is a crumpled, irregularly shattered pile of glass that turns out to be the entrance to the 9/11 Museum. It displaces a global emblem – a bronze sphere held up by a caryatid, which was damaged by shrapnel from the planes that crashed into the Trade Center. The sphere was moved to Battery Park, where it now valiantly shows off its dents and scars; the pavilion that has taken its place resembles a toppled building, but its interior is not the mangled mess left behind when the towers fell. It opens into another sublime immensity, a dim cavern or canyon that extends downwards for seven storeys until it reaches the raw foundations of Yamasaki's buildings, with only the barricade of a three-foot-thick slurry wall to stop the Hudson River from flooding in. During construction of the Trade Center, this ditch was nicknamed 'the bathtub', which does a disservice to its fortitude. The slurry wall is like the Hoover Dam in reverse: a membrane of reinforced concrete that keeps a river out, rather than holding a lake in. In these ominous depths we can watch and wonder at the battle between the violence of the elements and the ingenuity of the engineering that subdues them – a reprise of America's underlying triumph.

You make your way down, down, on sloping ramps and steep escalators, passing beside the preserved Vesey Street staircase, which was the route to safety for so many occupants of the towers. There are photographs of people stumbling down those stairs, enshrouded in white dust like walking cadavers; their scramble back to the street was not the archetypal American journey, which is a quest for the infinite or a race to self-betterment, a leap of faith not a jump to certain death. In a sequestered space is a repository for unidentified human remains, with a quotation on the wall from Virgil's *Aeneid* – 'No day shall erase you from the memory of time'. If only that were true: of course we will all suffer erasure. Uplift, however, is mandatory here. Then, at the lowest level, you have the experience of entombment. Despite Oprah's gesture towards the Christian heaven with its flocks of angels, this is more like the shady classical underworld, lacking any assurance that the shattered body will be pieced back together at the Second Coming.

The stages of the long descent are marked by salvaged emblems, refuse that has been organized into a sacred reliquary like those in Catholic churches, except that the tormented, death-defying saints are ordinary human beings – office workers, teams from the emergency services – who did not seek the martyred status they were awarded.

Some of the objects are fortuitously religious, which supports the official agenda of consolation and uplift. Near the entrance to the 9/11 Museum two forked columns of twisted steel that were once attached to the facades of the towers look, out of context, like Gothic arches. The nearby Woolworth Building was called a cathedral of commerce when it opened in 1913, but these butchered fragments no longer propound a gospel of profit. They testify instead to the combination of spiritual zeal and technical prowess that first impelled architecture to scale the heights. They are known as 'tridents', which stretches them between myth and technology: the word refers to the three-pronged spear imperiously wielded by Poseidon and borrowed by Britannia, but also to an American long-range ballistic missile launched from submarines that cruise in Poseidon's realm.

Further down stands a steel beam fused with a crossbar, unearthed two days after 9/11. During clearance of the site it functioned as a rusty crucifix, and every Sunday a Franciscan priest offered communion to rescue workers underneath it. In another subterranean expanse, a place of honour has been found for the Last Column, as it is respectfully called: a steel stump so deeply embedded in the bedrock that the workers trying to remove it deferred to its almost human tenacity and welded a flagpole onto it so that the Stars and Stripes could be hoisted aloft.

These battered leftovers function as icons – piety and politics fused and solidified in architectural form. Elsewhere the museum advances into abstraction. Lengths of steel from the impact zones where the planes tore through the buildings are included in the display, bent as if melting. In the museum guidebook a curator comments on their 'tortured' shape, says they are 'terrible to behold', but adds that they 'testify to the resilience that would characterize so much of the response to 9/11'. This optimistic reading overlooks a more painfully obvious point: steel may be hardy but it is insentient, unlike the creatures of flesh and blood who were incinerated here, or who helplessly challenged necessity by choosing to plummet to their deaths.

The exhibits arrange themselves into an impromptu history of art. We proceed, as if perambulating through the centuries rather than touring the wreckage of a single day, from relics like the accidentally consecrated arches and crosses to those brutally modern bars of buckled steel, which testify to the wrenching inquisition of matter that the Cubists undertook. Finally we arrive at what might be mistaken for a collection of Pop Art, arranged along a wall in glass cubicles like the household appliances of Jeff Koons or the flotsam and jetsam retrieved from street corners by Walker Evans and Robert Rauschenberg. The collection includes a red bandana handkerchief, a tattered $2 bill, a dog leash, and a pair of spike-heeled shoes, among a jumble of other carefully classified items – examples, perhaps, of the 'phenomena ... most unlike literature' that Barthes investigated in *Mythologies*, although narratives adhere to them all. The bandana was owned by an equities trader on the 78th floor, who used it, in the moments before he died, to cover his mouth from smoke inhalation while ushering colleagues to the stairs. The $2 bill came from the wallet of an insurance broker, another victim, who carried it everywhere as a remembrance of his happy second marriage. The leash belonged to a sniffer dog, a Labrador retriever crushed in a basement kennel after his police handler rushed upstairs. And the shoes were worn by a financial executive who tottered down sixty-two flights of stairs to the lobby, where she gratefully exchanged her heels for sneakers donated by employees of Foot Locker. These banal objects are not mythic; what makes them significant is a personal history. They are mementos of the dead or, in the case of the shoes, an improbable testimony to life.

Unaccustomed to disaster, Americans have decided that the entire site where the Trade Center stood is 'sacred ground', as if death sanctifies the place where it happened. Rules about the etiquette appropriate to the site have always been complicated and contradictory. On my first trip to Ground Zero, a month after the event, a rostrum had been built outside the fence overlooking the reeking, smouldering mess of tangled metal. An ocular puritanism prevailed at America's equivalent of the Wailing Wall. Police kept watch on the shuffling crowds, and sternly forbade photography. Even before the advent of the selfie, the prohibition seemed curious. We were permitted to look, but not through a lens. Was the camera too unfeeling an instrument? Were the cops concerned about the contagious good humour of happy snaps? The families of those who died gathered outside the fence in October 2011 for a concert at which the soprano Renée Fleming sang 'Amazing Grace', a hymn sung in thanks for the abolition of slavery. It was an odd choice: no one who attended seemed ready to believe that 9/11 had graciously freed the victims from the dire fate of being alive.

A year later, the moral guardians of the place took offence when the second *Lord of the Rings* film used Tolkien's title *The Two Towers*, as if the words were tragically trademarked. In 2013 two base jumpers parachuted off the tower that was being constructed on the site; the judge who sentenced them for 'unauthorized climbing' ruled that they had 'tarnished the building' by their sporty act. When the 9/11 Museum opened in 2014 with a cocktail party, relatives of victims protested that the event was a desecration. All these fulminations made a naive mistake about the nature of cities and of the buildings in them: both are places of passage, and the people who stream through never return.

Although their country's fabled Wild West was a battleground or a killing field, Americans prefer to think that they are living in a virgin land, an unspoiled place of fresh starts; New York wants to be a city without catacombs. In his criticism of Buffet's paintings, Barthes, paradoxical as ever, claimed that 'It is not up, towards the sky, that you must look in New York; it is down.' He meant that the primary purpose of the skyscrapers is to regularize city blocks and ease the circulation of men and merchandise. But the view downwards stops at street level, failing to penetrate the lower depths into which you terrifyingly travel in the 9/11 Museum.

Resurrection, however, happens nearby in the new skyscraper called 1 World Trade Center, as a lift hurtles up to an observatory on the

102nd floor at a rate of two thousand feet a minute. Marvels unfold in high definition inside a box that might be a commodious coffin tugged suddenly skywards. As soon as the doors of the lift to the viewing platform close, its interior walls turn into screens on which a montage of Lower Manhattan's history plays out. It starts deep in the granite bedrock, burrows up through the marsh that was drained to support the area's buildings, surveys unsettled nature and then glances at the growth of a straggling village surmounted by windmills and church steeples, after which the first skyscrapers can be seen sprouting. Just before the lift reaches its destination, a silhouette of the fallen World Trade Center appears, only to fade discreetly after a few seconds. We lower our heads briefly to acknowledge a tragedy, then blink.

The lift's descent, of course, is more of a problem: how can it not copy the toppling of the towers? But before the evolutionary saga resumes in reverse, gravity is airily repudiated, as the view on the lift's walls embarks on a swooping, swirling arc that might be an angel's flight path, after which the cabin gently restores us to ground level, not to Ground Zero. In vertical Manhattan, travelling upwards is always a sublimation; when you quit the heights and travel back down, you need to be assured of a soft landing.

The cities of ancient myth were dwelling-places of the gods, or citadels of holiness. One of the earliest American colonists, the preacher John Winthrop, revived that notion by telling his congregation, before they even arrived in Massachusetts, that their community in the New World should be 'as a city upon a hill'. American cities eventually became sites of man's self-deification, but they still sought the protection of seraphs like Bethesda, the Angel of the Waters who presides above the fountain in Central Park, or the indigenous prophet Moroni who stands atop the Mormon Tabernacle on its hill in Salt Lake City. In the west, cities grew up around Catholic missions and adopted as their patrons saints like Francisco, Diego and Barbara. When it was founded, Santa Fe's full name was La Villa Real de la Santa Fe de San Francisco de Asís: it has shed the references to royalty and to Assisi, but remains a synonym for faith. St Paul in Minnesota – first called Fort Snelling and for a while nicknamed Pig's Eye in homage to a Canadian bootlegger – finally made itself safe by adopting one of Christ's Apostles as its guardian. Even Philadelphia, sacred to brotherly love, took its name from an Asian settlement mentioned in the Book of Revelation.

Such auguries were no protection against the calamities that have recurrently overtaken these hallowed places: an earthquake and a fire in San Francisco, another fire in Chicago and another earthquake in the Los Angeles district of Northridge, floods in New Orleans and New York, and the economic devastation that has left Detroit to rust and moulder. One of myth's tasks is to reconcile us to our mortality; that undertaking is arduous enough, but how can it extend to eternalizing cities? Even if disasters pass them by, they must grow and change by demolition, and in being churned up and rebuilt they enforce the grim, unwelcome lesson of the individual's temporariness and expendability.

Other societies and cultures, which do not subscribe to the American myth of fresh starts and cosmetic makeovers, worry less about our existential infirmity. Half a mile from the World Trade Center, my favourite Chinatown restaurant lurks in a narrow, crooked alley where rival gangs once conducted their turf wars; the corner around which they charged at each other used to be known as the Bloody Angle, because of the gore that ran in the gutters there. The earth is a storeyed boneyard, and even New York is a necropolis, crammed with the corpses of those who have predeceased us.

BABEL-ON-THAMES

Myths often set a limit beyond which our understanding is not permitted to trespass. The Old Testament, for instance, imposes a divine ban on the construction of skyscrapers. The Tower of Babel was constructed by workmen from all over the world, who were able to collaborate because they shared a single language. It rose so high that God resented the intrusion on his aerial domain; he therefore confounded the workers by multiplying their languages. Scattered across the earth in tribes and factions with no common idiom, condemned to discord, they left Babel unfinished.

The myth links architecture and language, and superstitiously lames or trips up both. They are equally blameworthy because they are both methods of construction, which in different ways allow us to separate ourselves from nature and gain power over it. Although God bestowed the gift of speech on Adam and Eve, he planned to control what they said, and he also expected them to go on living in a rudimentary floral bower rather than erecting vainglorious towers. Yet there is more to the story of Babel than a nasty practical joke: it warns about the risks involved in our over-reaching. Architecture lifts us to heights that are physically if not morally dangerous, and language, which ought to be a medium of communication, is responsible for our misunderstandings and enables us to tell lies.

When steel, concrete, hydraulics and the granite bedrock of Manhattan made it possible to build high, Americans defied the biblical taboo, and buildings that deified magnates like Woolworth, Chrysler and Rockefeller prodded the sky above New York. Until recently, London was content to be surmounted by the churches of Wren and Hawksmoor – not because Londoners are especially God-fearing, but because their scurrilous, demotic humour snarls at self-promotion and over-achievement, in buildings as in people. The new skyscrapers in London's financial district have therefore been tagged with nicknames that tug them back to earth and stow them in the kitchen cupboard or the pantry: the cheese-grater, the can of ham, the gherkin.

The loftiest of them all, currently the tallest building in Europe, was at first referred to as the salt cellar, though its official name is The Shard. That too ought to be derogatory or diminutive, like the labels attached to its neighbours on the north side of London Bridge. A shard is a splinter, and a brittle one; in some cases, it is a piece of unearthed pottery that belonged to a larger vessel; it could even be one of the tribal dialects that replaced the universal language spoken at Babel. The architect Renzo Piano has built a fragment. But a fragment of what?

Piano startled the developer when they first met by declaring that he disliked tall buildings because they were egotistical – a rare moral scruple for an architect, and perhaps a little disingenuous. True, The Shard does not jab the heavens like the Empire State Building, which was meant to have a mast for anchoring dirigibles at its summit. High up, The Shard's panels of jagged glass open like the jaws of a silvery swordfish: they may intend to bite the sky, but they don't close on it. Rather than climbing aggressively upwards, The Shard seems to be letting a ladder down from above. It had risen twenty-one storeys into the air before its foundations were firmly planted, almost as an afterthought; seven hundred truckloads of concrete were then poured to anchor it in the marshy riverbank. Squeezed onto a narrow site, it makes light of its bulk and its height by playing hide and seek. As you approach, it crumples up and disappears into the dense, dog-legged alleys of Southwark; seen from further off, it mirrors and merges with the grey London weather, pretending to be transparent.

The Shard's metamorphic slipperiness recalls a comment made by Barthes about one of his mythical objects, the Eiffel Tower. 'This pure – virtually empty – sign is ineluctable,' he said, '*because it means everything.*' The Eiffel Tower is indeed empty, and its netted girders allow us to look through it. The Shard too remains pretty much unoccupied: there have been few takers for its apartments, which cost between £30 and £50 million, and a third of its commercial space is expected to stay vacant. Barthes rightly called the Eiffel Tower 'utterly useless'. Erected as a temporary folly, it was meant for demolition soon after the 1889 Exposition Universelle. Does The Shard have a use, or is it content to be beautiful? Its location – between the most functional of buildings, a hospital and a railway terminal, with a food market across the street – underlines how gratuitous and decoratively fanciful it is.

The building's promoters, while finding it difficult to rent office space, have had better luck selling the view from its 68th, 69th and 72nd floors. At that height, its slivers of glass narrow into a platform that juts out of the sky, allowing us to look back at the earth we have quit. Barthes said that 'every visitor to the Eiffel Tower makes structuralism without knowing it'. He meant that from the lookout you deconstruct Paris, taking it to pieces and then rearranging the facets, just as the component parts of a myth can be recombined at will. On the Eiffel Tower, Barthes remarked, the effort to identify landmarks means that tourists must perform 'an activity of the mind' known as decipherment. That is even truer at The Shard, which is so much taller than the Eiffel Tower and therefore renders the city that much more unintelligible.

From its viewing platform you can see London as a whole, which means that you see beyond it and watch it effacing itself. At its furthest edges, air and water take over from the sagging, over-burdened land. To the west, planes climb out of Heathrow, while to the east, the rotating gates of the Thames Barrier – modelled on the brass taps that used to turn off the supply of gas in British homes – are a reminder that we are camped on a floodplain which was once submerged and will be again. The earth is at best a runway, at worst a crowded life raft; either way, it is not much more secure than the jutting ledges of The Shard. The affluent evacuees from the lower world presumably don't mind, especially if they are drinking champagne – £80 a bottle when I visited, with only cash accepted – on the indoor lawn of Astroturf with which the uppermost viewing platform is carpeted. Here they can raise a glass to the success of their vertical migration, a trial run for a trip on Richard Branson's space shuttle.

Ticket-buyers to The View from The Shard are assured that this is 'The Only Place To See All Of London In High Definition'. The sales pitch cunningly appeals to our electronic tastes, but it's misleading. Although the vantage point is high, the view lacks the razor-edged clarity and microscopic detail of an HD image on television. Below, the city blurs indiscriminately, all its eminences equally abased. The axis of the old skyline extended down the river from the Houses of Parliament with their Gothic crockets to the grandiose baroque dome of St Paul's, linking church and state but keeping them at a distance. Seen from above, that diagrammatic groundplan of authority is smudged by haze, jumble, clutter. The gilded torch of the Monument, raised on its column as a memento of the Great Fire, appears to be grounded. Patches of bright green in parks and garden squares outshine the expanses of begrimed stone between them: in this most built-up of places, emptiness prevails. From so far above, Buckingham Palace is a stage set, with nothing behind it but gravel and grass. People are obliterated, and London becomes inanimate.

Because height is The Shard's prerogative, no other attempt at verticality counts; what matters instead is elongation. Trains on their elevated tracks are like tapeworms, and the roof of Nicholas Grimshaw's platform at Waterloo Station, once occupied by Eurostar, is a procession of armadillos. The only element of continuity, outlasting and overwhelming everything else, is the river. Suddenly the looping trajectory of the Thames in the credits for *East Enders* makes sense. In our limited views from the ground, the river seems to flow in a straight line. Viewed from up here, it regains power and like a bloated, muddy python it coils or writhes through a dry jungle of stone. The vista emphasizes patterned abstraction, and form, as always in myth, prevails over content.

The Eiffel Tower was for Barthes the purest and most vacant of signs. The Shard likewise is mostly empty, except for trippers looking at the view; it too means nothing and everything; and it may turn out to be as useless as that other high-rise relic, Centre Point, at the junction of Oxford Street and Tottenham Court Road, which is arguably central but definitely has no point. These negative attributes, however, mean that The Shard is at home in a city of a new kind. It is situated on an embankment that contains an open-roofed Shakespearean theatre where being rained on as you spend three hours standing is part of the fun; a docked Elizabethan galleon, like a set for a pirate movie; a decommissioned power station whose empty turbine hall now houses displays of extravagantly outsized art; a bridge that bounced excitingly underfoot when first opened; a tower that was once a factory where Oxo meat cubes were manufactured, though it is now full of galleries and restaurants; and a ferris wheel that sedately revolves and allows its passengers to review the floating world beneath them. Only Southwark Cathedral, squatting nearby, seems incongruous. In this city of kaleidoscopic delights, terror shadows pleasure: just below The Shard is a plague pit that has been converted into a black museum, the dank lair of spooks who are mostly unemployed actors. London was once a place of work, with the river as its commercial conduit, lined with wharves and warehouses. Now that the city's economy depends on expenditure and is always in need of new diversions, London has to be presented as a playground, a theme park, a magic kingdom.

Myths tell soothing lies to cover such economic upheavals, and 'mythical thought,' as Lévi-Strauss says, 'builds ideological castles out of the debris of social discourse'. As if to illustrate the point, the 34th to the 52nd floors of The Shard are given over to the Shangri-La Hotel, whose name – a transliteration of Shambhala, the esoteric paradise of Tibetan Buddhists – is taken from James Hilton's novel *Lost Horizon*. In the book, published in 1933 at a time of ideological friction throughout Europe, a seeker after truth is spirited away to a Himalayan Utopia where wise lamas preside over an idyllic meditative existence. Some disgruntled new arrivals, snatched out of the lower world, are unimpressed by Hilton's Shangri-La. Their smiling host calls the monastically austere accommodation 'simple, but I hope adequate'. 'Do we all have to line up for the bathroom?' asks one crabby guest, 'or is this an American hotel?' As it turns out, the hero takes a dip in a bath of green porcelain made in Akron, Ohio, after which he is 'valeted in Chinese fashion' by 'a native attendant', who cleanses his ears and nostrils and passes 'a thin, silk swab under his lower eyelids'. The altitudinous retreat exists to purge and enlighten its guests, not to pamper them, but its services sound very like those available at an expensive day spa. The Shard's Shangri-La, which promises 'Oriental elegance', recommends a dip in what it calls 'the infinity pool' on the 52nd floor. It's unclear what kind of infinitude the pool possesses; its waters surely cannot guarantee a life serenely extended to three hundred years, which is the bonus that Hilton's characters enjoy in their mystical hideaway.

Somewhat tactlessly, a restaurant on the 33rd floor is called Hutong: this was the name given to the alleys in which residents of Chinese cities like Beijing used to live, before their humble hutches were bulldozed to build skyscrapers. Having floated up to that exclusive altitude, the word has shed all memory of the downtrodden, populous earth. Barthes recalled that Guy de Maupassant used to dine at the restaurant in the Eiffel Tower because, although the food was poor, it was the only place in Paris where he did not have to look at the Tower itself. Hutong's customers have different motives: The Shard is not in their blind spot, and they eat there and drink cocktails that are said to be 'decadent' because they can afford to and others can't.

Shangri-La in Hilton's novel catered to the spiritually elect, not to an affluent elite. The Shard, financed by investors from Qatar, is a symbol of wealth, of ostentatious excess rather than renunciation, and – having weathered a bolt of forked lightning that struck it during a summer storm in 2014 – it brazenly refutes the biblical myth about the first overweening skyscraper and its inevitable doom. The Shard has arisen in a global capital where every language in the world is spoken; here the curse of incomprehension that halted work at Babel is waived. No matter if the Arab sheiks, Russian oligarchs and American CEOs who pass through don't understand each other, or if they're not understood by the Polish receptionists, Bolivian maids and Afro-Caribbean porters who wait on them. Money talks on their behalf, and in Babel-on-Thames the dollar, the pound, the Euro, the riyal, the ruble, the rupee and the renminbi all speak its slick Esperanto.

WRITING ON WALLS

The first writing on the wall, traced by a bodiless hand at Belshazzar's feast, announced the imminent fall of a city. It did so in letters of flame not ink; combustibility made it terrifying, and the inscription – MENE MENE TEKEL UPHARSIN – was all the more menacing because it was meaningless. Daniel decoded it, discovering a curse in every word: God had numbered the days of Belshazzar's reign over Babylon, weighed him in the balance and found him wanting, and divided his kingdom. The prophecy at once came true, and the king, according to the Bible, died that night.

Why should something written on a wall have such unsettling power? The Babylonian wall was internal, part of Belshazzar's banqueting hall. Such walls exist to divide rooms not to split realms in half, which in Daniel's reading was the purport of the fourth word; they demarcate privacy, and immure us with our secrets. No message from outside should intrude here. But the inscription suggests that walls have ears, eyes, even mouths that can utter commands and threats – and because Daniel read the words as an augury of doom, they serve as a reminder that all walls will collapse in the end.

Whenever Banksy stencils an image or a slogan on a wall in a public street, he recapitulates the story of the interrupted feast. His graffiti, like the fiery sentence that condemned Babylon, pronounce an anathema. He has decried our gormandizing by converting a Value bottle from Tesco into a container for a petrol bomb with a sparking wick, and by drawing an emaciated African waif with a begging bowl at his feet and a paper coronet from Burger King on his head. Once, mocking Western plenty not African poverty, he painted a trio of primitive hunter-gatherers in loincloths crouched in the grass as they stalk their prey. They aim a spear and a pick at a set of supermarket trolleys, all of them empty; discarded in the savannah, the carts look like beasts whose wiry bones have already been picked clean.

Rather than speaking on God's behalf, like the bodiless writer in Babylon, Banksy is flagrantly blasphemous. The false religion he assails is consumerism, into which all members of our society must be indoctrinated. One of his stencils on a wall in Islington therefore showed a group of children pledging allegiance to a Tesco flag: such corporations call their grandest outlets 'flagships', equivalents of the conquering armadas launched by imperial navies. The cult has its own version of the resurrection. Banksy's crucified Christ holds shopping bags stuffed with Christmas presents in his outstretched hands; a caption explains 'We don't need any more heroes, we just need someone to take out the recycling', which replaces the miracle of the uprisen body with the revivification of all that tattered packaging. Banksy's preference is probably for a more ancient, less consoling myth. In Bristol, on the rusty iron hulk of a ship that is now used as a nightclub, he painted a skeletal figure rowing a dinghy to ferry partygoers across the Styx. Sometimes the route to the netherworld is more direct: for a while, the wobbly Millennium Bridge in London had a sign stencilled by Banksy on its metal floor that read

CAUTION
CONCEALED
TRAP DOOR
IN OPERATION.

We may be able to do without walls, but we do need a floor beneath our feet.

To paint a wall is Banksy's way of toppling it, at least wishfully. In 2005 he worked on the segregation wall built by the Israelis to keep the Palestinians of the occupied territories at bay, using the slabs as his personal gallery. On one section he stencilled a pair of scissors eating their way along a dotted line, as if the concrete were as easy to slice through as paper. Failing that, he made the obtuse surface transparent. Scenic vistas of blue sky or snowy mountains or tropical beaches appeared, like openings in the wall. At a checkpoint in Bethlehem, the imaginary view was curtained like a picture window, with two-dimensional armchairs beneath it in which no one could sit. The stencilled figure of a girl was lifted upwards by the balloons she clutched, as if those puffballs could waft her weightlessly across to the other side. In another place, a boy stood holding a brush beneath a shaky rope ladder that he had painted all the way to the top: would he be able to scale it? A passer-by, watching Banksy at work, noted that he was beautifying the wall. Banksy thanked him, but the Palestinian observer did not mean to be complimentary. 'We don't want it to be beautiful,' he said. 'We hate this wall. Go home.' Although graffiti painting may qualify as art, it is primarily action – a gesture of defiance and contempt – and it should expect to be effaced, erased by the authorities it mocks.

In Jerusalem, believers go to a wall that was once part of Herod's temple to wail – to pray, chant, and beseech God to attend to their needs. The rest of us have it easier: holes in walls, shaped like thin mouths, promptly answer our prayers by dispensing money. Banksy fancies himself as an outlaw, a Robin Hood whose hiding place is not the woods but a dense, matted urban forest. His given name, rumour has it, is Robin, and early in his career he sometimes signed himself Robin Banx – a punning declaration of his affinity with the bank robbers John Dillinger and Clyde Barrow. But Banksy has no need to hold up cashiers; instead, in 2004 in east London he stencilled on a wall a cash machine with a litter of red ten-pound notes glued to the pavement beneath it – not legal tender because they portrayed the sly, sideways-glancing Princess Diana, rather than her glum mother-in-law. Banksy prepared a million pounds' worth of these Di-Faced Tenners, and intended to hurl wads of them from rooftops. Then, afraid of being arrested as a counterfeiter, he gave them away at a festival concert. But despite his misgivings, there is no way of undercutting the fictional logic of our economy, in which noble faces turn intrinsically worthless paper into a token of value: the people who took the notes committed fraud by crumpling them up until they were unrecognizable and using them to buy drinks. The Di-Faced Tenners are today worth far in excess of their nominal face value: one of them sold at auction in 2012 for £16,250. Without intending to, Banksy had demonstrated that successful artists have a licence to print money, and he may be laughing all the way to the banks he professes not to rob.

'A wall,' in Banksy's view, 'has always been the best place to publish your work.' The verb as used by him opens up a range of meanings: to publish means to place his work in the public realm and to gain publicity for it, as he did when he surreptitiously hung his images on walls in the British Museum, the Tate Gallery, the Museum of Modern Art and the Metropolitan Museum in New York. Yet after these acts of self-publication, he swiftly reassumes his private life. Concealment is a gimmick, a kind of trademark; it is also a supernatural privilege, the prerogative of a cat burglar, a guerrilla (Banksy's work clothes are camouflage gear), and of a god.

Technically, Banksy outdoes Belshazzar's portent. In the Bible, the words are formed by a hand that is cut off at the wrist. Banksy does not use a severed hand; instead he disembodies the hand altogether. To paint walls takes time, which puts him at risk of being noticed by policemen on the beat. He therefore prepares cut-out stencils, so he can quickly pin or tape them up, spread paint over them, remove the layer of paper and disappear. The procedure is controversial. The fly-by-night fraternity has an elaborate code of conduct: graffiti artists are expected to steal the paint they use, do their work freehand, and stay in place for the finishing touches despite the danger of arrest. Stencils cheat by abbreviating the process. Another nonchalant proviso obliges the daubers to accept the ephemerality of their work, whereas anything by Banksy is carefully removed from its wall and transferred to galleries or auction houses. There were complaints of 'disrespect' and even 'sacrilege' when Banksy broke another of the fraternity's rules by painting over some graffiti by his rival Robbo under a bridge on the Regent's Canal in north London. He made the insult more heinous by covering Robbo's work with an image of a decorator putting up wallpaper. Walls should be flayed by graffiti, not given the cushioning of an extra skin.

Perhaps the Babylonians were being gullible when they accepted Daniel's interpretation of the slogan on Belshazzar's wall and rewarded him with a scarlet robe and a chain of gold, as if conferring an honorary doctorate on an especially ingenious literary critic. MENE MENE TEKEL UPHARSIN continued to intrigue Talmudic scholars, who wondered whether the words were written backwards or with transposed letters, and puzzled over why they were arranged vertically not horizontally, in columns – which uphold buildings – not lines. The tag with which Banksy authenticates his work offers less of a challenge, but he does make conscientious efforts to be unintelligible. He might almost be using a foreign alphabet to sign his name (or his pseudonym, since he is apparently called Robin Gunningham). Without its spine, the B in his stencilled signature looks like E in reverse. The A and N are bracketed together, and the K, piggybacking on the N, is reduced to a beak. The S is unserpentine, closer to a C written backwards; the Y is recognizable, but that is not enough to make the interlinked chain of letters add up to a word. This signature, Banksy's trademark, vouches for his identity while at the same time obscuring it.

Daniel may have been overinterpreting when he came to the end of the cryptograph: he took UPHARSIN to be the plural of 'peres' and equated it with the Persians, who along with the Medes carved up the kingdom and killed Belshazzar. Banksy has an equivalent of this linguistic legerdemain: he is addicted to puns. He entitled his illustrated book *Wall and Piece*; in a related bit of wordplay, his statue of a policeman dressed in riot gear while riding a mechanical rocking horse is called *Metropolitan Peace*. Although the front cover of *Wall and Piece* shows a masked protester who seems to be hurling a missile, if you follow his arm around the book's spine you discover that he is holding not a rock or a grenade but a bunch of flowers. The substitutions demilitarize language. The war happens on walls, which remain intact; the policeman is a harmless big baby, and the act of protest is festive not riotous. *Existencilism*, the title of Banksy's second book, does not claim a tightrope-walking existential bravado for the graffiti artist. In it he reverts to irony – which is invisibility by other means – and like a crusty academician chides his colleagues for their poor draughtsmanship. Musing on the consumer economy, he complains about our obsession with branded goods and says 'I call it Brandalism' – arguably a worse vice than the vandalism of which graffiti artists are customarily accused.

Barcodes on merchandise can seem sinister. The data on the upright lines encodes a monetary value; supermarkets are prisons that guard their commodities behind bars. In another visual pun, Banksy therefore flexes the barriers and debars the regimentation of optical scanning. He barcodes the side of a parked circus van, then twists the parallel lines to leave a hole through which an escaped tiger lazily lopes to freedom. Jests like this question the linguistic metaphors that have economic and social power over us: why should bars made of ink have the forbidding rigidity of steel? Wildness wriggles through, and ambles away. Or else the dangerous beast is converted to cuddly mildness, its claws and fangs retracted. This is what happened high on a wall in Bristol, where Banksy's *Mild Mild West* portrayed a squad of riot police behind shields dodging a Molotov cocktail gripped by a teddy bear: a joke about activism, not a call to arms. In another ingratiating pun, Banksy calls his seasonal pop-up shop Santa's Ghetto. Santa usually officiates in a grotto, but that suggests a cavern – the word derives from a Latin transcription of the Greek word for crypt – which might be less convivial than a like-minded ghetto.

Despite these whimsies, Banksy knows how to cause offence, or to call the bluff of power. Hence his image of Queen Victoria, crowned and with orb and sceptre in place as she bestrides a high-heeled lesbian courtier who is kissing her sovereign's pudenda, not her hand. His statue of a whorish Lady Justice, exhibited in a Clerkenwell square, was exactly copied from the original above the Old Bailey – though Banksy pulled up the figure's skirt to reveal thigh-high leather boots, a thong, and a garter belt into which, like a pole-dancer, she had stuffed a handful of dollar bills. He has also defamed the totems of classical art. The sculpture he modelled on Rodin's *Thinker* was identified on the pedestal as *The Drinker* and given a traffic cone to wear like a dunce's cap. His Mona Lisa, stencilled onto a wall in Soho in 2001, was a terrorist who shouldered a rocket launcher; almost immediately, a spoilsport painted on a beard and turban and disguised her as Osama bin Laden.

But Banksy's irony always muffles his effrontery. In Shoreditch he gave the swaggering black-suited gangsters from Quentin Tarantino's *Pulp Fiction* bananas not guns to carry. The fickle transformations of iconology have taught him not to trust any signs, even his own. Meanings are unstable, and anything can be painted over or reinterpreted. As Banksy has said, Andy Warhol duplicated popular icons 'until they became meaningless'. After that, curators of junk like Banksy's own accomplice and imitator Thierry Guetta – whose tag is Mister Brainwash – made the same objects 'really meaningless', excerpts from a culture of stale quotations. 'Maybe,' Banksy added, '[this] means that art is a bit of a joke.' In his case, art is indeed a practical joke, with Banksy as both winner and loser: the inflated prices his works fetch on the market show how capitalism co-opts and perhaps corrupts those who threaten it.

'Art' is an anagram of 'rat', and a rodent – whose expressive output is its droppings – often appears on Banksy's walls with a pencil or crayon in its fingers, having emerged from its underground lair to survey a city it may one day inherit. Although Banksy sympathizes with such subterranean skulkers, his admirers prefer to think of him evangelically descending from on high. His friend Robert Clarke first caught sight of him in a New York flophouse in 1995; it was like those moments in Hollywood biblical epics when the shadow of the saviour, whose face we are not permitted to see, falls on the ungodly. 'Lo and behold,' the quivering Clarke remembers, 'he was framed in the office door and a radiant light was coming off him.' In his book about Banksy, he goes on to say 'No, no really!', but the disclaimer does not entirely dispel the religiosity of the encounter. Banksy's art, for Clarke, is 'Godgiven and righteous', and it preaches to our brazen latter-day Belshazzars.

Sometimes he appears to this apostle in dreams, like Christ after his disappearance from the tomb. In one of Clarke's woozy reveries, Banksy 'writes an oath with his finger on the sacred ancestral stones' of a cromlech. In fact he did better than that, constructing a Stonehenge of his own and then dooming it to decay. This non-primordial monument cropped up in a field during the music festival at Glastonbury in 2007. Instead of the priestly circle of pillars on Salisbury Plain – an open-air temple, in which rituals were presumably performed – Banksy's *Boghenge* used dwarfish portaloos, his version of the cramped boxes in which festival-goers were supposed to relieve themselves. Unevenly positioned, half-buried in the grass, the grey crates meant to contain bodily waste were left behind when the festival ended; like the stumps of Babylon's capsized towers, they waited to be reabsorbed into the surrounding landscape. Graffiti added by local amateurs soon covered them with creepers, tendrils and gaudily fertile blooms. Culture was re-ingested by nature – or had nature been made redundant by a culture in which art recycles everything, even ordure?

THE MIND OF GOD?

Pondering the mystery of Einstein's brain, Barthes regretted that what people revered was its 'clockwork-like mechanisms' and its capacity to reduce knowledge to a formulaic equation, $E = mc^2$. To formalize its status as an inhuman engine, the brain was cut out of its owner's skull immediately after his death in 1955.

Barthes believed that Einstein himself, regarding his own intelligence as somehow alien or at least extractable, had bequeathed it for scientific study, and reported that rival hospitals began squabbling over the prize as soon as his will was read. The very idea of such a bequest dismayed Barthes, because it deprived the genius of magic powers that resemble those possessed by genies. Popular images of Einstein showed him scribbling labyrinthine equations on a blackboard: was his fabled mind only 'monstrous', Barthes asked, because it could perform recondite tricks with numbers? In fact Einstein had no wish to be anatomized and dissected. The sorry truth is that during an autopsy his brain was stolen by a renegade pathologist, who sliced it into 240 pieces which he kept in a cider carton stowed beneath a beer cooler in his basement in Wichita, Kansas.

At least the brain of Stephen Hawking is not reducible to a calculator; it remains monstrous in what Barthes might have thought of as the best sense – overdeveloped, abstruse, and, as Wordsworth said about Newton's mind, capable of 'voyaging through strange seas of thought,/ Alone'. Hawking's brain has had as its lifelong mission an attempt to understand how and why the universe came to exist, and thereby, as he says at the end of *A Brief History of Time*, to 'know the mind of God'. It has explored these cosmic conundrums while entombed inside a body wasted and immobilized by motor-neuron disease. 'The supermen of science-fiction,' Barthes remarked, 'always have something reified about them', and Hawking is the valiant product of just such a reification. Withering in his wheelchair, using the last unparalyzed muscles in his face to select letters and slowly piece them into words on a screen, then relying on a computer-synthesized voice to utter them, he is almost entirely robotic.

As yet, however, Hawking has not formulated the equation that was to serve as his vaunted 'theory of everything', so the conclusion of *A Brief History of Time* now echoes a little hollowly. Given his low opinion of our prospects on an earth we have damaged beyond repair, it's odd that he looked ahead in that wilfully confident climactic sentence to 'the triumph of human reason'. It's even odder that he then, in a final flourish, set science to eavesdrop on God's thinking, since he does not believe in any such divine intelligence. In his view, our planetary system exploded into life, and it will die when the heat bleeds out of it; we are not the favourites of a divine parent but a muddling, potentially suicidal species in an innocuous suburban galaxy.

The ancient Greeks, as Hawking says in *A Brief History of Time*, also saw no need for a creator. What he omits to add is that they had their myths, and Hawking has his as well: in fact, in his vocabulary, theory is a synonym for myth. Do wormholes or white dwarfs actually exist? Shortcuts through space and collapsed stars cannot be observed; they are conjectures, actualized by metaphor. A theory, as Hawking says, 'exists only in our minds and does not have any other reality (whatever that might mean)'. Accordingly he measures time using imaginary numbers not real ones, and when describing the habits of particles he places them 'in imaginary time'. 'Any physical theory,' he admits, 'is always provisional, in the sense that it is only a hypothesis: you can never prove it.' He qualifies his contention that 'time and space should be finite without boundary' as 'just a proposal', almost plucked out of the air because 'it cannot be deduced from some other principle' and 'may initially be put forward for aesthetic or metaphysical reasons'. Is he theorizing or fantasizing? If you reverse time, as these mental experiments do, you soon use history up and launch yourself backwards into what precedes it – and that is myth, our best way of comprehending or at least conceiving of origins.

The suppositions of Hawking and his colleagues about black holes, big bangs, event horizons and so on vividly picture scenes that are unviewable; the initial explosion even has an optional soundtrack. The narrative that the astrophysicists assemble from these primal scenes is more chaotic and fatalistic than Genesis – where a presiding mind obliterates darkness, shapes the void into form, and allows the grand structure to exist everlastingly – but it unfolds as a step-by-step subversion of the authorized story. Eddie Redmayne, who plays Hawking in the biopic *The Theory of Everything*, makes this competition with the Bible explicit when, for the benefit of an unscientific girlfriend, he defines cosmology as 'religion for intelligent atheists'.

Barthes saw Einstein's quest for ultimate knowledge as a gnostic exercise. He was working towards an equation that might be 'the magic formula of the world', a mathematical equivalent of the last, most esoteric universal law that would reconcile relativity with quantum mechanics; though he failed to produce it, this only confirmed the daring of his endeavour by preserving 'God's share', which remained unknowable. Hawking has whittled away God's stock. His grandest cogitations often turn out to be nihilistic practical jokes, less sublimely terrifying than Einstein's belated recognition – expressed in a wartime letter to President Roosevelt – that nuclear physics could destroy the world. There is no such frisson of trepidation and possible temptation in Hawking, because he sees the outcome as absurd. When he calculates that 'if one took all the heavy water in all the oceans of the world, one could build a hydrogen bomb that would compress matter at the centre so much that a black hole would be created', the cosmic jest has its punchline in the parenthesis that follows: '(Of course, there would be no one left to observe it!)'.

Hawking's universe is frail, ephemeral. One metaphor likens the dying stars to balloons imploding, and another invokes soap bubbles. Infinitude dwindles into a speck when Hawking muses about using a black hole to run multiple power stations, a fancied solution to our need for new energy sources. 'This would be rather difficult,' he says with a ghoulish chuckle, because 'the black hole would have the mass of a mountain compressed into less than a million millionth of an inch, the size of the nucleus of an atom!' The end of the game arrives in those exponentiating noughts, which nullify the universe all over again.

By contrast with Barthes' comment on Einstein the gnostic, failure does not come about simply because man's mental reach exceeds his grasp. Far from acknowledging divine omniscience, the row of zeros reflects our littleness and our moral fallibility. The idea of creativity, the noble folly of artists who are tantalized by God's generation of life, provokes one of Hawking's sourest jests. In his opinion, computer viruses are the sole proof we have so far given of our capacity to manufacture something that is autonomous, the uncontrollably vital offspring of our brains – and it is possible that a genetically engineered virus ordered to attack human bodies rather than electronic circuits could finish our species off. 'Maybe it says something about human nature,' Hawking has remarked, 'that the only form of life we have created so far is purely destructive. Talk about creating life in our own image.' We are worms or wriggling snakes, not the sapient beings who were put in charge of Eden.

In the 1951 science-fiction film *The Day the Earth Stood Still* Sam Jaffe plays a saintly facsimile of Einstein, with frizzy hair to suggest a buzzing cerebral cortex. He is called away from the blackboard on which he is chalking his runes and sent off to do God's work: a threatening ambassador from outer space has touched down in Washington, and it is the professor's task to broker an interplanetary peace. For Hawking there can be no such link between physics and religion (which probably means that no theory can cover everything). After the peroration in which he challenges the mind of God, he explains in an appendix to *A Brief History of Time* why Einstein edged the biblical God out of his universe.

Hawking then gives short biographical accounts of Galileo and Newton, two cosmologists whose God-given minds were housed in the bodies of unheroic, averagely faulty men. He emphasizes Galileo's embarrassing surrender to Catholic orthodoxy, and underlines Newton's 'talents for deviousness and vitriol', which led him to ruin the careers of competitors and write rave reviews of his own achievements under assumed names. Theories, Hawking says, sometimes contain 'a fatal flaw', and theorists, it might be added, are hardly immune. Hawking's first marriage broke up because his wife, as she said, tired of worshipping 'the ground under his wheelchair'. His second wife, hired as a nurse, had less interest in devout adoration, and in *The Theory of Everything* she is seen regaling Hawking with a montage of lascivious *Penthouse* pin-ups: he drools, giggles, and programmes his synthetic voice to announce 'I've been looking for a model of the universe and now I've found her!' In 2004 Hawking's daughter lamented that 'fame and money' had morally unsettled him. 'My brothers and I,' she recalled, 'were useful only to be shown off as beautiful blonde children, so he could be even more of a superstar.' And stardom, as Hawking knows better than anyone after having studied the lifespan of astral bodies, is a fizzy, overheated, unstable condition.

In Barthes' opinion, Einstein was posthumously demythologized. Hawking, however, has begun behaving mythologically – or perhaps monstrously – while still alive. He dematerialized into a hologram for an episode of *Star Trek*, and in a television sketch in 2015 he ordered his wheelchair to rear up into one of the Cybertrons from Michael Bay's film *Transformers* so that he could zap a prattling carer and a nun who objected to his atheism. Recently he combined narcissism and altruism by trademarking his image. Einstein wanted his body (brain included) to be cremated and the ashes secretly scattered, but Hawking is cannily making plans for his afterlife. He already appears on T-shirts, hoodies, mouse pads, laptop bags, coffee mugs, posters, jigsaws and a *Simpsons* action toy. A caricature of his body may well outlast the work his brain has done, so he quite reasonably seeks to share in the business of exploiting it.

Vitruvian Man was the measure of a universe in which he was central: in Leonardo da Vinci's diagram he reaches out to touch its extremities, which remain enclosed within a perfect circle. In Hawking's case the analogy between physiology and physics is very different. No longer promoting man to parity with the gods, he dramatizes our helpless insignificance in a modern universe that is drifting away from us. His account of his doctoral work, undertaken after he received the news that he was likely to be dead in two years, sounds like a self-diagnosis: 'in 1965 I read about Penrose's theory that any body undergoing gravitational collapse must eventually form a singularity'. He was able to reverse 'the direction of time in Penrose's theorem, so that the collapse became an expansion'; he also managed to extend the brief time the doctors allocated to him, but he could not arrest his gravitational collapse. We watch it happening in *The Theory of Everything*, where time's arrow is speeded up by prosthetics. False ears, kneecaps, shoulders and hands are successively fitted to Redmayne so that his head, arms and legs seem to wizen, leaving him crumpled and deflated in a wheelchair several sizes too large.

Hawking's wizard-like persona matches his Gothic or spectral cosmology. Taking over Paul Dirac's theory about the electron's partner, known as an anti-electron or positron, he gave it a shadowy, sinister inflection by declaring that 'every particle has an antiparticle, with which it can annihilate'. The verb is intransitive, though it soon becomes clear what the antiparticle intends to annihilate. 'There could,' Hawking surmised, 'be whole antiworlds and antipeople made out of antiparticles.' Foreseeing a danger, he warned, 'if you meet your antiself, don't shake hands! You would both vanish in a great flash of light.' He did meet his own doppelgänger, in the youthful, personable form of Eddie Redmayne, to whom he donated his croaking voice (though Redmayne, he joked, 'unfortunately did not inherit my good looks'). Was this extension of himself a man 'angelized' by technology – made 'disincarnate' and turned into software, as Marshall McLuhan hoped we would be in the electronic age – or 'a demon in a false body', which is how the blue people in James Cameron's science-fiction film *Avatar* refer to the digital soldiers with whom they do battle?

A handshake between self and antiself might have been awkward, but Hawking's encounter with Redmayne did produce a great flash of light – the sunburst that is known as cinema. As for whether they both vanished, it's more likely that self and antiself changed places. Hawking's less admirable traits – his reputed avarice and crankiness, his questionable record as a husband and father – disappeared in that dazzling moment, as did his cheerless atheism. When *The Theory of Everything* ends, he has vanished into the body of Redmayne, who smiles as his children run around in circles in a landscaped garden that resembles the universe before its patterned planetary orbits were dislocated by Galileo, Newton, Einstein and Hawking; paraphrasing God in Genesis on the seventh day, he says to his improbably devoted and forgiving first wife, 'Look at what we created.'

3 *In the Pantheon*

AN ALIEN FROM WINDSOR

The French, who killed their king and exiled their emperor, have ever since kept an envious eye on the British monarchy. Soon after the coronation of Elizabeth II, Barthes reported that his compatriots were 'pining for fresh news of royal activities'. In the absence of Windsor-related tittle-tattle, he supplied the need in his essay about a regal cruise around the Mediterranean in the summer of 1954. King Paul and Queen Frederica of Greece were the hosts, and the guests on their yacht *Agamemnon* included the Comte de Paris, the pretender to the French throne, and Umberto II of Italy (who had been barred from setting foot in the country he regarded as his realm, and therefore had to be picked up in Corfu not Naples, where the voyage began). Among the hundred other passengers was Infante Juan Carlos of Spain, who met his future wife, a Greek princess, on board.

At Versailles before 1789, kings and queens amused themselves by masquerading as peasants and milkmaids; on the Greek yacht, these relics of defunct or expiring dynasties spent ten days impersonating bourgeois holidaymakers. Visiting Santorini, they rode on donkeys rather than in golden coaches. Courtly decorum was waived, except for a ban on bikinis. Barthes, who took for granted the death of God, was able to gloat over another demise: the trip demonstrated the fate of that ancient, semi-sacred being he called 'the God-King'. King Paul had evidently forgotten that Agamemnon was a murdered monarch.

But the obituary for royalty was premature. Only a year before, Elizabeth II had been seated in state in Westminster Abbey, handed an orb and sceptre, and anointed with holy oil by an archbishop. During the ceremony, she appeared to be in a mystical trance, enskied not merely enthroned. Impersonated by Helen Mirren in Peter Morgan's play *The Audience*, the Queen tells two of her astonished prime ministers – politicians whose temporary power depends on a mandate from voters, not the superstition of worshippers – what the occasion meant. In one of her weekly audiences with Gordon Brown, she refers to the coronation as a consecration 'in God's house', and she informs the startled John Major that 'God's *will*' awarded sovereignty to her. Later in the play she again invokes her divine protector when Major announces his government's intention to decommission her yacht. Coming soon after the fire at Windsor Castle in 1992, this must have struck the Queen as a final insult. On board *Britannia*, she could indulge the illusion that she ruled the waves. When she forfeited that allegorical vessel, she seemed to be shrivelling into one of the washed-up retirees on board the *Agamemnon* – has-beens crammed onto what Barthes in his essay described first as a 'modern Ark where the main variations of the monarchic species are preserved', then as a reservation that keeps the remaining Sioux Indians corralled as an 'ethnographic curiosity'.

In an irritable moment in Morgan's play, the Queen tells Major, 'I am the Crown'. Before the coronation, she needed much rehearsal to ensure that she could walk while wearing the onerous headpiece, like a model taking deportment lessons with a book balanced on her head. Now it has grown into place and, thanks to her adamantine helmet of tightly permed white hair, she looks as if she has it on even when she is bareheaded. Annie Leibovitz, arriving with her troop of eleven assistants at Buckingham Palace for a portrait session in 2007, glimpsed the Queen's sense of divine entitlement when she made the mistake of suggesting a decoronation. Leibovitz fancied photographing her on horseback in the state apartments, but had to make do with the Queen at floor level wearing the robes of the Order of the Garter. When the sitting began, she tried to warm up her wary subject by marvelling that she did her own hair and make-up, rather than requiring the team of *Vanity Fair* stylists who might have fluffed up her cast-iron curls and thinned out the mask of powder on her unamused face. Leibovitz next asked the Queen to remove her tiara, saying that she would look 'less dressy' without the 'crown'. Princess Diana, who knew that her position was a role that required an appropriate costume, would have understood the request: sending a Victor Edelstein gown to be auctioned for charity, Diana remarked, 'When I put this on, I actually felt like a princess.' But the Queen bridled at the suggestion. 'Less dressy?' she shrilled. 'What do you think this *is*?' Imagine the Statue of Liberty's reaction if a stylist had said, 'Honey, let's lose the torch.' The Queen then let out a cackle like the rat-tat-tat of a firing squad. She was not just wearing clothes; her costume invested her with authority, perhaps with holiness.

Such haughty reactions are rare, perhaps reserved for upstarts from the republic across the ocean: the Queen also scowled when George W. Bush, formally welcoming her to the White House, remembered that she had paid a previous visit to the United States in 1776. Americans, after all, not content with rejecting monarchy, have made free with its titular flummery. Michael Jackson reigned as the King of Pop, Queen Latifah is a sassy, buxom rapper, and the platform-heeled singer Prince is, in his own estimation, a princeling. Those appropriations must annoy a family whose privileges actually depend on the same onomastic magic. Prince Edward, for instance, was due to be renamed Duke of Cambridge when he married, but wheedled to be made Earl of Wessex instead. The earldom was a pure invention, presiding over a region that could be found on no map: Edward – once fondly dubbed Barbara Windsor or 'Babs' by his theatrical chums, in homage to the squealing *Carry On* actress who now impersonates the first Queen Elizabeth in advertisements for online bingo – came across it in the cast list of the film *Shakespeare in Love*. He persuaded his mother to pluck it out of the air and confer it on him. Legitimacy is insecure if it depends on such conceits.

The cruellest humiliation meted out to the divorced Diana was to revoke her designation as Her Royal Highness, as if some transformative spell resided in the abbreviation HRH. While married, she was officially known as The Princess of Wales; divorced, she became Diana, Princess of Wales. Her head could not be cut off like Anne Boleyn's, so she was deprived of her definite article and its punctilious capital, while a comma reduced her title to an afterthought. She retaliated by crowning herself 'queen of hearts', without capital letters – not the murderous matriarch who issues orders to the axeman in *Alice in Wonderland* but the nation's agony aunt, absorbing sympathy from her admirers and redistributing it to the needy.

In her television address the night before Diana's funeral in 1997, the Queen had to remind the fractious masses that she was 'your Queen'.

With the tabloids orchestrating discontent and accusing her of cold-heartedness, it sounded like a call to order, issued to the lachrymose mob seen over her shoulder outside the gates of Buckingham Palace, and she went on to enjoin the crowds to be 'British' – meaning cowed and respectful – on the morrow. All the same, I wonder about the ambiguity of that possessive pronoun. If she is our Queen, then it is we who own her. In *The Audience*, the elderly Queen warns her friskier adolescent self about the constitutional contract: 'They just expect you to do exactly as they want,' she says. It is the complaint of a divinity who on occasion must wish she were not the object of so much fervent belief and submissive adoration.

Mentally inaccessible, the Queen is also in theory physically untouchable. 'I did but see her passing by,' said Robert Menzies, the Australian prime minister, 'and yet I love her till I die.' Quoting Thomas Ford, a minor sixteenth-century versifier, Menzies adopted the persona of a courtly lover: professing spurious emotions about an astral beloved, he expected no reciprocation. In 1992 another Australian prime minister, Paul Keating, was accused of lèse-majesté – the wounding of majesty – when he gently placed his hand on the Queen's back to guide her through the throng at a reception. Did anyone expect that she would slap Keating's face, or even react with a slight shudder as does Helen Mirren, again on duty in Stephen Frears's film *The Queen*, when she wipes her ungloved hand after Tony Blair kneels and over-literally kisses it? Despite manhandling by Keating and a sisterly squeeze from Michelle Obama, who stooped from a teetering height to give her a cuddle in 2009, the Queen's aura remains intact, reinforced by our reverence.

She is obliged to be as fixed and stable as the profile that stamps value on the coins and banknotes of her realm. Icons are usually inanimate, like the carved Madonnas carried through the streets on festive days in Spain and Italy. The Queen does her best to be a votive object, a grudgingly mobilized sculpture, especially now that, aged ninety, she proceeds with slow, stern implacability through the routines that fill up her year. She functions as a sign, which for preference is non-verbal: the words she speaks – the dreary governmental agenda recited at the opening of every parliamentary session, the Christmas broadcast, even that supposedly heartfelt tribute to Diana – are usually written by others. When unscripted, she confines herself to banal small talk. Without needing to read Barthes, she has become an expert semiotician, a transmitter of speaking looks: a glance, a politely dismissive nod, sometimes a fixed glare, and on very rare occasions a wordless noise. When David Cameron told her the results of the referendum on Scottish independence in 2014, she retained her neutrality by responding, as he indiscreetly reported, with a feline purr. In 2009 she even gruffly barked, to express her opinion of Silvio Berlusconi's obstreperous shouting at a G20 photocall.

'I have to be seen to be believed,' the Queen apparently remarked when stipulating that she must be visible when out in public: seen, that is, not heard, like a well-drilled Victorian child. Hence the picture windows of the cars she travels in, and the slow, stately pace – nine miles an hour, sometimes only three – maintained by her drivers. Hence also the clothes she wears, which are semaphore by other means: ensembles of blockish colour, with matching dresses, coats, hats and gloves, to ensure that she can be identified at a distance like a traffic signal. Understandably enough, Rolf Harris spent one of the portrait sittings he was granted in 2005 painting her dress not her face. The Queen remarked that she could have sent the garment on a hanger and saved herself the bother of turning up.

During his sessions at Buckingham Palace, Harris did his best to get a rise out of the Queen, wondering as he flicked his brushes whether he might slosh paint over her – not the wounding but the splattering of majesty, arguably a more heinous crime. At one point he asked whether she minded the smell of turpentine. The Queen, unacquainted with its resinous stink, hovered between wariness and menace: 'Well, we'll tell, won't we, soon?' she replied. She got through the sittings unscathed, but Harris's banter – about pets relieving themselves on the carpet and the stench of dissected horses in the studio of the equine painter Stubbs – flirted with indelicacy, and his initial efforts, which had to be painted over, hinted at caricature: he afflicted the Queen with the buck teeth of the *Spitting Image* puppet, and admitted that the coarse, muddy face which first appeared on his canvas should have belonged to 'a pork butcher from Norwich'.

Caricaturists have made valiant efforts to unsettle the Queen's unblinking rigour, like tourists teasing a statuesque mime on a pedestal in Covent Garden or Trafalgar Square. The *Spitting Image* puppet afflicted her with a bulbous nose, a shelving lower lip, a mouth swollen as if by Botox, equine teeth and a chin that sagged into slack folds. In 2012 Banksy joked about royal eugenics by giving the Queen the face of a scowling chimpanzee, adorned as usual with crown, earrings and a spangly necklace: an ape is here the mother of us all, with only jewellery to distance her from the jungle. He has also depicted her in profile as on a postage stamp, but he adds a gas mask that gives her what looks like a pig's snout or, more kindly, the elongated head of a horse. As worn by riot police, the mask signals depersonalization and oppression, and it implicates the Queen in a charade that conceals raw, ruthless power. Yet the joke cannot harm its victim: under the mask, the Queen's actual face is another mask, impenetrable and impervious.

In Alan Bennett's *A Question of Attribution*, an investigator quizzing the Soviet informer Anthony Blunt – then respectably installed at court as Keeper of the Queen's Pictures – asks, 'What's she really like?' It is a pointless question: as a nonpareil, she is only like herself, and metaphor rebounds from her august presence. Unlike the devious Blunt, Bennett's Queen never betrays herself, or anyone else. In a discussion of portraiture that doubles as a commentary on Blunt's other career as a spy, she speculates about the secret selves of the characters in her portrait gallery, then adds, 'I don't know that one has a secret self, though it's generally assumed that one has.' Her habit of speaking impersonally – 'One likes to know what one's doing,' she says, or, in a reference to chicken, 'One has just had it for lunch' – renders her opaque: I in this case truly is another. Blunt, at once obsequious and subtly impudent, replies, 'The only person who doesn't have a secret self, Ma'am, is God.' Surely she is not as po-faced as the deity?

On her own initiative, the Queen joked about her sanctity at the opening of the London Olympics. She allowed an effigy of herself to parachute from a helicopter into the arena, accompanied by Daniel Craig's James Bond (who this time actually was On Her Majesty's Secret Service). To use two sceptical terms coined by Shakespeare in his history plays, a king or queen is 'monarchized' or 'royalized' by our consent or obeisance. For the Queen, the vertical transit moves in the opposite direction: she floats down from on high and, from behind a barricade, smiles on her subjects as she hands their floral offerings to an attendant.

Despite that landing in the Olympic stadium, her exact status remains indeterminate. Rewriting the national anthem, the Sex Pistols asked God to save the Queen because 'She ain't no human being'. In 2015, interviewed by *The New York Times*, Helen Mirren called the royal family 'aliens', exempt from the nuisances that make us human by collectivizing us: they have never had to stand in a queue, and when they drive down the street the traffic is stopped to let them through.

Barthes referred to the God-King, and Gore Vidal, pondering the American presidency, switched the compound back to front and described the incumbent as a 'man-god'. President Kennedy's 'death in public' reminded Vidal of the sacrifices staged by primitive tribes, when victims were slaughtered to ensure that the crops grew. Why does a state need a head? Only so that it can be chopped off to cancel the whole ornate imposture. A republic is supposed to dispense with personification: according to the Latin etymology, it should consist of 'public things', the aggregate of us all. In Morgan's play the Queen calls herself 'a tribal leader in eccentric costume' and reveals that among her titles is Kotoku, 'the White Heron', Paramount Chief of Fiji. Pacific islands lack written constitutions, so perhaps as Kotoku she was a candidate for some regicidal rite; Fiji in any case is now a republic. In Frears's film she grieves over the killing of a Highland stag, a top-heavily antlered sacrificial beast that she sees as a kindred spirit, like the 'monarch of the Glen' in Landseer's painting. Once at least, the memory of the guillotine seemingly perturbed the actual Queen. At a preview of a Buckingham Palace exhibition in 2011, she was overheard protesting when she saw a decapitated mannequin wearing the Duchess of Cambridge's wedding dress. She called it 'horrid', then 'horrible'; a veil and tiara floating in the air above where the head should have been struck her as 'creepy', as if she were confronting the ghost of Marie Antoinette.

Barthes was astonished that 'our kings', as he put it, clung to their 'mythical character' in a secular age. The Queen, however, has camouflaged herself in ordinariness. She leaves swank to the likes of David and Victoria Beckham, who once dressed in gaudy regalia and perched on gilded chairs to receive the homage of guests at a party in their Hertfordshire mansion, nicknamed Beckingham Palace. Roger Allam, playing the Queen's private secretary in the Frears film, hesitantly outlines the guest list for Diana's funeral, which includes 'actors of stage and screen and other … celebrities'. He pauses for a muted grimace before whispering the last, vulgar word. Mirren acidly purses her lips, while Sylvia Syms, cast as the Queen Mother, asks with quavery-voiced disbelief, 'Celebrities?', like Lady Bracknell querying the propriety of a handbag as a birthplace. Documentary footage later shows Tom Cruise and Nicole Kidman, Tom Hanks and Steven Spielberg – people Diana had met on receiving lines but regarded as her peers because they were fellow luminaries – entering Westminster Abbey for the service. This flashy new aristocracy, regularly topped up by exhibitionists from reality shows, has ousted the dowdy ancestral establishment, and there may be historical justice in that. Royal personages are revered automatically, for no other reason than that they took the trouble to be born. Celebrities are admired because they are beautiful and perhaps even talented; they stop short of attributing their advantages to God's will, and can be replaced whenever we tire of them.

Barthes ended his essay about the pretenders holidaying on the Greek yacht with a sideswipe at Juan Carlos, then apprenticed to Generalissimo Franco. He warned that such upstarts, 'confident of their restored divinity', might tamper with democracy by 'engaging in politics'. In fact, not long after his coronation Juan Carlos salvaged democracy in Spain by thwarting a military coup, but those words are still worth remembering, especially in view of the debate about Prince Charles's opinionated memos to Cabinet ministers. Are we ready for the succession, or reconciled to it? Perhaps *The Audience* – revived in the West End in 2015 with Kristin Scott Thomas while Mirren was appearing in it on Broadway – should have been called

The Audition, since the Queen's imitators are multiplying: her teenage self has also been reincarnated in a film about the night she spent out on the town incognito on VE Day in 1945. If we must be deprived of her, what we want is a facsimile, not a more biologically authentic heir.

AIR FORCE ONE × 2

Power refuses to think in binary terms: at its most single-minded, it demands priority and pre-eminence, and ignores whatever might be second best. For that reason, a monopolistic numeral identifies Air Force One. Hardly a first among equals, the presidential plane is one of a kind. Like the country whose head of state it carries, it is exceptional, and exceptions are always made for it by air-traffic controllers, who instantly clear it for take-off or landing. Here is America with wings, avian as well as aeronautical, capable of out-flying the beaked, pinioned eagle – a predator with twin bundles of olive branches and spiky arrows clutched in its claws – that appears on the Great Seal of the United States.

Until 1943, when Franklin Roosevelt flew to Casablanca for a wartime conference, the American presidency was a desk job, tethered to Washington DC. During the Cold War it became a global office, and Air Force One makes that universality manifest. The first President Bush, who commissioned the current double-decker version of the plane to replace the humbler 707 he inherited from Ronald Reagan, remarked in a *National Geographic* documentary that Air Force One projects the 'majesty' of the United States around the world. A Freudian slip, surely – republics should be unmajestic, and this one was meant to be the paradise of the common man – but it told the truth. Housed at Joint Base Andrews in a fortified hangar that the documentary describes as a 'sanctuary', guarded by snipers and sniffer dogs, Air Force One is evidence of dominance and intimidation, hierarchy and exclusion; it symbolizes pomp not populism. In a competing assertion of spiritual power, the Alitalia plane used by the Pope has been given the call sign Shepherd One, which does not induce the same awed reaction. Good shepherds should keep watch over their flocks at ground level, not half a mile above it. Fighter jets, rockets and satellites crowd our contemporary sky, and leave no room for divine emissaries.

Acknowledging that the American republic expanded after 1945 into a permanently embattled empire, Air Force One is a flying bunker, kept ready for the prosecution of war. Every flight is classified as a military mission, even if the president is on a trip to raise campaign funds; itineraries are planned by military aides at the White House, who nominate 'contingency hospitals' in each city visited. There is an operating table on board, discreetly stowed away like a Murphy bed, and the *National Geographic* documentary reports that the Secret Service when travelling always 'packs enough fire power for a small army'. Even the sedentary, earthbound experience offered by the film is edged with alarm. 'Share now in a rare privilege,' says the grave-voiced narrator. 'Ride this plane.' Of course we never will, but what would come close to such an experience? Being pummelled by g-forces on a roller coaster – or maybe playing a video game, which might enable us to discover whether Air Force One has the capacity, so far unused, to discharge missiles as well as to dodge them, and whether it really can withstand a nuclear blast.

Although the founding fathers would not have approved, this is the incumbent's triumphal chariot. For extra effect, President Lyndon B. Johnson installed a leather 'king chair' on board his version of Air Force One, with a hydraulic lift that enabled him – though he was already six feet four inches tall – to hover in mid-air as he harangued the congressmen whom he invited into his cabin. When Johnson's flight back to Texas touched down after Richard Nixon's inauguration in 1969, he insisted on removing his throne, along with the monogrammed towels in the bathroom. In the republic over which Johnson had presided, some things were definitely not public, whereas others, which ought to have remained zipped up in privacy, were selectively exposed to public view: he often invited colleagues at adjacent urinals in the US Capitol to admire his penis, which he nicknamed 'Jumbo' – an organ as elephantine as a 747. More wistful than boastful, Barack Obama said, 'The plane is really nice' in a speech to donors during his re-election campaign in the summer of 2012. 'It really is,' he went on, counting the years or perhaps months that remained before he would have to resume taking commercial flights. 'It's a great plane.'

Symbolism aggrandizes the individual. Ever since the 1960s, the American president has been described as 'the most powerful man in the world', even though fortunately none of those to hold the office – a succession of tricky fixers, slippery philanderers, blunderers and waiverers – have availed themselves of the power invested in the box of nuclear codes that accompanies them everywhere. How then can their power be made manifest? American presidents often jog to demonstrate their fitness, though they are seldom seen doing anything more strenuous: not for them Vladimir Putin's bare-chested horseback riding, or the sessions of judo in which he sends opponents crashing onto the mat. A president's best chance of being physically impressive is in bounding optimistically down the stairs as he leaves Air Force One. The height and the steep angle of those treacherous stairs prove that the presidency is a heady, perhaps hubristic office: after the Messiah-like proclamations of inauguration day, the alternatives are a tragic fall or a comic tumble. In 1975 in rainy Salzburg, Gerald Ford skidded on a wet step at the bottom of the stairs and landed on the tarmac with a thump, forcing his wife to shelter him with an umbrella while a military official hauled him upright.

Air Force One is a metaphor – literally so, because metaphors are transporters, agents of metamorphosis. A metaphor consists of tenor and vehicle: a subject borrows the attributes of an object, as when Shelley likens a skylark to a high-born maiden in a palace tower. In the case of Air Force One, tenor and vehicle remain incommensurate. The plane borrows America's attributes – its size, its might, its technological supremacy – but can any president dare borrow those attributes from the plane? It may be dangerous to invest it with such a heroic identity, rather than letting it be a vehicle in the most humdrum sense, a mere means of transport.

In fact, Air Force One's solitary integer is misleading. Nothing exists alone: the president has a deputy, a vice-president who is ready in case of need, and his plane has a duplicate, a twin which, to preserve the myth of autonomy, cannot be called Air Force Two. The planes are both known as Air Force One – or rather one of them assumes that call sign after it is boarded by the incumbent. To clarify matters, he presumably changes into a nylon flight jacket on which the aquiline presidential coat of arms is surmounted by stitched letters that remind him where he is by spelling out 'Air Force One'.

The stand-by plane is at best a proof of American superfluity and at worst, like the vice-president, an insurance against mishaps. In the event of technical embarrassments, another personification of the United States of America – the words are printed along the plane's side, above a Nike-like flash that perhaps represents blue-sky thinking, the national creed – can always trundle into view, five storeys tall and a city block long (or, in some more enthusiastic descriptions, six storeys tall and as a long as a football field).

So far, George W. Bush is probably the only president to have used both planes on a single journey. At Thanksgiving in 2003 he flew to Baghdad, where he spent two and a half hours posing for photographs as he dished out portions of turkey to the troops who were fighting his war. To ensure that the trip remained a secret, he had established an alibi by retreating to his ranch in Texas, supposedly to spend the holiday with his family. The night before Thanksgiving, he travelled back to Washington on the first Air Force One – though it was not called Air Force One on this initial leg, which the logbook described as a routine trip home for maintenance, because the president was pretending not to be on board. The second plane was waiting in a hangar at Joint Base Andrews, fuelled and provisioned for the onward flight to Baghdad. Bush entered it by the back stairs, disguised by a baseball cap. That skulking between planes, the brim of his cap pulled far down, was an odd manoeuvre and very unlike his usual strutting: he was playing a game of hide and seek with his two Air Force Ones, and duplication hinted at duplicity, surely unworthy of a warrior chieftain.

The *National Geographic* documentary admits that Air Force One has an 'Achilles heel'. The metaphor does not refer to some chink in the plane's armour, like the heel of the great warrior that was vulnerable because his mother Thetis held him by it when she protectively dipped him in the Styx, leaving one spot on his body defenceless against the poisoned arrow that eventually killed him. The plane's weakness is an absence not a defect. Despite its battery of technology, it lacks the means to make the airborne president visible to those he is supposed to protect. On the morning of 9/11, after being bundled aboard his plane in Sarasota, Florida, Bush had to land in Louisiana to tape a speech for broadcast on television. Explaining his cross-country digressions before he returned to Washington in the evening, he later said that he did not want to give America's enemies the satisfaction of killing him. Except for his touchdown in Louisiana, he spent the rest of the day either up in a sky that had been emptied of other planes or, when he stopped at a nuclear bunker at Offutt in Nebraska, deep underground – omniscient because invisible, or running for cover?

Although the presidential plane only flies when the commander-in-chief is on board, he is of course not in command. When Obama boarded Air Force One for the first time, travelling from Chicago to Washington, he shook the hand of the pilot and complimented him for looking the part, 'like Sam Shepard in *The Right Stuff*': in the film of Tom Wolfe's book, Shepard as Chuck Yeager breaks the sound barrier while remaining laconic, nonchalant and down to earth. Actually, the pilot who flies Air Force One is nicknamed Top Gun for the duration of his time in the cockpit; it's lucky that the new president was greeted by a Shepard lookalike rather than a clone of Tom Cruise, who plays the hepped-up naval aviator known as 'Maverick' in Tony Scott's film *Top Gun*. Obama's offhand remark was charmingly deferential, yet in retrospect a little troublesome. Did he realize that the power he had assumed was a masquerade, a performance that might be better left to movie actors?

Wolfgang Petersen's film *Air Force One*, released in 1997, sought to repair another breach in the national myth by making its fictitious president worthy of the plane, on which he even doubles as pilot. Harrison Ford plays President Marshall, who flew combat helicopters in Vietnam and was awarded the Presidential Medal of Honor for valour in battle by one of his predecessors; his name suggests martial prowess as well as anticipating the air marshalls who after 9/11 began to travel on civilian flights, guns at the ready. This militarizing of the office occurs as well in Roland Emmerich's *Independence Day*. President Whitmore, played by the not particularly strapping Bill Pullman, is a former Gulf War pilot who, after escaping on Air Force One when aliens aim a death ray at the White House, re-enlists and flies on a combat mission against an extraterrestrial foe. Samuel L. Jackson as President Moore in the 2014 film *Big Game* has fewer resources. He is twice forcibly ejected from Air Force One when terrorists shoot it down – once in an evacuation pod and again after he returns to hide in the wreckage, in an ejector seat. He has to be saved by a Finnish boy who is out hunting deer. *Big Game* was produced in Finland, and has no interest in flattering America. On the film's poster, the president and the boy stand back to back as Air Force One crashes in flames behind them. The young hunter gets ready to fire off an arrow from his bow; the politician, unarmed and still dressed in his business suit, tries to look sturdy and self-possessed, though his tie flaps excitedly in the wind whipped up by the crashing plane – not quite a substitute for the flaunting American flag.

Such indignities are ruled out in Petersen's *Air Force One*. Here the plane is taken over by hijackers from Kazakhstan during the return flight to Washington from Moscow, where Marshall has just inconveniently made a speech in which he vows never to negotiate with terrorists. He can hardly renege on this undertaking, even though his wife and daughter are on board; he therefore fights, not by remote control as commanders-in-chief usually do when they authorize the use of smart bombs and drones, but with his fists, the furniture, and a machine gun. He kills one terrorist with his bare hands in a galley walled with a glass cabinet of refrigerated soft drinks: here – augmented by some cartons of Budweiser stacked in the baggage hold, on which the camera pauses for an idyllic moment of product placement – is the American cornucopia he has sworn to defend. Politics and pugilism join forces again, and Marshall both regains control of Air Force One and rehabilitates the United States, which ever since Vietnam, according to jingoists, has been held to ransom by ideological crazies from cockamamie countries.

Marshall begins as the kind of president any of us might like to be, treating the executive branch and its perks as a licence to daydream. On the way to the airport in wintry Moscow, he suggests a whimsical detour on the way home: 'Let's go to Barbados'. Here, in theory, is true power, unhindered by responsibility or the need to court public opinion. Even after the hijacking, this imaginary president sometimes behaves as if he were an absolute monarch, distributing honours and appointments like party favours. A secretary points out that he can still send a message back to the White House by fax, since it's only the plane's voice lines that have been disabled by the terrorists. 'If this works,' Marshall tells her, 'you get to be Postmaster General!' It's no surprise that Donald Trump, demagogically campaigning in 2015, cited 'Harrison Ford on the plane' as his ideal president. Ford's reply after hearing the accolade was scornful, sad and more than a little anxious. 'Donald,' he said, 'it was a movie! It's not like this in real life – but how would you know?'

Air Force One also notices the insubstantiality of the office, which depends on verbal spells, oaths and ceremonial reminders. To keep his eavesdropping subordinates in the White House informed, Marshall recites a synopsis of the plot so far to one of the terrorists, his voice raised to reach a cell phone secreted in his pocket. 'Listen to me, you know who I am, I'm the President of the United States,' he says. He is announcing this for the benefit of the Cabinet members in the situation room at home, and perhaps for his own benefit as well. The terminology is solemn and sacred, which is why the terrorist Korshunov, played by Gary Oldman, sneeringly deploys it in full: 'We now hold hostage the President of the United States of America,' he tells the vice-president. During a bout of fisticuffs near an open cargo door, Marshall tumbles out of the plane and briefly flaps about in limbo, clutching the fuselage with one frantic hand. A loyal aide, played by William H. Macy, begs the terrorist's permission to drag his boss back inside: 'Let me save him, he's our president for God's sake!' He is allowed to hold the metaphor together by reuniting tenor and vehicle, but the desperation of his plea is telling. Is it only appearances that he wants to salvage? God is already dead, so why should the president expect to survive? The urgency of the appeal may derive from the fact that the vice-president, waiting at the White House to take over, is a woman – Glenn Close, coiffed for the role in a wig that Benjamin Franklin might have worn.

Macy's exclamation suggests that although the man being buffeted in mid-air is mortal, the office he holds makes him a demigod. The presidency is a myth: like Shakespeare's hollow crown, it consists of form with variable content, or with no content at all. It sheds its expendable, fixed-term incumbents, and in the same way Air Force One is successively depleted or emptied of meaning throughout the film. A pod that ought to contain the president is released; fuel is dumped; staff members queue at the cargo door and float away on parachutes. Dean Stockwell plays a Secretary of Defence who has his own reading of the constitution, and prefers to sacrifice the plane and the current president rather than making concessions that might allow a resurgence of the Soviet empire. 'The presidency is bigger than any one man,' he tells a more humane sceptic. 'Didn't they teach you that at Yale?'

Reverse the proposition and it logically follows that the one man is smaller than the presidency. It's startling to see how roughly Marshall is handled by the Secret Service when the first shots are fired on the plane. They grab him and hurl him out of range, treating him like an inert bundle, just as on 9/11 they stormed into Vice-President Cheney's office, scooped him up under both arms and ran with him to a bunker. When, hidden in the baggage compartment, President Marshall finds the cell phone that allows him to call home to alert the Cabinet, he is suddenly disempowered, reduced to impotence in the absence of assistants or underlings to execute his orders. He can't even remember the White House phone number, and has to obtain it from directory information; when he places the call to 1600 Pennsylvania Avenue and identifies himself to the switchboard operator, she thinks he's a crank, yawns, 'Get a life', and refuses to put him through. Is he, like Harrison Ford, merely a meta-president?

His vice-president would prefer it if he hadn't tried so hard to live up to the aura of the indomitable office, and she is shocked when told that he has stayed on the plane rather than bailing out in the pod. Such courage is unconstitutional: 'He has no right to take chances with his life,' she says. A president who wants to be an action hero has almost committed an impeachable offence. She would probably also have disapproved of his decision not to escape by parachute when he had the chance. His wife and daughter are being held hostage on board, and he says 'I won't go without my family' – a monarchical scruple, and a misinterpretation of his role.

The fictitious Marshall is an even more recklessly existential president than Kennedy, whose brinkmanship during the Cuban missile crisis excited Norman Mailer. Marshall orders his escort of F15 bombers to fire at Air Force One, confident that the plane will resist the impact but wanting to create shockwaves that will help him in his battle with the hijackers. Luckily myth can suture contradictions together, so the gung-ho Marshall is simultaneously exceptional and ordinary, propulsively airborne and grounded in the tame suburbs. George W. Bush relied on a baseball cap to transform him into an innocuous nobody when he commuted between Air Force Ones on his way from Texas to Baghdad; as proof of his own humdrum Americanism, Marshall takes his baseball glove along on his diplomatic journey to Russia, and when he boards the plane for the homebound trip he settles down to watch a videotaped World Series game. The chief terrorist sarcastically informs the White House that he is holding hostage Marshall's family, his staff, his classified papers and – most shamingly of all – his baseball glove. Such insults cannot be tolerated: the glove is at once switched from a green signal to a red one, from a signifier that evokes summer afternoons, the little league and hot dogs in the park to a signal that makes sport a rehearsal for war. A general in the situation room bristles. 'The President,' he vows, 'will get back his baseball glove and play catch with this guy's balls.'

A last showdown in the cargo bay settles the matter. The leader of the terrorists is wearing his parachute, ready to jump off as Air Force One lunges out of control. Marshall activates the parachute and yells 'Get off my plane!' as if a hijacker were simply a passenger without a valid ticket. A strap from the cargo net happily breaks the intruder's neck; Marshall watches his corpse spiral into oblivion. One more semiotic emergency remains. With failing engines, a ruptured fuel tank and a damaged rudder, Air Force One cannot be landed – surely a defeat for the country with which the plane is synonymous? But Marshall restores national honour: attached to a zip-line, he is yanked upwards towards a hovering Hercules aircraft, which is comfortingly named Liberty 24. He manages the feat alone, rather than being cradled like a baby in the arms of a rescuer, as his wife and daughter were; virile and self-sufficient, he still honourably embodies America.

Air Force One, however, ditches, splits apart, and dives head first into the Caspian Sea. The vehicle can be allowed to founder, because the tenor, only a little the worse for wear after two hours of fisticuffs, remains intact. With the president on board, the pilot of the Hercules sends out the message that Liberty 24 is now Air Force One. The succession is technological: the plane is dead, long live the plane.

JUDY AND JUSTITIA

Here is a choice between paired allegories of justice, not quite equally balanced. On the one hand, a serene Roman goddess; on the other, a wisecracking Jewish grandmother. In London, a bronze angel balances on the globe above the Old Bailey; in Los Angeles, a tiny animated statuette presides in a television studio. The Romans imagined Justitia to be a woman because her gender guaranteed that the law's exactions would be tempered by solicitude and emotional insight. Is Judith Sheindlin – who has been crankily adjudicating petty squabbles between litigants on her daytime show *Judge Judy* since 1996, and who now earns close to $50 million a year for her injudicious grimaces and sarcastic put-downs – a legitimate descendant of the matron with a blindfold over her eyes and the scales and upraised sword in her evenly equilibrated hands?

Sartorially, there is a tenuous connection. Justice atop the Old Bailey wears a long dress, and Judge Judy, in the opening credits for her show, stands on a pedestal wearing a white ball gown – even though her usual costume for a day in court is a pair of slacks covered up by a black lawyer's robe, out of which peeps a quaint, dainty, primly starched lace collar.

In our first brief glimpse of Judge Judy as a statue, she does hold the customary symbolic trays with their balanced weights, which in her case are definitely not kitchen scales: she brags that she has not cooked food in twenty-seven years. No sword is visible, perhaps because its job of hewing and slicing is done by Judge Judy's razor-edged tongue. In place of the weapon, she grips an illuminated globe, as if she had borrowed the planetary sphere beneath Justice at the Old Bailey and switched on a light inside it. Another iconographic substitution explains why the sword has become a bulb. No sooner do we see Judge Judy – smiling with uncharacteristic sweetness as she beckons us into her presence – than our gaze is shifted sideways to the blue-tinted sculptural face of the Statue of Liberty, crowned with forbidding spikes: the light in Judge Judy's hand is an allusion to the torch held up by the statue in New York harbour to enlighten and admonish the world.

It's a strained compliment, because Judge Judy is hardly a libertarian and takes a dim view of the wretched human refuse that has washed up on her country's shores. She regularly moans, 'This is some good America' as she denounces welfare cheats and other parasites who misappropriate the taxes the government extorts from her, or use their welfare cheques to pay for visits to a tattoo parlour; such sentiments explain why excerpts from her shows crop up so often on conservative websites, where they serve as parables about the shiftlessness of the underclass. 'If I were running this nuthouse,' she sometimes opines when considering the state of the nation, 'we'd build more jails.' The Statue of Liberty has a stern face, but her message is a welcome to all. Judge Judy, on the other hand, calls herself 'an ecumenical abuser', equalizing the transgressors who stand before her when she upbraids them as deadbeats, losers, lowlifes, grifters, hustlers, punks, scammers, addicts, slobs, pigs, bums, idiots and morons. 'Whaddaya want from me?' is a recurrent line, delivered with an indifferent shrug. 'I'm not here to make you smart,' she adds when rebuking someone who has been hoodwinked. For a while she advised plaintiffs whose cases she dismissed to consult a less censorious rival, Judge Glenda Hatchett, the star of a show that was subsequently cancelled. Judge Hatchett, she used to say, is 'a great gal, she likes to help people – I don't. I've got five children and twelve grandchildren, I don't need more people to help.' In Judge Judy's creed, generosity begins at home and stays there. 'Not in my America,' she frequently remarks, slamming the golden door behind her as she struts out of the courtroom.

The Statue of Liberty broadcasts hope, whereas the opening credits of Judge Judy's show are underscored by a jazzed-up quotation of the four-note motto that begins Beethoven's Fifth Symphony, often said to represent fate knocking on the door. That sound, peremptory and alarming, is also heard as Judge Judy orders litigants to pay attention: lacking a gavel, she raps on her desk with a pen, very near a microphone.

So why has Lady Justice been nudged into proximity with Miss Liberty? Possibly to identify Judge Judy as a New Yorker, a proud daughter of Brooklyn (though now richly resident in Greenwich, Connecticut, and in Florida during the winter). Her programme is actually made in a studio on Sunset Boulevard in Los Angeles, and for a few weeks every year Judge Judy travels west in her private jet to officiate. But before and after every commercial break, touristic video clips of Manhattan – the arch in Washington Square, Central Park, and of course the Statue of Liberty with torch aglow – explain her accent, her fondness for Yiddish slang, and her boast that interrogation by her is almost as painful as circumcision, along with the combination of pessimism and resilient wit in her grimly jaunty worldview.

Beyond that, the New York landmarks dissociate her from California and its therapeutic cults of healing, wholeness and wellness. Sob stories do not interest Judge Judy. 'He's *depressed*?' she bellowed at a mother who made excuses for her light-fingered son by adducing his shaky mental state. 'He's not depressed, he's a *THIEF!*' She would rather send people to jail than to rehab, although her power is restricted to awarding damages up to five thousand dollars. Toned physiques, fluffy coiffures and dazzling dental work do not impress her. Why, she wondered in one programme, was a witness smiling so inanely? 'I'm just a happy person, Judge,' he chirped. 'Get unhappy!' she growled back at him. Plaintiffs whose clothes are too casually alfresco for court are liable to be asked, 'Where did you think you were coming today? To the beach?' Her favourite mantra, often repeated to empty-headed litigants, is as prophetically doom-laden as the pronouncement of a biblical sage: 'Beauty fades, dumb is forever.'

Judge Judy, born in 1942, has not altogether kept faith with the first part of her maxim, and she looks noticeably older in programmes taped fifteen years ago than in recent episodes. Nor does she entirely shun the beach, an arena for bodies unafflicted by the guilt and shame that she tries to inculcate. In 2012, cruising around the Bahamas on her yacht, she posed for snapshots in a white halterneck bikini. She later added she would probably not wear that garment again: California's fleshly vanities and cosmetic emendations cannot stop time, which is marching us all – Judge Judy included – towards a final judgement.

In the credit sequence, Judge Judy tweaks the iconography of Justitia. Marbleized, she wears the blindfold that is the sign of judicial impartiality. But when she casts off the stiffness of statuary, she pulls up a corner of the mask, peeps out, and knowingly winks: if justice were truly blind, court shows would have to be confined to the radio. With her fixed, inquisitorial gaze, Judge Judy is a camera with X-ray capabilities. She orders witnesses to stare directly back at her when testifying, as if they were undergoing hypnosis. 'Don't look at the heavens,' she told an evasive fellow who could not meet her gaze. 'God is not going to help you. Only the truth will set you free. Look in my eyes!'

She has no qualms about laying down the law physiognomically or even phrenologically. Crossed arms – the body language of truculence – are disallowed, as are hands stuffed into pockets. A defendant pouring water from a jug on the table is liable to be told, 'People who lie, their mouths get dry.' A woman's reddening chest also counts as evidence of mendacity. Sizing up a defendant, Judge Judy once remarked, 'That's the guiltiest face I've seen all day.' 'Who are you?' she barked at a witness on another occasion. 'I'm his mother,' said a bashful woman, glancing with protective concern at an ill-favoured man who was standing before the court. 'You want to acknowledge that?' demanded Judge Judy. 'Get used to the fact that your son's no beauty!' Her morality is harshly Judaic, not Christian: turned inside out, we expose our sins to public view. Glands or genes are no excuse. An overweight adolescent 'looks,' she once said, 'like he's never missed a meal'. She asked a diminutive bully in another show whether he might have a Napoleon complex because he was so 'short of stature'. 'I don't find you particularly attractive,' she told a preening male miscreant. 'Maybe she did,' she added, nodding at the besotted plaintiff who had loaned him money, 'but I don't.'

Judge Judy's verdicts are pronounced by her smirking or snarling mouth, her exasperated rolling eyes and her irately furrowed brow. Expressing aversion is easier than establishing accountability, since the people who come before her have perfected a language that denies causal connections and thereby fudges guilt. A teenage driver, asked who bought the beers that led him to crash his car, relied on the past perfect continuous tense to absolve him: 'They had been there,' he answered. 'They came from the beer fairy?' said Judge Judy, who does not believe in such diaphanous interventions. 'Someone got you down on a couch, like a goose, and poured Bailey's Irish Cream down your throat?' she demanded. The passive voice also comes in handy for wrigglers and quibblers. 'It happened,' said a drug dealer in explaining to her why he had fathered a child. 'Weather happens,' she shot back. 'You're supposed to use *judgement*!' In her view, everyone should have his or her homunculus-like Judge Judy implanted to bark prohibitions internally.

Provoked by a lazy and dishonest defendant, she turned to her placid bailiff – who passes the time chewing gum and doing crossword puzzles – and asked, 'Aren't you glad you're not a violent person?' What she meant was 'Aren't you sorry you can't be a violent person and get away with it?' Her father and brother were dentists. Consequently, as she often says when mentioning their profession, she knows all about the infliction of pain: explaining her handling of a slippery witness who presented in evidence letters that were clumsily forged, Judge Judy said, 'When she tries to put something over on me, I put my heel on her throat.' 'I eat car salesmen for breakfast,' she snapped at another shifty, sweating defendant after ascertaining where he worked. 'It's my sport. It's my joy in life.' 'There is no question in my mind,' she told another blinking defendant, 'that I would send you for a frontal lobotomy.'

During her earlier career in the family court in New York, Judge Judy believed she was performing triage – hectically coping with cases of alimony, spousal abuse and child neglect, sometimes at the rate of forty a day, and binding social wounds as she did so. Triage and trial: the words are connected, as are the procedures. Both determine just desserts, assigning a degree of urgency to injuries or separating right from wrong. But should a judge be as fraught and hustled as a parademic in an emergency room? 'Gotta go,' Judge Judy told a journalist who was interviewing her during a fraught session at the family court in 1993, 'I've got a world falling apart here.' She still relies on homilies about responsibility to make that disintegrating world cohere, and when unwed couples who have separated ask her to rule about common property she upholds the sanctity – or at least the old-fashioned legal convenience – of marriage. Sterilization is her recommendation for the idle, promiscuous underclass. 'You have enough children,' she told a twenty-one-year-old

African American who had fathered ten children with 'about four' mothers. 'Keep it zipped, sir,' she ordered a divorced husband with children scattered throughout Delaware, Florida and Georgia. 'If you want to pollenate half the civilized world, make sure it's geographically suitable.' Her emasculating edicts probably went unheeded.

Fame has made Judge Judy fantasize about an enhanced authority: she is no longer a mere triage nurse, hurriedly applying bandages at the scene of an accident. When a man in a harassment case complained that a former girlfriend was constantly telephoning to threaten that 'a higher power' would sort him out, Judge Judy snapped, 'She was referring to me.' She once lamented the lenient convention that fines criminals or suspends their sentences rather than sending them to prison, and she changed the gender of maternal Justitia in doing so: 'That wouldn't be the kind of justice system I'd create if I was king of the universe.' On another occasion she warned a male bully, 'Here I get a chance to be macho!' A long and unusually patient exchange with a goofy defendant called Jason allowed her to indulge another reverie. Her taxes, she said, paid for his public defender when he was arrested on a drugs charge, and if she ran the country he'd have to reimburse the government. 'So is that why you don't run it?' asked Jason. 'Oh, but I like to think I do,' said Judge Judy very softly. 'For an hour a day, I do run the country.' 'Gee,' Jason marvelled, 'that must be good for the head.' 'Yes Jason,' she rejoined with a thin, mean smile, 'it's very good for my head.'

Satirists like to imagine that they are presiding on judgement day, after the world has irrevocably fallen apart. Yet their railing seldom reforms their unregenerate victims. No matter how brutally Judge Judy treats the miscreants who come before her, they emerge victorious, because any financial indemnity is paid by her producers. If the law's point is to identify culprits and exact punishment, in this forum it is flouted: the worst that can happen is that losers will be embarrassed. Often, deprived of other powers, Judge Judy reverts to the name-calling of the school playground and wags a finger as she chants, 'Liar, liar, pants on fire'. The offenders seldom crumple. I have only once seen her dumbfounded: it happened when the father of ten with approximately four babymamas insolently drawled, 'This may be your show, but it's my episode.' Do we watch to see justice being done, or in the hope that the whole onerous, pedantic system – the 'weighing operation' that Barthes, in his comments on justice in *Mythologies*, associates with bourgeois morality and the petty exactitude of shopkeeping – might be overturned by a riotous disbeliever? Judge Judy's rulings are said to be final, but there is always a cheeky epilogue in which the litigants – their backs turned to a portrait of Lincoln, the president who purportedly never told a lie – sum up their experience by remarking, 'Whatever' or 'It is what it is' before strolling off. 'What do you want me to do?' Judge Judy asked an aggrieved man whose car had been totalled in a collision with an unlicensed and uninsured driver who despite his lack of a licence had driven himself to court that morning. 'I can't execute him,' she added with a regretful glance at the defendant. 'The only thing I can do is humiliate him.' She has no black cap to don; at best she sometimes has the chance to wield a plastic swatter with which she briskly smites passing flies.

Perhaps the spectacle that keeps us watching is that of judicial morality collapsing, reduced to ineffectual fury in a society that has cast off ancient inhibitions. Myths, from the *Oresteia* of Aeschylus to Kafka's *The Trial*, establish the primacy and fixity of law, which ignores individual differences and personal quirks. Today everyone is an unreliable narrator with a self-interested, self-excusing story to tell, and the lawgiver – like Judge Judy when she shouts, 'Can't you see my mouth is moving?' or, more succinctly, 'Shuddup!' – has trouble compelling obedience. Psychotherapy has replaced sins with syndromes, for which it prescribes soothing cures in sun-kissed clinics: Judge Judy frequently has to interrupt the maudlin reminiscences of litigants by saying, 'This is not some psychological show, this is a court!' But it's a court mocked up in a television studio and, because the medium in which she operates has redefined reality as a performance and made visibility the supreme value, those who misbehave expect to be celebrated not castigated for their antics.

Barthes thought that agony aunts were only pretending to sympathize with the heartaches of those who confided in them; their real task was to enforce society's 'constitutive moral dogmas'. Since the dogmas no longer have any force, the agony devolves on Judge Judy, who recently dismissed a counter-claim for pain and suffering by telling a startled woman, 'You're being a pain and it's me who's suffering!' Gods and goddesses must spend much of their time asking why they bothered to create our messed-up world.

Yet Judge Judy may be a symptom, not the remedy. In mid-afternoon the audience that keeps up her ratings consists of those who are watching television rather than earning a living or exercising to stave off obesity. 'Get a job,' she once ordered a lazy young woman. Because the idea seemed strange, she then spelled it out. 'That means you're gonna have to leave your mother, you're gonna have to get off your couch and get outta the house – you're even gonna have to turn off *Judge Judy.*' It was a risky remark, because if all her constituents followed her command, she would be out of a job: her income depends on our unregeneracy. After living for so many millennia in fear of divine retribution or secular reproof, we have at last escaped from the infantile belief that a superior power is sitting in judgement on us, and can settle down on our sofas to enjoy the spectacle of our own folly.

NARCISSUS ON A STICK

In his essay on the Eiffel Tower, Barthes noted that it exists to be looked at, while also serving, once you ascend it, as a lookout, like an eye or a camera lens. Uniquely, it overcomes 'the habitual divorce of *seeing* and *being seen*'; doubling as a thing to be viewed and as a voyeur, it is saved from what Barthes called 'the pure passivity of the visible'. The tower, he concluded, possesses 'both sexes of sight', like an upstanding iron androgyne.

In 2010, when Apple released the iPhone4, everyone in the world acquired this enviable capacity to be at once subject and object. The new phone had a front-facing camera, and adolescent early adopters soon learned how to hold it out at arm's length and let it focus automatically while they pouted or smirked or grimaced for its benefit as they photographed themselves. Generally an outstretched arm appeared in the frame, awkwardly exemplifying what Marshall McLuhan meant when he said, back in the 1960s, that our technological media are 'extensions of man', prolonging the reach of our sensory organs. The phone is an elongated ear, the camera a protruding eye. With the assistance of that extended arm and a telescopic stick that elongates it even further, the long-range ear and the retractable eye have now joined forces; instead of eavesdropping on the rest of the world or surveying it, they turn backwards to gaze in wonderment at the body to which they are remotely attached.

More than a fad, the result has been a new human function, commemorated by a neologism. 'Selfie' became the *Oxford English Dictionary*'s word of the year in 2013, after being used seventeen thousand times more often than in 2012. The statistics for 2014 made those numbers seem paltry: the word popped up ninety-two million times on Twitter, a fivefold increase over the previous year. Revealingly, 'selfie' is a diminutive – probably originating in Australia, where relatives are rellies and sandwiches are sarnies – which gives it a wry familiarity: to call selfies self-portraits would sound pompous, and those who take them tend to giggle apologetically during or after the little rite.

The attraction of these trivial, ephemeral things is easy to understand. Ever since Narcissus stared at his own face in the water of a pool, we have been tantalized by the possibility of overcoming the blind spot in our optical system, which prevents us from seeing or truly knowing ourselves. In the myth, Narcissus bent down to kiss the handsome face that so fetchingly eyed him from beneath the water. Dismayed when the surface shattered and the object of adoration fled, he pined away.

Christianity attached a moral to the fable. In *Paradise Lost*, Eve starts as a female Narcissus, enchanted by her winsome reflection in a pool and alarmed by the very different face of Adam, so square and masculine. As Milton saw it, she has to make the transition from self to other by subjugating herself to her partner, a biologically complementary but mentally superior other half. Freud, writing about narcissism in 1914, reinforced this stern judgement. He treated narcissism as a perversion, which misdirected erotic energy. If we are to attain adulthood, love of an image must give way to love of an object, a person who is not yourself; anyone who cannot make the transition is becalmed in an infantile or at best adolescent state, incapable of loving but needing 'to *be* loved'. Freud thought that the narcissist aspired to 'the immortality of the ego, so gravely threatened by sheer reality'. Oscar Wilde had already pointed out that 'Nero and Narcissus are always with us', and his alliteration hinted that they are one and the same. Does self-love furiously revenge itself on a world that is less than infatuated with the sight of its reflected face?

When glass was first coated with an amalgam of tin and mercury in the sixteenth century, mirrors placed on view a self that was variable, as moodily changeful as the weather. The ego is singular, convinced of its uniqueness, but we can have as many selves as we can take selfies. 'Look in thy glass,' Shakespeare tells a lover in one of his sonnets, 'and tell the face thou viewest/Now is the time that face should form another'. We are all actors, able to multiply ourselves by literally making faces.

Mirrors, however, do not have memories, and reflections in polished glass are immediately wiped away, like the facsimile that breaks up when Narcissus tries to kiss it. The iPhone's little lens preserves the image, and transfers it to the public domain. Without putting down their cameras, selfie-takers can turn themselves into pin-ups on Facebook, Twitter and Instagram, where as if posing against a lamp post on a street corner they wait to receive wolf whistles in the form of upturned thumbs and goofy grinning emoticons. It is like being your own paparazzo and publicist; if you spend long enough performing for your camera, you can both star in and direct the film of your own life. The cult of 'technical, scientific progress', Barthes claimed, had as its aim the 'unlimited transformation of nature'. He regarded this as a cheating illusion, but the 'perfectible mobile world' he scoffed at now exists, mobilized and supposedly perfected by our versatile, hyper-intelligent phones, and the demand of Barthes' bourgeoisie for 'an unchanging humanity, characterised by an indefinite repetition of its identity', is actualized whenever someone confirms and celebrates his or her existence by taking a selfie and sending it out to be re-tweeted.

Those whose role in life is to be looked at resent the innovation, especially when they are forced to rub shoulders with a camera-wielding stranger inside the frame of a selfie. Prince Harry refused to pose for selfies in Australia in 2015, and advised those with smartphones to take 'normal' photographs. The Queen told the American ambassador that she finds the mania for selfies 'strange', because those who take them do not make eye contact with her during the few brief moments when they have the chance. But the frontal gaze involves keeping a distance, which dooms the selfie-taker to invisibility; the matey etiquette of the form requires you to be side by side with your new best friend. In France, sight may have two sexes, but in Britain and its former dominions it has two social classes, and French coition is debarred by British reserve. The selfie, however, is no respecter of rank, and two young women from the Australian hockey team, nuzzling shoulder to shoulder at the Commonwealth Games in 2014, found that an intruder behind them had trespassed on their selfie. On the other side of a mesh fence was the Queen, wearing a green outfit that tallied nicely with their team uniforms and smiling as she passed by, perhaps relieved to be relegated for once to the background.

With a little elasticity and the help of a bathroom mirror, you can spread much more than your face around the world. In 2013 Kim Kardashian posted on Instagram a saucy selfie in which one of her breasts and both of her buttocks fought to free themselves from a skimpy leotard; only one of Kim's eyes was visible, ogling her reflection through a waterfall of newly blonded hair, but the iPhone she held stood in for the other. Of course she totted up innumerable 'likes', and the rapper Kanye West, then her fiancé, promptly passed the salacious image along to his ten million followers on Twitter. Kim's body, or the erogenous zones that swallowed her shrinking thong, had become public property by being 'shared' – that most unctuous of words – with an avid world. Luckily there are no emoticons with excited penises or lapping tongues – not yet anyway.

The incident recalled Kim's hard-boiled wisdom in an episode of her family's reality show, *Keeping Up with the Kardashians*. Kim's sister Kourtney was distressed because a tabloid had bought a sex tape she had made with a discarded lover. Kim advised Kourtney to chill: 'Everyone has sex with their boyfriend, everyone takes pictures.' Their mother Kris shook her head and insisted, 'Not everyone takes pictures!' But Kris was behind the brazen times, and Kourtney's husband, far from being offended by his wife's on-camera mating, merely enquired, 'Was that before your boob job? Is that why you're mad?' His logic was impeccable: it is only a problem to be seen and heard in flagrante if your silicone implants are not proudly in place.

In 2014 Kim was responsible for the selfie's autoerotic consummation, a closure of the circle that joined Barthes' 'two sexes of sight' and mimed a gravity-defying merger of bodily orifices. The image was not strictly a selfie: Kim had some help from Jean-Paul Goude, who restaged his earlier photograph *Champagne Incident*, taken in 1976 with a black model. Dressed to resemble an African tribal carving, with a pineapple-shaped topknot of hair and some looped strings of beads to lengthen her neck, Kim posed in profile, her celebrated rear end jutting out into the semblance of a sideboard, its edges bevelled or photoshopped into regularity. Her hands fastened around a bottle of champagne whose cork had just eased out, spilling an excited froth onto her black gloves; by some tricksy miracle, the contents of the bottle shot straight up in a phallic jet, then disrupted the laws of physics by bending into an arc above Kim's head and coming to land, after some rococo wiggling in mid-air and a final excited splash, in a glass that was poised on those ample buttocks. The trajectory of the white foam began with a male eruption and ended as a female intromission: here was Magna Mater self-inseminating, without recourse to a turkey baster. There may have been nothing quite so mythologically indecent since Titian painted the making of the Milky Way, when fluid that squirted from the breasts of Juno cooled into stars and dripped to earth to shoot upwards again as lilies. But Juno gave birth to a galactic smattering of worlds and fertilized a garden, whereas Kim, to judge from her satisfied expression, was merely pleasuring herself. In case her husband felt excluded, another digital wizard in early 2015 supplied him with his own equivalent to this feat. A snap of Kanye smooching with Kim was altered so that Kanye now clasped a duplicate of himself. Groin to groin, firmly planting his hands on his alter ego's buttocks, he kissed his own ardent, yielding mouth.

Behaviour like this is so odd that the ancient myth cannot account for it. The Renaissance theorist Alberti called Narcissus 'the inventor of painting', the art that attempts to fix the crinkly, unstable surface of the pool. But the self-portraits of painters, mostly made after hours spent staring sideways at their reflection in the mirror, are not like selfies. Rembrandt or van Gogh train a pitiless gaze on themselves, scrutinizing their puffy flesh or ravaged expression. The longer you look at yourself, the more estranged you are from what you see: who is this stranger? The selfie, which relies on a machine to do the looking and compresses the portrait session into a split second, has no time for such appraisals. Instead it concentrates on the filtering and finessing that touch up the image and prepare it for the delectation of others.

Selfies snatch moments, discontinuous and unconsecutive. In Paolo Sorrentino's 2013 film *La Grande Bellezza*, the hero – a depressed socialite who moodily reappraises his life as he reaches his sixty-fifth birthday – visits an exhibition of photographic self-portraits, thousands of them, arranged in chronological order as murals in a palatial Roman courtyard. Each image records a day in the photographer's life. His father, the artist explains, began the documentation when he was born, and he took it over at the age of fourteen. The result may look like a series of Facebook walls, but these are not selfies. As he advances into middle age, the exhibition shows time stealthily altering a face whose owner elasticizes it to show that it's still alive. Despite his efforts to animate his slack features, we follow the advance of mortality as it gnaws from within. The subject, who began to die on the day he was born, cannot hide behind the play-acting and attitudinizing of those who take selfies. Sorrentino's hero is moved almost to tears by what he sees. But a tragic selfie is a contradiction in terms, and it's unlikely that the young, who now use their cameras to show off their happiness, will want to document the memento mori of their ageing faces.

While being sealed in introversion, the selfie also caters to an extroverted desire to be seen and if possible admired. Uploaded, it abandons privacy and courts publicity. This kind of display comes easily to actors, who are professional dissemblers with faces they have trained as masks. James Franco, an inveterate selfie-taker, insists that he is not only being vain. 'Selfies,' he has said, 'are avatars, Mini-Mes that we send out to give others a sense of who we are.' But his statement oscillates ambiguously between mysticism and science fiction. If you're a Hindu, an avatar is an incarnation of the divine; if you're thinking of James Cameron's film of the same name, an avatar is an alias that replaces a real person in an electronic forum. Mini-Me, to complicate matters further, is a cloned homunculus in the Austin Powers films. Does Franco's comment admit that selfie-taking is a parody or an outright deception? Not entirely: the Hindu meaning of 'avatar' reminds him that his own face when projected onto a screen has an existence beyond him, like a soul released from captivity. Franco takes the selfie to be a sign that 'our social lives' are becoming 'more electronic'. Perhaps society and community are now only virtual realities: our phones project images into a limbo where they play games with so-called friends whom we may never have met and who may not even exist.

Another excerpt from the daily routine of the Kardashian clan, photographed in 2014, offered a preview of this future. The setting was a luxurious beige nursery, where Kim and Kanye appeared with their infant daughter. Kim cuddled the baby, but with no evidence of maternal affection on her face, which turned aside to look at the iPhone she was using to take a selfie. Meanwhile Kanye's gaze was fixed on the image of Kim and their daughter framed on his iPad. Out of sight over his shoulder, another photographer recorded the scene, in which the members of a nuclear family redefined for the electronic age ignored each other while concentrating on their gadgetry. Perhaps Kanye should have been photographing himself, because his avatar on this occasion was eerily absent. Although the room had a mirrored wall, Kanye, standing in front of it, was not reflected in it, which led spook-hunters on the Internet to speculate that he might be a vampire. Water could hardly be blamed for rippling and ruffling when Narcissus tried to kiss it, but imagine the rage of a narcissist who can't see his face in the glass!

Has the new technology extended our reach, as McLuhan wished, or closed it down? Insulated by electronics, we have relationships with others that are deflected or mediated. Selfies address a personal question to impersonal strangers: their posturing puts the self out to tender as they ask, 'Is this who I am?' The question assumes that identity is conferred from without, so that you decide who you are by adding up the number of 'likes' that any particular persona tots up. The habit is dangerous, physically as well as morally. In the summer of 2014 two Polish tourists linked arms and smiled for a holiday snap. Unfortunately they were standing at the edge of a cliff on the rocky Portuguese coast and, when they stepped backwards to give the lens held out in front of them a better view, they tumbled to their deaths. More recently a young man was gored to death when he paused to take a snap during a bull-running festival in Spain, and a Japanese tourist was killed after falling on some steps at the Taj Mahal and fracturing his skull while he smiled into his camera. Some casualties are brazenly careless: young Russian daredevils are frequently electrocuted when they clamber on top of railway carriages to pose for their cameras.

Guileless selfie-takers often supply prosecutors with evidence to be used against them. In 2014 two young Germans in Singapore were sentenced to imprisonment and a flogging after they painted graffiti on a parked train; they were convicted because of a self-timed photograph they took at the depot. In the Norfolk town of King's Lynn a befuddled criminal posted a self-portrait on his Facebook page, together with an announcement that he was off to rob the local Tesco supermarket. Oddly enough, he was startled to find the police waiting for him at the scene of the as yet uncommitted crime. In Pittsburgh a young man killed a former friend, then posed the body in a chair and smugly photographed himself with his victim. Attaching his name, he posted the image on Snapchat, which promises automatic erasure after a few seconds. An acquaintance reacted quickly enough to take a screenshot and contact the police, who took the malefactor into custody. More innocuously, a group of backpackers were arrested in 2015 because they had outraged local spirits by stripping naked for a collective selfie on top of a sacred mountain in Malaysia.

Did all these self-incriminating law-breakers think that the camera confers immunity from prosecution? The selfie is the perfection of solipsism: we assume that the rest of the world will share our high opinion of ourselves, and don't allow for the possibility that we might be viewed more sceptically. Obsessed with who we are, we forget where we are; rapt in self-consciousness, we squander our chance of attaining self-awareness.

KHAOS THEORY

The Christian myth tells a chaste story about a heavenly family whose sexual arrangements are a little curious. God the Father begot a son without female assistance; a ghost then implanted the embryo in the womb of a married virgin, whose husband took the miraculous event on trust. The Greeks were less embarrassed by the sexual energy that thrills through nature. The gods who lived on Olympus caroused, committed adultery, and when in the mood for exogamic intercourse swooped down in animal form to seduce naive earthlings; with their tiffs, tantrums and vendettas, they were no better than the rest of us, just larger, louder, richer and, being immortal, longer-lived.

Idolatry comes easier to us than idealism and, despite Christian disapproval, the alternative classical pantheon has made frequent comebacks. The Renaissance marked its first return, when fleshly figures like Botticelli's personification of spring or Titian's voluptuous Venus challenged Gothic austerity and emaciation. The French revolutionaries disestablished Christianity and instead celebrated Feasts of Reason, recruiting nubile young girls to represent values that were resolutely secular; for one such festival, the high altar of Notre-Dame was covered with a model of a Greek temple, on which an allegorical maiden stood to recite an ode to liberty. In Wagner's *Tannhäuser* a Christian minstrel scandalizes his colleagues by holing up in a mossy mound known as the Venusberg, where he dallies with the love goddess.

Today the home of these lusty classical deities has shifted from Mount Olympus to the Hollywood hills, above a city founded by Catholic missionaries and named after Our Lady and all her angels. It is hard to find seraphs in Los Angeles, though there are starlets aplenty; in place of the Virgin who gave birth to a chastely begotten son we must make do with the Kardashians, an unholy family that consists of five alliterating sisters, Kim, Kourtney, Khloé, Kendall and Kylie, mass-produced by a mother called Kris, who once worked as a flight attendant.

The father of Kim, Kourtney and Khloé was an Armenian lawyer, part of the team that defended O. J. Simpson at his murder trial – a landmark in the moral history of the 1990s – and succeeded in persuading a jury to acquit him. Kendall and Kylie are the daughters of Bruce Jenner, a former Olympic athlete who, at least until he changed gender, did not quite qualify as divine, perhaps because his name lacked the magic K. The Kardashian women have more or less exclusive rights to that letter, which is their monogram. K is shorthand for thousands of currency units and for calorific measurements on the Kelvin scale; in the private alphabet of the Kardashians, it signals loot and heat, money and sex, the symbiotic ideas that are their governing principles. Kris's son Rob remains a lacklustre and depressively overweight slacker, a wannabe whose life might have been illustrious if he had been christened Kaleb, Kraig or even Kevin.

Kim, Kourtney, Khloé, Kendall, Kylie and Kris share a single aim in life, which is to be fabulous; they therefore rightfully belong to 'the age of fable', which is the title Thomas Bulfinch gave to his mid-nineteenth-century compilation of Greek myths, intended as a primer for readers of what he called 'elegant literature'. The Kardashians are a throwback to that fabled heyday when spirits made a habit of sorties to earth, usually to enjoy illicit sex. Their existence is one long, unrolling red carpet on which they statuesquely pose, showing off Botoxed brows, chiselled noses, capped teeth and silicone-augmented curves. These rarefied creatures eat dainty meals of scrambled egg whites, steel-cut oatmeal, undressed salads and guacamole dip, which they wash down with a contemporary equivalent of the nectar the Olympians imbibed – sometimes a passion-fruit iced tea or an açaí berry smoothie, on more festive occasions an appletini or a pitcher of midouri sours. Because they lead charmed lives, human sorrows do not impinge on the sisters: when their father died of cancer, Kim, Kourtney and Khloé collectively recall that 'our mom ... always wanted us to look our best, and so we went to buy clothes for the funeral'. Retail therapy was a sure cure for the pain of bereavement.

Cameras cling to the Kardashians like the adhesive fabric of their frocks, recording their business meetings, spending binges and photo-shoots, their love-making marathons, pregnancy tests, and the birthing of their babies. Images of them proliferate on magazine covers and billboards, on the labels of the clothes in their boutiques, and on the vials and tubes of eye cream, skin bronzer, sunless lotion tan extender, body mist, belly wraps and leg spray that they sell. 'Sometimes,' the sisters chorally chirp in their book *Kardashian Konfidential*, 'it seems like we're everywhere at once!' Only supernatural beings can make such a boast.

The Kardashians are exponents of a physiological paganism, which cultivates the body rather the spirit or – God forbid – the mind. Kourtney did attend a Methodist college in Dallas where, as she remembers, she 'learned to do my own laundry' while 'going to Blockbuster and making cupcakes'; she majored in stagecraft, and for a graduation project 'had to light a body form' – an apt apprenticeship for a career of semi-clad self-exposure. While studying, she doubled as an educator: 'These friends of mine said they'd never had a bikini wax. I was, like, "*Seriously?*" It was unbelievable.' It is unclear whether the co-eds in Kourtney's tutorial earned credits for depilating, but the fastidious Kardashian nymphs, unlike their predecessors in Greek mythology, never mate with shaggy satyrs. In *Keeping Up with the Kardashians*, Kim sent her terms and conditions to a prospective date: a go-between was told to warn him that 'Laser hair removal is, like, a requirement.'

The sisters may lack talent but they have a genius for marketing, and their reality show has perfected a formula for transforming mere existence into entertainment. Here we have an endlessly unspooling saga that consists of family confabulations, shopping excursions and cosmetic touch-ups, briefly rendered more dramatic by foolish tiffs or nonsensical intrigues. Kim has a tantrum when some red wine is spilled at her housewarming party, then calms down. Khloé loses her engagement ring in the laundry, then finds it again. The sisters conspire to arrange a date for the sulky, unsociable Rob, then spoil it by turning up to spy on him. Kourtney masterminds a scheme to stop Kris smoking, then weans her by buying fake cigarettes made of honey and marshmallow. Misunderstandings are fomented only to be overcome in a polymorphous hug on the sofa. Why do millions watch, as they have been doing ever since 2007? Because, minus the gilding and the glamour that make it a show, reality for many people is something similar: an epic of trivia.

Of course it is scripted, but that only confirms television's power over us. In the 1950s, sitcoms like *Father Knows Best* and *Leave It to Beaver* established the official version of domestic bliss in the snug suburbs. All conflicts were cheerily resolved by the end of each half-hour episode; advertisements for cleaning products, kitchenware and pancake mix merged with the house-bound action, suggesting that the good life was available for purchase. The Kardashians, however, do not leave the exploitation to Westinghouse, General Foods or Purina Dog Chow, which sponsored the first sitcoms. For them, the family doubles as an industrial operation, with their lives as merchandise. Many of the factitious plots in the reality show concern their pop-up shops, which they try to transplant from California to Miami and even New York. In one episode, Khloé visits a boutique kept by Kris, pounces on a covetable item and squeals, 'I *love* that bag!' in an ecstasy of cupidity; Kris parts with it, beaming, 'Enjoy your bag' as Khloé leaves – a little parable of happiness pursued and attained in the consumerist era. Kardashian DNA has its own unique encoding, and the sisters declare in their tribute to Kris, 'We're quite sure we inherited our shopping gene from her!'

Keeping Up with the Kardashians assumes that this is the kind of existence we all desire. The show's title is a pun: watching, we keep ourselves informed about the Kardashians while enviously trying to keep pace with them. Their output of how-to manuals and interactive games points the way. Kris, as the matriarch, advises on preparing communion meals. Her table settings are elaborate – Hermès dishes, glasses by Baccarat – but her food is comfortingly elementary. Her recipe book talks us through preparing Cream of Wheat: you open a box, pour its contents into a pan, turn on the heat, stir, transfer the porridge to a plate, and as a personalized final touch you sinfully sprinkle sugar on it before tottering to the breakfast nook in your high heels. More ambitiously, in 2014 Kim launched a smartphone app entitled *Kim Kardashian: Hollywood*, which allows those who download it to accumulate K stars, awarded for patiently enduring lectures by stylists, publicists, denturists and cosmetologists. At a certain point the game gets real: you can only edge nearer to Kim – buying knock-offs of her clothes, or holidaying in the resorts she fancies – if you start spending actual money, and initial estimates suggested that the fans who mimic her laid out $85 million in the first year alone.

The vices that Christianity listed as deadly sins – all of them deriving from the idolatry of the self – have now been redefined as virtues. Wrath, avarice, pride, envy and lust are all on display in the various Kardashian households, and the spurious little dramas incited by the reality show exist to accentuate them; gluttony is missing, debarred by their diets, and their assiduous self-promotion means that they can hardly be accused of sloth. In a novel that claims to be jointly written by Kim, Kourtney and Khloé, their imaginary sister Kamille summarizes the hard work, some of it surgical, entailed in being a Kardashian. 'Ohmigod!' she screeches as she races through her 'frantic to-do list: total body and face wax; mini-pedi; haircut; facial; a two … no, three-day cleanse'. Luckily Kamille has already undergone LASIK vision correction, and at some point she may have to endure labiaplasty, a cosmetic procedure frequently recommended by the Kardashians.

'It all began,' the sisters concur, 'with Kim's bootylicious butt': everything followed from the revelation of that fabled rear end. Kim is a modern reincarnation of the Callypygian Venus, a Roman copy of a Greek statue that shows the love goddess pulling up her smock and staring over her shoulder at her beautiful buttocks. In one episode of the reality show, she is persuaded, supposedly against her better judgement, to strip for a *Playboy* centrefold. She feigns horror, which she then downgrades to coy reluctance; minutes later she agrees to negotiate with the doddering Hugh Hefner. Finally, having teased us through several commercial breaks, she agrees. A rhyming couplet seals the deal: 'I'm doing it with class,' she purrs, ''cos I gotta big ass.' On another occasion, Kourtney cattily remarks that Kim's bottom might have become a bit too callipygian – or, to quote Kourtney exactly, she may have too much junk in her trunk. Khloé dismisses the objection, adding another rhyme for finality: 'Her ass makes money, honey.' Barthes said that myth enabled mute objects to speak, and in these impromptu poems Kim's backside attains what he called 'the oral state'.

Her union with Kanye grafted together two fetishized body parts: the expansive bottom was now capped by an ever-expanding swollen head. In his own opinion, Kanye is 'the number one most impactful artist of our generation', comparable – as he has claimed at various times – to Andy Warhol and Walt Disney, to Jim Morrison and Jimi Hendrix, and to Steve Jobs, Nike and Google. 'I am Shakespeare in the flesh,' he once declared. 'I am a god,' he adds in one of his songs, which goes on to describe a conversation with Christ. For Kim, his proposal of marriage might have come from the Holy Ghost: she reported that 'It was, like, an out-of-body experience'. The sensation, professionally defined as autoscopy, can't have been new, since leaving your body in order to look back on it is what happens when you take a selfie.

This particular psychic flight occurred in a San Francisco baseball stadium that had been cleared of people, except for the full orchestra Kanye hired to accompany him as he asked for Kim's hand, and the television crew that was recording the occasion. Like a dictator, Kanye insists on being surrounded by either a resonant, echoing emptiness – as in that vacated arena – or an indiscriminate but unanimous mob, which must be kept at a respectful distance. On tour in Melbourne in 2014, he felt slightly unwell while shooting hoops on a basketball court. An emergency was declared: he was rushed to hospital and unloaded onto a stretcher by parademics. But treatment could not begin until his security team moved in to clear the waiting area and the consulting rooms, banishing fifty patients – including some with appointments for MRI scans – so that Kanye could be attended to on his own. His symptoms, it turned out, were imaginary. Fame of this kind indulges in a reign of terror, intimidating fans not seducing them. Kanye halted one of his Australian concerts when he spotted 'two people who don't wanna stand up'. He glared at the refuseniks, and only relented when one of them displayed a prosthetic limb, the equivalent of a doctor's note.

Referring to his union with Kim, Kanye explained, 'I just wanted to make something awesome and be awesome and change the world, and that's exactly what I plan to do.' The world he vowed to change has been powerless to resist. Their nuptials in 2014 involved a more than royal progress across Europe. After Kim's bachelorette party at the Eiffel Tower, a private tour of the Château of Versailles and some shopping at Givenchy, the couple advanced to Florence, where they were married at the Belvedere fortress, which was built by the Medicis. Local dignitaries with a sense of their city's cultural history were scandalized, but wasn't the Italian Renaissance the era of Machiavelli and Lucrezia Borgia? For their honeymoon, the newlyweds transferred to a country hotel in Ireland, but left prematurely when they found the mobile phone reception unreliable: disconnected from their Twitter followers, they must have felt that they were in a Celtic version of the Bermuda Triangle. They backtracked to Prague, where they went for a photogenic stroll in matching leather pants and, mindful of endorsements, paid a visit to an Armani shop.

Naming their daughter North, Kim and Kanye deviated from the family's partiality for the letter K. North was Kim's choice because this compass point signified 'highest power, the most high'; having ascertained that 'the sun rises in the east and sets in the west', she identified the baby as 'our north star'. That magnetic attraction deviates off course when you remember that the child's full name is North West, but this may be further evidence of the universality of her parents. In 2015 Kim ordered a film crew to down tools so that she and Kanye could retire to an adjacent bathroom to copulate. She was ovulating, she explained, and wanted to seize the moment; sources with privy information later reported that Kim was pregnant again, and in due course she gave birth to a son called Saint. When the time came for Saint's first photoshoot, Kanye – who designed the baby clothes and directed the proceedings – described himself as the infant's 'creative director'. Reproduction is not enough: whatever Kanye begets qualifies as a work of art. Judge Judy may feel that the world is falling apart, but elsewhere in Los Angeles a new solar system is being spawned and the human race is being saved from extinction. The Italian health minister Beatrice Lorenzin has said that hers is 'a dying country', because of a declining birth rate that it shares with other European nations. Should we look to Kim and Kanye as agents of regeneration?

Probably not, since the Kardashians have redesigned the body and rewritten biological rules. 'I styled my mom,' Kim once remarked: the daughter created her parent, the so-called 'momager' who oversees the careers of her offspring. When Kourtney turned broody and pined for a second child, Khloé had a swift suggestion: 'Ohmigod we're gonna have to, like, sew up her vagina.' Kim prescribed something more drastic for her boxer Rocky. Explaining that 'I don't like big balls on a dog', she had her woebegone pet castrated, though as compensation he was fitted with silicone implants, known as neuticles – a 'boob job for a dog', the vet explained.

Rocky received moral support during the procedure from Kim's crestfallen stepfather Bruce Jenner, who subsequently abandoned the effort to be a paterfamilias and in his mid-sixties moved over to join the oestrogen-rich majority. He began to grow his hair, dosed himself with female hormones, had his Adam's apple flattened and, after ten hours of 'facial feminization surgery' and a course of breast augmentation, relaunched himself as a woman in April 2015. At the time, paraphrasing Kanye's comment on his merger with Kim, Bruce vowed 'We're going to change the world.' It was not enough to reconfigure his body and replace his wardrobe: he expected nature to undergo a makeover, and the singer Katy Perry praised him for 'evolving everyone right now with all of his wonderfulness'. Accepting an award for courage in July 2015, Bruce, now renamed Caitlyn, placed on display a persona in transit – a statuesque baritone dressed in a slinky white goddess gown with a waterfall of reddish hair – and vowed 'to tell my story the right way, for me', which served as a promotional boost for the self-celebrating reality show *I Am Cait*.

Fabulations about the rest of the clan continue to spread in tabloids like the *National Enquirer*, which reported in one of its weekly updates that Kylie was having her bottom resculpted to compete with Kim, who planned to make an 'artistic moulding' of her own nether region as a gift for Kanye. In 2015 the *Enquirer* also confided that Kylie was showing a baby bump, and passed on the equally spurious information that Khloé was expecting twins: hysterical pregnancies for the benefit of overexcited fans. A parody of the family's show by the Chicago comedian Fawzia Mirza went further by inventing an extra sister called Kam, a lesbian disowned for being unfabulous. Drunk in a rough bar, Kam rails against her siblings: 'The Kardashians, the Kardashians – are they *Star Trek* characters?' Speculating along similar lines, the rapper Snoop Dogg unchivalrously classified Caitlyn Jenner as 'a science project'. Transit between genders, a mutation between species: such metamorphoses have always been the stuff of myth.

Kris and her daughters have created Khaos, which is the title they gave to the shop they opened in Las Vegas in 2010; they may also exemplify a chaos that, like the weather in mathematical theory, disrupts the sane predictability of normal life. Late in 2014 Kim posted online a portrait from the *Champagne Incident* session in which she showed off her naked behind, slick with oil and mythically bulbous, and added that she hoped it would 'break the Internet' when it was re-tweeted. In contemporary terms, that malfunction represents the collapse of society, but Kim found the prospect thrilling: for the Kardashians, elevated above mortal status by their spike-heeled shoes, society is where other people live. Even so, these women set a standard of normality in our addled world. 'She was into normal teenage things, she used to watch *Keeping Up with the Kardashians*' – that was Sahima Begum's baffled comment on her fifteen-year-old sister Shamima, who in early 2015 sneaked away from home in the East End of London with two schoolfriends, flew to Turkey, then crossed the border into Syria, where all three girls joined the army of Isis, the self-styled Islamic State, or at least volunteered to serve as underage comfort women for its fanatical warriors. Shamima's interest in the show might be comprehensible if she had seen the Kardashians as symptoms of Western depravity, but she was a wide-eyed follower rather than a disgusted critic. Perhaps, since stardom seemed to be a remote prospect, she calculated that martyrdom was the next best thing.

In Barthes' day, the merchandizing of the female body was confined to the pornographic underground. But he did write an essay about the face of Greta Garbo, which for him counted as a mythical object – another pure sign, and therefore an object of adoration. *Queen Christina* ends with the monarch sailing into exile; in stoically expressionless close-up, Garbo stares for several minutes at the Swedish coast as it recedes into an irretrievable past. Her make-up in that scene, Barthes noted, has 'the snowy thickness of a mask': this is less a painted face than one set in plaster, idealized and perfected. For Kim Kardashian, such an impasto is something quite ordinary, applied each morning by her 'glam squad' and refortified every few hours. 'My makeup was amazing yesterday,' she once reflected. 'Even if I scratched my face with a big nail it would have stayed on. … I can't believe how cement it was.' Garbo's beauty is like snow, sadly liable to melt, but the indestructible, impervious Kim has a surface of calcinated mortar.

Closing his essay with a philosophical cadenza, Barthes contrasted Garbo with Audrey Hepburn, a favourite in the mid-1950s. He offered a loftily abstract choice between the immateriality of a Platonic essence and the existential instability of Sartre's very different contemporary creed. 'As a language,' Barthes wrote, 'Garbo's singularity was that of the order of the concept, that of Audrey Hepburn is of the order of substance. The face of Garbo is an Idea, that of Hepburn an Event.' The Kardashian face, however, is plural not singular. Neither an icon like Garbo's nor a happening like Hepburn's, it is a brand, a commercial logo with a price tag attached, in theory available to all who buy the bronzers, moisturizers, exfoliators, lip-plumping shimmer gloss and film-noir eyeliner that the Kardashians sell. Myth, Barthes argued, can 'corrupt everything', and in an act that mimics rape it 'carries [meaning] away bodily'. As these metaphors suggest, a mythic character is a happy harlot, belonging to whoever will pay: the sacred image has arrived at what Barthes called 'its final prostitution'.

DAEMON DOGS

Myth, Barthes warned, begins its work of social conditioning early. In an essay on toys, he noted that the playthings sold in France treated children as dwarfish adults, whose games – at least in those innocent pre-electronic days – trained them for the functions they were to fulfil in the stratified, sexually separatist world of their bourgeois parents. Boys began their professional apprenticeship by experimenting with chemistry sets and medical kits, or learned the tricks of less exalted masculine trades from models of trains and petrol stations. Little girls rehearsed for their future roles by bathing, dressing and perming the hair of dolls that served as parthenogenetic babies. Toys like these, Barthes said, turned childhood into a drearily dutiful 'microcosm of the adult world'.

A recent fad complicates his theory: certain female celebrities are in the habit of carrying dogs around with them, using their handbags as portable kennels. What kind of genetic charade is it that muddles up the different realms of childhood play and adult responsibility, as well as toppling the proper boundaries between human and animal? Cocottes have always had poodles in attendance, but it is only recently that the animals have taken an equal share in the social lives of their owners. The fad may have begun with the model Anna Nicole Smith, who at the age of twenty-six married the oil billionaire J. Howard Marshall, eighty-nine and mentally incompetent, after they met in the 'titty bar' where she was lap-dancing. She fed the old man Valium and scraps of raw bacon, and sometimes parked him outdoors in the rain in his wheelchair; when he obliged her by dying, she attended his funeral in a backless and near-frontless white wedding gown, with a yapping dog tucked under her arm. The indecorous squirming and squealing of her pet expressed Anna Nicole's attitude to the ceremony even more pointedly than the dress she wore: it signalled her refusal or incapacity to behave like a sober adult and exhibit the customary emotions. Why should we accept the social regimentation that begins with toilet training, since dogs see no need to abide by such rules? Anna Nicole later adopted a miniature poodle called Sugar Pie, which needed Prozac to regulate its moods and had a psychotherapist on standby to deal with its whimpering anxiety. Not that it had much cause for complaint, considering its home comforts: it slept in a boudoir not a kennel, on a wrought-iron bed with pink faux-fur upholstery and a feather-decorated canopy top, and it shared its owner's calorific meals. After Anna Nicole's death, her publicist Howard Stern inherited Sugar Pie and reported that he was 'transitioning her to dog food', which must have been penitential.

At least the toys Barthes wrote about were figurines, appropriately costumed for work: soldiers in uniform, nurses or beauticians in smocks. But the breeds of dog now photographed on red carpets cannot be mistaken for tiny people; in fact their species is sometimes questionable. The ditzy heiress Paris Hilton collects chihuahuas that look like wingless, bug-eyed bats, and also favours Pomeranians that resemble balls of fluff afflicted with hysterics. Mariah Carey has an entourage of more recognizably canine Jack Russells, though unlike most dogs they have a full-time chauffeur who ferries them to appointments with their stylists, groomers and therapists, and when necessary takes them to the airport. As a conveyance, a handbag is beneath their dignity. Mariah's dogs, she once tweeted, 'live on private jets'.

Many of us moralize or allegorize our dogs: fond, familiar names like Buddy or Fido make them embodiments of virtue. American presidents traditionally install a pet in the White House to signify that it is a family home and not only an executive office, and they expect the incumbent of the First Kennel to embody national values. Gerald Ford's golden retriever was named Liberty, and Reagan had a dog of the same breed called Victory. Exercising Victory must have been like taking an aircraft carrier for a walk; I hope that no leash restrained Liberty from pursuing happiness and seeking out aromatic trees on the White House lawn.

For Paris and Mariah, however, christening is not generic, nor does it hand out merit badges. Paris bestows names as if sprinkling stardust from a magic wand. Her most famous chihuahua was called Tinkerbell, which suggests a pedigree stretching back to gauzy fairyland; another dog, known as Ariel, had the same provenance. One of her Pomeranians was called Mr Amazing when she acquired him, but she changed that demotic name to Prince Hilton. Another Pomeranian was entitled Prince Baby Bear, which confusingly elevated him to the hereditary aristocracy while exiling him to an altogether different, gruffer and shaggier species. A third nurseling, more fashion-conscious and street-smart, was dubbed Harajuku Bitch. Its first name referred to Tokyo's version of 1960s Carnaby Street, the second was a slangy endearment from the American ghetto: was there room inside the tiny cranium of a chihuahua for a teenage fashion victim and a gangsta moll to cohabit? Paris has also commodified her pets. Two of her dogs are labelled Dolce and Prada; they are accessories, like the handbags in which they travel.

Mariah's litter consists of Dickensian eccentrics, separated from the common herd by middle initials and flattered by ceremonious forms of address: Jill E. Beans and Squeak E. Beans, Pipitty Jackson and Mutley O. Gore Jackson III. The Good Reverend Pow Jackson is the first Jack Russell on record to have received holy orders and taken a vow to minister to mankind, which he presumably does by licking. Sometimes Mariah invites her fans to suggest names, and one recent arrival risked being called Beau T. Ful, though Mariah vetoed the proposal. After so much inventive drollery, it is startling to discover that her first Jack Russell was simply called Jack. Was that the best she could do, or did the tautologous name admit the absurdity of the whole business? 'One takes refuge in tautology,' said Barthes, 'as one does in fear, or anger, or sadness. ... One kills language because it betrays one. Tautology is a faint at the right moment ... it is a death, or perhaps a comedy.' In this case it is certainly a comedy, though it also evinces the desperation sensed by Barthes. The choice is grim – between dismissively assigning a dog a name that is no more personal than a number and endowing it with a fanciful title that derides it for being merely a dog, transforming it into an attendant, a flunkey, a bitch-in-waiting.

Paris has constructed what she calls a 'mini doggie mansion' for her brood. This scaled-down replica of her own house has wardrobes for the gem-encrusted outfits worn by her dogs, and a spiral staircase up and down which they can scamper; a chandelier shines its spangled light on them, and they sleep in punning cots designed by 'Chewy Vuitton'.

Mariah's canine regime is more strenuous. Not left to expend surplus energy in romping, her pets are forcibly inducted into their owner's high-maintenance routine of athletic workouts: she sends them to a spa called Barkingham Palace, where they are treated to body wraps, blueberry facials, Thai massages, and a tender squeezing of their anal glands to ensure friction-free bowel movements.

Eventually the silliness becomes spooky, uncanny. These yelping, skittering creatures might be what Philip Pullman in *His Dark Materials* calls daemons – manifestations of a hidden self, like the ermine cradled by the lady in a Leonardo da Vinci portrait. If so, the dogs Paris dandles exactly correspond to her undersized soul. In Mexican folklore chihuahuas were supposed to be psychopomps, guiding the spirit into the afterlife as jackals did in ancient Egypt, so perhaps they are helping her to practise for her descent into a glittery grave. Dogs have shorter lives than we do; the lifespan of celebrities, consigned to oblivion as soon as we tire of them, is even shorter, so it is just as well that Paris is thinking ahead.

Our special friendship with dogs is one of civilization's mysteries. Somehow we managed to charm a wolf into taking food from our hands and then snuggling up to us. After that first victory, a godlike power of genetic manipulation has enabled us to produce an uncountable variety of breeds from a common ancestor. With dogs, we can enjoy relationships that are truly egalitarian: they judge us by the way we treat them, not by our position in the world or our income. Although Queen Victoria named her successive Scottish collies Noble and the current Queen registered a corgi born in 1971 as Windsor Loyal Subject, these quadruped courtiers do not bow or curtsy; Bo the Portuguese water dog is equally unimpressed by Barack Obama's power as commander-in-chief. Yet this unbiological kinship is now reaching its perverse terminus. Evolution has gone backwards, and the self-centred despotic infant described by Freud as 'His Majesty the Child' has been replaced by Prince or Princess Puppy, liable to have hysterics if not promptly fed and watered or kissed, cuddled and papped. Pomeranians fit this regressive fantasy, because their history reverses the law of organic growth. During the nineteenth century, inbreeding caused the average size of Poms to decrease by half, as if they were being forcibly compressed. Miniaturized, they have become culinary morsels, consumerist treats. At a canine Halloween parade in New York in 2015, the star was a Pomeranian that had been squeezed into a waxed-paper cone along with some cardboard French fries and punningly labelled 'Pom Frite'. It worried Barthes that 'the adult Frenchman sees the child as another self'; it's a good deal more bizarre for an adult American woman to see a chihuahua or a posh Pom in that way. But Paris and Mariah are reluctant to renounce self-centred infancy, and they pine for the permanent childhood that their querulous babies enjoy. Evidence of maturity, moral or physical, is immediately punished: Paris got rid of Tinkerbell when the dog outgrew her handbag.

Pets like this are no one's best friend. Their actual purpose is to dramatize disaffection with the human race or dislike of it. Paris and Mariah are following the lead of Leona Helmsley, the widow of a billionaire New York hotelier, who punished her relatives by bequeathing $12 million to Trouble, her Maltese terrier. Leona, a notorious harridan, tyrannized and persecuted her staff; she disdained any notion of an obligation to others, and once remarked that paying taxes was for 'little people'. More than a love-token, her bequest to Trouble was an ultimate act of misanthropy: her will directed that the dog should be installed in a private suite in a Helmsley hotel in Florida, with security guards to protect her from being kidnapped and held to ransom.

Trouble eked out a miserably sickly old age in her gilded kennel before being transferred to the Helmsley family mausoleum. By all accounts she was an inoffensive creature, but her function was the same as that of the Staffordshire bull terriers or rottweilers that strut down our meaner streets beside their thuggish masters and ventilate aggression through razory jaws. Typically named Terror, Killer or Asbo, these attack dogs are descendants of the bull terrier kept by Bill Sikes in *Oliver Twist*, which paddles in blood after Nancy's murder and, when Sikes dies, commits suicide by dashing out its deranged brains on a stone. Trouble had no need to snarl and bark; without baring her teeth, she signalled a quieter, deadlier animosity on her owner's behalf. Marie Antoinette thought that starving people should eat cake.

Leona Helmsley might have sarcastically prescribed a diet of dog food for the disadvantaged.

We are entitled to take pride in having coaxed another species from wildness to domesticity. Instead, whether in Beverly Hills or on a south London council estate, we envy animals for being blindly impelled by instinct and appetite. The snobbery of the leisure class and the rankling resentment of the underclass here reach an accord. It doesn't matter that some dogs have Instagram accounts like Paris's brood or are manicured and blow-dried like Mariah's. Their eating habits remain gross, and they sniff the sphincters of other dogs when they meet rather than shaking hands or kissing cheeks. With chihuahuas frenetically yapping on one side and bull terriers gutturally rumbling on the other, we are stranded somewhere between the nursery and the jungle.

4

Forms and their Content

A VIRAL DESSERT

Defining myth as 'a form of speech', Barthes did not specify what kind of speech it was. Sometimes he saw myth as a specialized idiolect destined for use by politicians and bureaucrats, like the covertly imperialistic vocabulary he discerned in French reports on politics in colonial Africa. On one occasion in *Mythologies* it is dialect: Barthes believed that the peasant Gaston Dominici, accused of murdering three British tourists, was denied a fair trial because his bourgeois judges did not understand his rural accent and therefore mistrusted him. Elsewhere myth is wordless, a mechanistic chatter and clatter like that of the pinball machine in Arthur Adamov's 1955 play *Ping-Pong*, whose 'network of language situations' Barthes defended. Unstoppably voluble without necessarily being articulate, myth can speak in gobbets of sound that make little sense.

Barthes did warn that myth was 'stolen language': an enigmatic phrase, which hints that myth steals meaning from language or wantonly alters it. An example? Well, if you didn't already know, you might find it hard to guess the meaning of the recently invented and trademarked word 'cronut', the tag for an object that is mythologized by its oddity, its elusiveness and its expense. The word's first syllable evokes Cro-Magnon, once the designation of our brutish-looking ancestors, and 'nut' in conjunction with 'cro' suggests an item of hardware such as a crowbar, probably wielded as a weapon.

In fact, the cronut is a fluffy pastry, a croissant-donut hybrid confected in New York in 2013 by the pastry chef Dominique Ansel. Having created the thing – basically by frying croissant dough, though he indignantly denies that the process is so humdrum – Ansel then had to christen it, which he did by mashing together the two constituent words, as if language were as malleable as batter. Such coinages are known as portmanteaux, metaphorically evoking a suitcase that opens into two parts and then clamps shut again. Verbally, Ansel's recipe follows the rules of Jabberwocky, Lewis Carroll's nonsense lingo, where one of the portmanteau words is 'slithy', an adjective that merges 'sly' and 'lithe'. Our hybridized world contains portmanteau people – 'Brangelina' for instance, or 'Kimye', short for the Kardashian-Wests – and the same merger, again enforced by sex, creates portmanteau dogs like the dorgi, cockerpoo and labradoodle; we should not be surprised by crossbred food.

Time magazine allowed the cronut onto its list of the year's twenty-five best inventions, though its birth was hardly a Eureka moment, comparable with the blending of oil and egg yolk to make mayonnaise or the stiffening of egg whites with sugar to make a meringue. Ansel found he had rivals, who claimed to have got there first. They established their originality by repositioning the syllables of the compound: a word, as Barthes said, is a 'sum of signs', and there are no rules against different ways of adding that sum up. A chef in Massachusetts claimed she had begun selling what she called 'dosants' five years earlier, and a baker in Ohio pointed out that his 'doughssants' had been on the market for more than twenty years. It's unfortunate that 'dosants' suggests medicinal doses, while 'doughssants' – with its anglicized spelling of 'dough' and the double 's' that it carries over from 'croissant' – is fussily un-American. An outlet in Singapore dodged the prohibitions of the cronut trademark by labelling its product the 'crodo', which rhymes with 'dodo' and therefore suggests that the pastry may be several centuries beyond its sell-by date. The Japanese may be wise to unpack the portmanteau: with an implicit bow, they address the product as Mr Croissant Donut. In Britain, Greggs the bakers call their version 'Greggnuts'. That sounds testicular and embarrassingly personal; in addition, all those glottal 'gs' lodge a choked obstruction in the throat. This grafting of syllables and ingredients looks likely to continue indefinitely. In 2015 a bakery in the upcoming London district of Shoreditch invented the 'cruffin', which merges the croissant and the muffin. In the verbal contest at least, Ansel remains ahead.

The name of the miscegenated pastry should not matter, but the cronut owes its allure to the high-toned language lavished on it. Ansel refers to his 'baking philosophy', and asserts that his mission is 'to bring you constant creativity'. The patissier thus poses as a deep thinker, at once an experimental scientist and an iconoclastic artist, who can render the simplest procedures obscure by deploying an unexpected word. His cronut dough, we're told, is 'laminated', which is a pseudo-metallic way of saying that it is layered; during preparation it is 'proofed' – another startlingly rigorous term, as if the uncooked mess has to undergo some intellectual trial before it is fit to be fried, sugared, filled with cream and glazed. Supposedly it takes three days to make a batch of cronuts, and this labour theory of value justifies a price of five dollars per item.

The finicky climax of the process is the injection of flavour. Before that, despite the lamination of the dough and the grapeseed oil in which it spits and sizzles, it is form without content, like a Nando's chicken that has not been basted. And of course Ansel does not pump anything as namby-pamby as jam or custard into his creations. The flavours change monthly, and they amount to an almost psychedelic array of multicoloured illusions, all crossbred like the cronuts into which they are syringed. The blends have included rose vanilla, blackberry lime, fig mascarpone, Valrhona chocolate champagne, peanut butter rum caramel, raspberry lychee, Morello cherry with toasted almond, and passionfruit caramelia (which may well be a portmanteau of 'caramel' and 'camellia'). Just as we are told to listen for entirely imaginary musical 'notes' of fruit or flowers as we sip wine, here we are challenged to analyse the cream as it trickles into our throats. Those kaleidoscopic mixtures recall Willy Wonka's implosion of a three-course meal in Roald Dahl's novel: at his chocolate factory, a single stick of chewing gum contains the flavours of tomato soup, roast beef accompanied by a baked potato, and blueberry pie with ice cream. This streamlines the process of eating dinner, but wouldn't it be more satisfying to have the dishes themselves, rather than simulations of them?

Oddly enough, consumerism, which classifies everything we buy as ersatz nourishment, finds something a little indecent about the act of ingestion, and prefers to think that food is programming sensations or, like a psychelic drug, successively triggering ideas. Ansel designs his culinary novelties for the mind, not for the mouth. Yellow peach black tea was the flavour during one summer month: the play of adjectival contrasts is chromatically pleasing, though in effect the mixture would produce a brownish murk. That may be why customers are advised not to investigate the cronut's interior, supposedly because cutting will crush the laminated layers. If we must slice through the precious item, we are told to use a serrated knife to keep the contents from squeezing out. To preserve the mystery, we are expected to visualize the paradoxical flavours rather than actually seeing those rainbow coalitions of blackberry and lime or chocolate and champagne.

Perhaps the cronut is primarily a verbal experience. Ansel has a habit of relying on words to make you salivate. Another of his portmanteaux is the frozen 's'more', a contraction of Oliver Twist's request for 'some more'. This is based on the marshmallows toasted by campers huddling around a crackling hearth in the American wilderness, although Ansel adjusts the rustic delicacy for urbanites: fire gives way to ice, though a flame applies a finishing touch. S'mores are made by covering Tahitian vanilla ice cream with a kindling of chocolate wafer chips, like an experiment in cold fusion. Then the core is 'enrobed' in a marshmallow that has been somehow 'modified', after which a blowtorch applies a blast of oxygen and methane gas. Finally, to complete the cycle that leads from nature to culture and back again, the frozen square is impaled on a twig of smoked willow. Are we in humid Tahiti, at a campsite in the forest, or perhaps in the changing room of a clothes shop that sells robes rather than drab everyday garments? Metaphor here runs wild: the s'more is well named, because it is the perfection of superfluity.

Ansel's website describes the cronut as 'the most virally talked about dessert item in history', which exemplifies the verbal overvaluation that kneads this doughy lump into a myth. The boast about history also reveals that, for the cronut's chroniclers, the world began with the launch of Twitter and Instagram. As for the idea of a viral dessert – well, it is true that online gossip transmits misinformation as if spreading germs, but a virus was a disease long before it became a malady that afflicts computers or a contagion that spreads on social media, and the metaphor should probably keep away from food. Most curiously of all, in this estimation the cronut's triumph lies in being talked about, not eaten. That may be because, despite a worldwide craving, it is not easy to get your hands on one. Ansel's bakery produces roughly 350 a day for sale to those who trek to his shop on Prince Street in Lower Manhattan, where the staff impose a limit of two cronuts per person. A pre-order list is open online, but it fills up weeks in advance, and Ansel – making inefficiency contribute to the excitement of this tortuous mythological quest – warns that the system 'may be timed out because of the inflow of customers'. You can also join the queue that forms outside the bakery at around 7 a.m., or earlier over the weekend: in an affluent society, where we have too much of everything, it is modishly retro to be seen on a breadline, like clients at a soup kitchen or starving Third World refugees.

A code of behaviour is suggested for those who queue at dawn, and the website requests that 'you keep your voice level to a minimum'. This allows neighbours in SoHo to sleep, but it also suits the reverential nature of the vigil. You are outside a church waiting to take communion, and when the cronut eventually pops into your mouth you have to think symbolically. It is not quite the same as a wafer's transubstantiation into the body of Christ, but you need to be an earnest believer to bring back to life the rose bushes, fig trees, tea plantations and passionfruit vines that have contributed their elusive essences to this circle of moist-centred dough. After extending the wait to buy a cronut to weeks (if you place an advance reservation) or at least hours (if you choose to queue), the bakery suggests that you should eat it the moment it comes into your possession, because of its abbreviated shelf life: it is a matter of urgency to return the fluffy thing to the nothingness from whence it came.

A limited supply intensifies demand. Cronuts have been resold on the black market for $100 each, and bidders at a charity auction once paid $14,000 for a dozen of them. Without being quite so desperate, I have made repeated attempts to buy one. The first time, the Prince Street bakery was closed because of health violations after the discovery of a smattering of little black mice pellets, not meant to be sprinkled on the cronuts. I tried again on subsequent trips to New York, but no matter how early I arrived, the daily allocation was always sold out. After my most recent disappointment I began to wonder whether the cronut might be a supreme fiction, a purely conceptual sweet. That would be the ultimate demonstration of a myth's potency – to make people worship the idea of something that, like God, is simply not there.

I suppose Ansel's cronuts must exist, because a smattering of the cores gouged out during the cooking process fell to earth in a Manhattan park in 2013. Known as 'concretes', they might have been the pebbly litter of an asteroid. A thousand of these missing centres were mixed with brown-butter caramel custard, then sold for $4.50 each to benefit charity. Myths can browbeat us back into childhood; under the influence of this one, the faithful happily paid money for holes and munched on chunks of delectable cement.

UTTERLY OYSTER

Since the 1950s, what Barthes called mystification – exemplified by the deifying of the Citroën as a Déesse or the frothy spirituality attributed to Omo – has come to be known as branding. Rather than alluding to religion, the word invokes the branding of cattle, which are held down while a monogram that signifies ownership is seared into their flesh. The aim is certainly proprietorial, but the violence of the act seems too blatant for an economy that aims to seduce consumers. Commercial branding therefore relies on subtler tactics: it incites poetic reveries that flit around a product without ever fastening onto it.

What, for instance, does a trip on a bus or train have in common with an oyster? Nothing at all. Nevertheless, in 1998 Transport for London – once called London Transport, before the nouns were transposed and the preposition inserted to make the business sound more devoted to its mission – hired an expensive team of experts to confer an identity on its new electronic ticket. The branders decided that it would be called the Oyster card, and in doing so they proved the truth of Barthes' contention that anything at all can be a myth.

Tickets have not always needed such fanciful designations. On the London Underground, they used to be thumb-shaped stubs of cardboard with prices printed on them, collected at the end of your journey by uniformed inspectors sitting in sentry boxes. On London buses they were strips of paper, churned out by conductors from a hurdy-gurdy they wore around their necks. Now you carry a pre-paid plastic card with no visible evidence of value on its surface; an electronic pad reads it, does a quick calculation to assess whether you can afford to travel, and decides whether to admit or debar you. No human interaction takes place, unless you need to 'seek assistance' – as the bossy little sign on the closed gate orders – which is generally a euphemism for your lack of credit.

When Jean-Paul Sartre first ventured down into the New York subway in the 1940s, he came up against an existential frontier. He baulked at dropping a nickel into a slot to operate the turnstile that would let him onto the platform: to do so, he feared, meant sacrificing individuality in order to be 'elevated … to the impersonality of the Universal', changing from a person to a unit. His scruples may have seemed absurd at the time, but the 'readers' now installed in train stations and on buses in cities around the world insist on electronic reconnaissance and recognition. It's open to question whether we are elevated by the procedure: surely it is more like a demotion, since we are submitting to scrutiny by a machine. The brisk automatism of the procedure is what makes the Oyster card's designation seem so otiose and obscure.

The Oyster's branders took a positive pride in the whimsicality of the name they selected. At least the New York equivalent, the MetroCard, gives you some clue about its purpose: the receding perspective of the letters on the card suggests rapid transit, and a black magnetic strip at the bottom could be tarmac or an electrified rail. Instead of the MetroCard's insignia of speed, the Oyster card makes do with a gently curving white roundel, which might be suggesting that velocity ought to be reduced while negotiating a bend.

The colour scheme of the Oyster is equally odd. The card is azure deepening to navy blue, while the electronic readers with which it has to make contact are a glaring yellow. Again the scene is unearthly: it suggests a cloudless summer afternoon ignited by a flaring sun, although London's skies are usually ashen, just as its river looks as if teabags are stewing in it. One slightly desperate conjecture suggests that the branders meant to invoke the Thames and its oyster beds, but these were closed to fishermen a few years ago because of depleted supplies. The yellow readers are stamped with a flick, a comma-like graphic gesture that tells us to press the card into contact. That icon is a good deal fishier than the card's merely notional oyster: it resembles a tadpole, though with a square bookish head grafted onto it – a sign that this larva is literate and spends all day speed-reading the payment history of our cards as we hurry past.

The idea of the Oyster may have been lifted from the alliterating Octopus card used on public transport in Hong Kong. At least the octopus has a metaphorical affinity with the activities it brands: it is tentacular, and in Cantonese the card's name means 'reaching in all directions', so the network is envisaged as a mollusc with its eight arms flailing. The Oyster card is less adventurous. The bivalve mollusc to which it refers is a stay-at-home creature, clenched and almost anally retentive – surely the very opposite of what a transport system needs to signify. The octopus forages with its suckers, omnivorously sampling lesser fry, but the oyster is more timid: it clutches its pearls like an affronted dowager, tightly locks its door against intruders, and when venturing out keeps a wary eye on anyone who might be wielding the kind of knife that can prise open its hiding places to steal its goods. Come to think of it, the card may after all have some affinity with the citizens who carry it! The same goes for the gemstones that some oysters contain. Transport for London supplies the grime at no extra charge; it's up to us to turn the specks of it that adhere to us into profit or even beauty as we make our way through the city. And because the molluscs are so busy coping with friction and irritation, oyster beds might resemble London tubes or buses – wards crowded with neurotics, some of whom may be artists with the ability to transform their tumours into jewels.

The branders, keen to ease the stress of city life, probably reckoned that calling the card Oyster would vouch for safety and security. For the same reason the German horologist Hans Wilsdorf decided in 1926 to name one of his Rolex watches the Oyster: it was hermetically sealed, dust-proof and water-proof, and it went on implacably ticking when tested during a ten-hour cross-Channel swim. That particular triumph, however, does not carry over to the Oyster card, which is a flat surface that cannot be sealed. Nor are the tunnels through which its users travel dust-free, and they are also liable to leak in bad weather.

'The world,' we are told by the proverb, 'is your oyster', and that may be another of the Oyster card's gambits. But a world modelled on an oyster would be a stuffy, solitary place, not at all like the thronging metropolis that Transport for London opens up to us. On his first visit to New York, Dickens was intrigued by the city's sinister oyster bars. They were located below street level, and had to be entered down flights of steps; inside, customers ate behind curtains in booths or cubicles. 'The swallowers of oysters,' Dickens surmised, copy 'the coyness of the thing they eat.'

He might have been describing the deportment of people on a crowded tube, who erect cellular defences around themselves and direct their eyes to a neutral space in mid-air, as if everyone is in an impregnable shell.

In the loftiest social circles, the oyster's self-enclosure signifies discretion. In the early 1950s Crawfie, the governess who had looked after the little princesses Elizabeth and Margaret Rose, wrote a mawkish memoir about her young charges. Outraged by this indiscretion, her former employer, soon to be known as the Queen Mother, sent her a letter warning that 'People in positions of confidence with us must be utterly oyster.' Oyster cards, however, are less taciturn, and can't always be trusted to respect the privacy of their owners. Computers retain the details of our travel for up to two months, and during that period the police can ask to search through the stored data to check on our whereabouts; the plastic oblong in our wallets does the work of a surveillance camera.

For a while in 2008, cheeky Londoners teased the inflexible system by scissoring the microchip off their Oyster cards and fixing it to a wristwatch or adding it to a charm bracelet: they wore the card as an ornament, which spared them the clumsy routine of removing it from a pocket or purse for validation at the station gates or the bus door. But instead of outwitting the electronic readers, they had anticipated the next stage in the rite of passage described by Sartre when he entered the New York subway. The Oyster card is our ticket to ride into a future of utter impersonality. Transport for London has done away with the human beings who used to sell tickets and check them; what logically follows is to make the card itself obsolete by inserting its microchip beneath our skin. The calculating intelligence hidden in those yellow discs will then be able to scan our bodies and determine our life expectancy as passengers or customers. Have we 'topped up', fuelling ourselves like vehicles for shorter or longer journeys? Already an invisible eye assesses our worth, the narrow gate opens its jaws to let us in, and an escalator sends us down to circulate inside London's fetid, windy intestines. Oysters are best consumed raw, still living as they slip into our gullets; the Oyster card takes its revenge on their behalf, easing our entry into a system that eats us alive.

NOOKS AND KOBOS

God's death left other would-be gods with a tenuous lease of life. Barthes disposed of monarchs in his essay on the Greek cruise, and in 1967 he got around to the presumptuously omniscient figure he called 'the Author-God', another mythical potentate whose power depended on bluff. Authors inscribe words on a page in the belief that they are chiselling their thoughts into durable stone. Yet, as Barthes pointed out, these know-alls are absent from their writing, unable to stand guard over whatever it was they thought they meant; the reader is entitled to interpret their words at will, which does away with the idea of an authorized version. Barthes downgraded authors to 'scriptors', who collaged together scraps of language and manufactured 'texts', which like textiles were a fabric of threads that could be unpicked and rewoven by readers and critics.

He thought of this as a liberation: he wrote at a time when 'Literature', to which he awarded an officious capital letter, was 'abolishing ... its condition as a bourgeois myth', a credential of social superiority. Theodor Adorno enforced that abolition by decreeing that there could be no more poetry after Auschwitz; given the evidence of human foulness, 'belles lettres' had to be stripped of any claim to beauty or nobility. Barthes devoted one of the essays in *Mythologies* to the case of Minou Drouet, the child poet whose literary works were probably forged by her mother. Minou interested him because to share the popular belief in her innate, precocious genius was 'to posit literature once again as a gift of the gods' – for Barthes, an absurd overestimation. In his essay on Dumas' *Lady of the Camellias* he described the ingenuous Armand's vision of the courtesan Marguérite as 'the moment when the argument [between the different kinds of love they profess] really becomes Literature'. The naive young man has conferred respectability on the soiled, unworthy object of his desire and canonized her, whereas in truth she belongs, like a text, to whoever cares to have his way with her.

Although Barthes rejoiced in the death of the author, he preferred not to contemplate the death of the book; it was left to Jacques Derrida to declare that 'the end of linear writing is indeed the end of the book'.

Asked about this prognosis in 1971, Barthes replied, 'I cannot see the death of the book because that would be to see my own death, which is to say that I can hardly speak of it, except mythically.' Why 'mythically'? Presumably because beginnings and endings are events we can only imagine, and Barthes surely never foresaw being struck down by a laundry van outside the Collège de France in Paris; he died in 1980 a month after that accident, aged only sixty-four. Although the printed book still clings to life, the outlook for its future is increasingly gloomy.

Those cumbrous tomes are quietly disappearing – transcribed onto microfilm as public libraries clear their shelves and install computers, or dwindling to fit inside an electronic gadget that replaces the page with a screen displaying backlit digital print. Yes, books have their inconveniences. They do weigh us down: they have bulk, which is why in the bourgeois society decried by Barthes they double as furniture. More importantly, they have gravity. Dense with ideas, storing experience, they aim to be as solid as the reality they describe, and their volume testifies to the work that went into making them. It was not enough for Balzac to write his novels; he printed them as well, because he wanted to contribute to the process by which a mechanical press reproduced and multiplied his words. He even slept in the factory, to keep company with the machines that were his helpmates. But now the books with which he wanted to replenish the world are being transferred to some notional cybernetic cloud where they wait to be recalled, page by page, for perusal in e-readers. These slim slabs of plastic consume the hefty novels and loquacious Shakespearean plays that are fed into them. One of Amazon's Kindles, which weighs just 6.34 ounces and is 0.3 inches thick, was called the Voyage. Just what kind of voyage is it possible to take in such an airy, insubstantial vessel?

I tried out an early e-reader a few years ago. What I read was print without an imprint, words that hovered in a grey cloud on the screen, remote from the indentations of the press or the flourishes of human handwriting. There was no chance of a dialogue, which is what I loved when as a student I wrote my name in the books I owned and annotated them as I went along. The format kept the words out of reach behind glass, which prohibited marginal scribbles or enthusiastic underlinings. The page was also squeakily, repellently clean. Ink reminds us of mess, spillage, false starts, crossings-out and the need to refill the well – all the lively uncertainty of thinking and writing. The electronic text lacked texture, despite the manufacturer's flavoursome description of the display as 'plain vanilla'; when you hold a real book, your fingers and even your nose tell you that you're dealing with an organic product, the pulped derivative of a tree. Milton defined a book as 'the precious life-blood of a master spirit', and it does match our bodily substance – paper like skin, binding like nerves, a spine that functions as a backbone, a dust jacket that serves as protective outdoor clothing.

It's an additional benefit, in theory at least, if you have to cut the pages before reading them. The container is naturally retentive, guarding secrets that belong in the master spirit's consciousness, to which we can only gain access by slicing open the folds. Our own minds are supposed to have a cutting edge, like that of the blade we have to use before we start reading. Or perhaps we need a knife, fork and spoon: Walter Benjamin liked the idea that we can 'devour' books – an odd metaphor, as he remarked, but an apt one, because eating is a magical practice, a literal incorporation, as we absorb 'the spirits of things eaten' along with our prescribed daily intake of minerals, vitamins, carbohydrates and saturated fats. Remembering Milton's image of the spirit's blood, it's possible that to read might even be a vampirish habit.

E-readers, however, are inedible, juiceless despite the current that activates them. After a couple of ham-fisted hours I unplugged the one I was testing and went back gratefully to my favourite book, a copy of the complete Shakespeare that I won as a school prize in the 1960s. It has aged with me, its margins filling up with layered notes; its cloth cover is frayed like thinning hair to expose the cardboard underneath, and the spine is as unreliable as my own lower back. I may outlive it but I will never exhaust it, and to read it you do not need a connection to the electricity supply. Even Barthes – whose own books were short or fragmentary, sometimes mostly made up, like *Mythologies*, of very brief aphoristic essays – allowed himself to be impressed by the 'sphericity' of the great nineteenth-century novels, 'plane projections of a curved and organic world', overpopulated and bulbous like what Shakespeare called 'the great globe itself'. The e-reader's screen has no such spatial extension: it is flat, it stops at the margins, and if it gets much thinner than Amazon's Voyage it risks disappearing into the same limbo to which it has despatched all those inconveniently heavy volumes, loose baggy suitcases into which all the uproar of life and the noisy vigour of language are packed.

Encouragingly, the prototype of the book has not been easy to discard. The e-reader I tried out was an iLiad, which spelled its name that way because it claimed kinship with the iPod or iPad as well as with Homer's epic, and the metaphorical stylus with which I pretended to turn the non-existent pages was shaped like a pen. A competing device is called the Kobo, a scrambled anagram of 'book', while the name Amazon chose in 2012 for its new reader with built-in LED lights was the Paperwhite: the fibrous, pulpy stuff, refined to smoothness and bleached to remove impurities, is still the standard to which the grey screen aspires.

Announcing the new Fire HDX tablet in 2014, Amazon's founder and chief executive Jeff Bezos said that 'the team has packed an incredible amount of technology and innovation' into the product – yet in spite of all this novelty, the device clung to a very old-fangled name. Tablets were sheets of ivory and wood on which scribes wrote; Hamlet calls for his 'tables' so that he can scribble down his discovery about the smiling villainy of his uncle. Even tabloid newspapers, hardly synonymous with literature, have a lineal connection to those ancient surfaces, whose purpose was to record thoughts that had to be preserved, saved from the breathy amnesia of speech. Thanks to such metaphors, computers still pay homage to a physical presence that electronic equipment has actually overcome. What could be cosier than the notion of a laptop, almost as comforting as a lapdog? The word ingratiates by suggesting that this is not office equipment, like the clunky computers called desktops: instead a laptop is meant to be held close, cradled like a pet or a baby.

E-readers are marketed with similar cunning. Barnes & Noble calls its product the Nook, which rhymes with 'book' and also conjures up the reclusive corner in which we do our reading – curled in a favourite armchair, or in one of the private compartments in American libraries that are known as carrels. Closed off from the idle chatter of those who are living not reading, we engage in a silent dialogue with a writer, which may be why Amazon downloads e-books from a soft-spoken source that it calls Whispernet. Although e-readers allude to nooks, crannies and cloistered mental spaces, they are better suited to trains or airline seats with minimal elbow room than to libraries, and they do bring a sotto voce privacy to such congested public spaces. A neighbour can't easily read over your shoulder if you are holding one, and because there is no book jacket on display no one can judge you by appraising your choice of reading matter. Female commuters were apparently glad of the chance to download E. L. James's *Fifty Shades of Grey*, rather than having to be seen on public transport with the thick, incriminating paperbacks.

The e-reader has sneakily borrowed the myth of clarification that makes all printed books, no matter how profane and trashy, remote offshoots of the Bible – a word that derives from 'biblos', meaning papyrus bark. 'Dominus illuminatio mea' is the motto of Oxford University Press. With the e-reader, divine illumination changes to electrification, or perhaps to arson: Amazon named its device the Kindle to evoke the moment when the mind strikes sparks from words, and the Nook contains a gently radiant lamp called a GlowLight. The light and heat become more intense in the Fire HDX: perhaps a hint that paper is flammable, and a pious admonition to get rid of it in the interest of ecological health. New technologies are cruel, and while intromitting books e-readers are also burning them, turning words into shuttling electrons, hot because they are mobilized as they speed through the air or down the wires.

Bezos boasted that the new Fire tablet has 'an incredible HDX display, a powerful quad-core processor, a 70 per cent faster engine, exceptional audio, and faster wi-fi'. How can our eyes, ears and minds keep up with such a barrage of instantly connected audiovisual signals? It is not only the book that is threatened with redundancy; the human reader will have to work hard to compete with this e-avatar. Barthes complained that the medical scrutiny of Einstein's brain assessed thought as 'the measurable product of a complex (quasi-electrical) apparatus'. Today the engine that, as Barthes said, 'transforms cerebral substance into power' is no longer a physical organ: we are on the point of outsourcing our native intelligence to Apple and its newest, smartest products. All the same, I do not intend to junk my tattered Shakespeare, which if carefully handled will, I hope, not fall apart before I do.

VAPING

Barthes was often photographed gripping a Havana cigar, the end of which he had usually chomped off with his teeth. He knew that he was brandishing 'a bourgeois emblem', as he said when commenting on Brecht's fondness for the same prop: the cigar used to be shamingly associated with captains of industry, who resembled their own factory chimneys as they puffed out acrid fumes. The social semiotics of smoking worried Barthes more than the danger to his health, but he pondered the theoretical dangers in a rhetorical question, asking 'Are we no longer to smoke cigars, to enter into the metonymy of the social Fault, to refuse to compromise ourselves in the Sign?' A metonym is a part that stands for the whole, so the social and political gaffe was scaled down to a figure of speech. Having made the act merely linguistic, Barthes allowed himself this compromise with capitalist swank. He pleaded that a cigar 'gives pleasure', and thought that the acts of sucking or chewing on it and gesticulating with it were 'the ambiguous flowering, half functional and half ludic, of the signifier'. Forget about making the tobacco burn or inhaling the smoke: what matters are the signals the smoker sends out, as if he were a Native American chieftain fanning his campfire.

In other portraits Barthes appears with a pipe – less of a threatening truncheon than the industrialist's cigar, and consecrated to more highbrow uses by generations of Oxford dons. In his book on photography, Barthes contradicted Magritte's assertion that a painted pipe is not a pipe because you can't put tobacco in it. A cigar could dwindle to a metonym, but a photographed pipe was, he said, 'always and intractably a pipe', and its fixity vouched for 'the funeral immobility at the very heart of the moving world'. There was an inadvertent premonition in that remark: on the night of his death, he smoked six successive pipes after dinner, which might have brought on his final collapse. He was also partial to consumerism's most dangerous trophy, the cigarette, which – in the words of a scientist at an American institute that researches tobacco control – is 'still the most satisfying and deadly product ever made'. The apple that grew on the tree in Eden symbolizes sin but is not to blame for our mortality; about tobacco there can be no such doubt.

Barthes admitted that a cigarette was for him a fetish, like the wand flourished by a 'feitiçeiro' or enchanter. Trying to understand the magnetism of a lover's body, he guessed that it had something to do with the loved one's 'way of spreading the fingers, while talking, while smoking'. The equation links sexual attraction with articulacy, and takes it for granted that conversation involves the exchange of smoke. But unlike Bogart and Bacall, Hollywood stars no longer flirt inside a cloud of cigarette smoke apparently exhaled by their overheated bodies, nor do they use ashtrays as metonyms for double beds. Nowadays intellectuals in Left Bank cafés also have to exercise their minds without flourishing a tube of burning tobacco to dramatize the electrical flashes inside their heads. Smoking has been punitively marginalized, confined to the shivering doorsteps of office buildings.

Even so, consumerism can hardly allow us to be cured of a vice that has been so lucrative. Cigarettes have therefore had a second coming – a rebirth in virtual form as e-cigarettes. These are only notionally electronic, though their vaporizers rely on a battery, and they are hardly cigarettes, since they do without both tobacco and fire; instead they come with atomizers to heat a liquid, along with mains-plug chargers, LED lights and cartridges that serve as mouthpieces. The kit supplies the unreformed with their fix of nicotine, while ensuring that they absorb nothing more harmful than a spray of flavours that include vanilla and chocolate, cherry and mango, or coffee and piña colada – though the raunchiest brands do brew up reminiscences of Marlboros and Camels. You can now perform the old, bad, deadly and foul-smelling ritual metaphorically: rather than smoking, you are vaping.

Back in the 1970s, the comic strip *2000 AD* predicted that life would be like this when the twenty-first century arrived. In the strip, the hard-boiled private eye Sam Slade smoked as a credential of toughness. But the publisher of IPC Comics didn't want the character to set a bad example, so Sam was issued with a robotic cigar called Stogie. This obnoxious android occasionally jumped free from his imprisonment between Sam's teeth, stood upright on his thin wiry legs, and delivered homilies in a Cuban accent: 'We don need no steenkeeng eelecktroneek cigarettes, hombre. Peoples have been suckeeng on my battery-powered butt for over thirty years.'

Although Stogie remains safely in the future, in 2004 a Chinese pharmacist patented non-flammable cigarettes, pipes and cigars, all guaranteed free from tar and carbon monoxide. The Hong Kong company that sold them was called the Golden Dragon Group (Holdings) Limited, but because dragons breathe fire they were no longer appropriate as spirit animals; the corporate name was therefore changed to Ruyan, which means 'Resembling Smoking'. The resemblance is teasingly close. Ruyan tries hard to deny that its devices are counterfeits, and is careful to duplicate form while detoxifying content. Its e-cigarettes imitate actual tubes of paper plugged into a cartridge that pretends to be a cigarette holder, its pipes have stems and bowls of rosewood or agate, and in America its e-cigar retains a certain brawny plutocratic mystique by being called the Ruyan Vegas.

Those who are frank about the physical need to which they are surrendering refer to the e-cigarette as an electronic nicotine delivery system, though that has ENDS as its gruesome acronym. More stylish users describe it as a personal vaporizer, as if it were contributing to intimate hygiene or rehydration. The element of performance that was so important to the act of smoking remains intact, because the liquid puffed out as vapour is odourless propylene glycol, also used to produce fog in theatres and at rock concerts. An American teenager told *The New York Times* in 2015 about his excited reaction when he saw a friend brandishing one of the devices: 'I was, like, "Dude, why do you have a lightsabre?"' It is something of a stretch to turn the knobby little baton into the laser-beamed shaft deployed by the Jedi in *Star Wars*, but cigarettes have always aroused the erectile imaginations of young men.

LiquiPal advertises its product as a marvel of 'pure, precision technology'. Language does the purifying, and the precision technology is the jargon that labels the e-cigarette's components. As with the cronut, portmanteau words are favoured. The refillable tube that holds the liquid is known as a 'cartomizer', compressing 'cartridge' and 'atomizer'. A more guileless-sounding alternative is 'clearomizer' or 'clearo', because the tank is transparent and contains no soaked polyfoam. Interestingly, these portmanteaux chop off the first letter of 'atomizer': the initial 'a' – in words like 'analysis' or 'anatomy', and also in 'atom', the smallest of particles – is the sign of reduction and destruction, a lethal minus inherited from the Greeks; it is concealed for fear that we might remember those science-fiction invasions in which earthlings are 'atomized' by extraterrestrials with ray guns. As an antidote to that 'a', the vocabulary of vaping attaches the modish initial 'e'. As in 'e-mail' or 'e-ticket', it signals modernity while vaguely testifying to ecological virtue. It is also attached to ingredients like the vaporized liquid, which owes nothing to circuitry, transistors or microchips. This pharmaceutical concoction is no more electronic than a drink of water, but vapers call it e-juice. Perhaps the 'e' stands for emulation.

Any oral fixation is necessarily linguistic, and vaping goes beyond simply huffing and puffing through the atomizer in your mouth: it's necessary as well to talk the vape talk. In California, according to a BBC report by Owen Bennett-Jones early in 2015, vapers in bars, lounges and arty hang-outs have elaborated a glossary to define their connoisseurship. They carefully calculate nic levels, and debate the virtues of sub-ohm rechargeable mech mods and metal rebuildable atomizers. Because technological innovation follows the hasty pace of fashion, eco wool and steel mesh have given way to drip tips and wire coils with dual silica wicks. Flavours grow ever more floridly verbose. One example given by Bennett-Jones is organic kosher shazamazam, a 'grape and apple combo' that blends propylene glycol, vegetable glycerin and sucralose, with – according to the Drip Society – a possible tincture of nicotine. Teenagers favour grosser-sounding concoctions with names like Unicorn Puke and Hawk Sauce. Taste is subjective, so the labels on the bottles of liquid are playgrounds for metaphor.

It was shrewd to choose the word 'vaping' for the activity and its accessories. Vapour is milder than smoke, less dense and stifling, and there is no suggestion that it can be traced back to some conflagration in a woodpile, a furnace, or your seared throat and blackened lungs. Still, the history of the word has its embarrassments. In the medical jargon of the early nineteenth century, the vapours were fluttery disturbances of the organism's weather that caused young women to swoon. Over-anxious to detach cigarettes from their carcinogenic reputation, the promoters of vaping have labelled their own product with a name that once covered a range of nervous maladies corresponding to depression, PMS or bipolar disorder. 'Vapid', the adjective that lurks in the vicinity, is even more unwelcome. Applied to drinks – and by association to the e-juice poured into cartotanks or clearos – it means flat and stale; something that has vaporized must have breathed out whatever goodness or vigour it once contained. Rather than a chimney, the e-smoker resembles an aerosol bottle spritzing the atmosphere. The smoker at least stoked up an internal combustion engine, and in fits of coughing signalled that a motor was still effortfully working. The vaper, by contrast, exhales nothing but warm air.

For Barthes and his post-war contemporaries in Paris, smoking dramatized our existential dicing with death. Sartre, who was seldom photographed without his pipe and in addition got through several packets of Boyards a day, declared in *Being and Nothingness* that the habit was 'the symbolic equivalent of destructively appropriating the entire world'. When he lit up, he fancied that he was making a funeral pyre of obtuse material reality; no atomizer could do such a thorough job of incinerating the 'consumed solid' or stage such a 'crematory sacrifice'. Barthes was never so ridiculously Moloch-like, but he thought of his pipe, like one of McLuhan's media, as an extension of himself, and said that a smoker and the tube of tobacco plugged into his mouth are 'glued together, limb by limb, like the condemned man and the corpse in certain tortures, or even like those pairs of fish (sharks, I think ...) which navigate in convoy, as though united by an eternal coitus' – a connection that is at once erotic and toxic.

Given this Wagnerian anticipation of death, Barthes would have scoffed at e-cigarettes as cowardly things. Vaping lacks the reckless sensuality he valued. All the same, he often referred to the process, most tellingly when he explained how myth removes objects from their proper place in time and uproots them from their origins. Because of myth, Barthes said, 'history evaporates', and – repeating the insistent phrase – he professed to find something 'miraculous' in what he called 'the evaporation of history'. What better example could there be than the e-cigarette, which has mythically wished away all the venal iniquities of Big Tobacco and denied responsibility for the millions of patients who have expired in cancer wards? At least that is what it thought it had done, before a British report suggested that new generations of young people were being introduced to addictive nicotine by this supposedly harmless fad.

Barthes called myth 'a language which does not want to die'. Smoking, too, is just such a language, and it has made the same sly protest against its extinction. Although the habit has been condemned, the murder weapons it so profitably deployed have made a comeback as electronic toys. Vapour, however, weightlessly blows away. Barthes with his pipes and cigars preferred residue, embers, ash – the fallout from our vices, and evidence of our enjoyable bodily existence. Better to burn up than to dissolve, leaving only a flavoured haze behind. 'The function of myth,' Barthes warned, 'is to empty reality: it is, literally, a ceaseless flowing out, a haemorrhage, or perhaps an evaporation.' Myth, it appears, is vaping by other means.

A MIRAGE

Cities have always grown slowly, accumulating human stories that pile up on the earth like the stacked storeys of buildings and entangle beneath it like the intertwined roots of plants and trees. Dubai, which shimmers unstably above the forgetful sand, has no such grounding: it is like a bubble that encloses empty air in a thin film of transparent liquid. A couple of decades ago, this was a dusty encampment on the edge of the desert; then the crouched skyline suddenly bristled with cranes that nodded and swivelled around the clock as new hotels and corporate offices scaled the sky, welded together by harried labourers flown in from India and Pakistan.

Geography was hurriedly revised, with God's first draft overwritten by real-estate developers. On reclaimed land in the Persian Gulf, the fronds of a floating palm tree house a tourist resort. Eroding dunes have miraculously turned into lushly pampered golf courses, and a slab-like diagonal building pitched at a sick angle contains a piste where you can ski indoors all year on man-made snow that mocks the tropical humidity outdoors. Yet something is missing – a reason for being, a predestining myth to establish the necessity of the place and supplant the actual story of Dubai's origins as a market frequented by a vagrant population of pearl-divers, camel-drivers, Bedouin nomads, fishermen in dhows, and refugees from tribal feuds in adjoining countries.

Cities usually save themselves from contingency by nominating a mythical patron or progenitor. Lisbon was first called Olissipone in homage to Odysseus who, according to the legend, strayed this far west during his dilatory journey home from Troy, and Julius Caesar was once given credit for building the Tower of London. Rome takes pride in the wolf-suckled twins who were its founders, while Berlin – reluctant to accept the suggested derivations of its name from a dialect word for a swamp or a logjam in a river – claims to have a bear as its titular defender. Nature supplies a blessing for Buenos Aires. Cincinnati and Washington nominate political mentors, just as Leningrad did when Soviet atheism banned the worship of St Peter. Who or what protects Dubai and, apart from its tax advantages, endows it with a sense of mission?

Early in the twenty-first century, lolling on a beach beside the Gulf, the Mayfair gallery-owner John Martin experienced a revelation. 'What Dubai needs,' he decided, 'is an international art fair.' At the time, there were other things Dubai needed more urgently: some walkable streets, traffic regulations for its marauding jeeps, or perhaps a bookshop. But it soon acquired its art fair, which, in the words of Martin's publicists, was meant to establish this improbable outpost with its artificial landscape as 'the most important centre in Asia, likely to rival London and New York within a decade'.

Dubai's neighbour Abu Dhabi, which not long ago consisted of a few straggling villages and a smattering of date farms, showed the way by trading oil for culture. An arid island off the coast has been set aside as a cultural precinct, due to house the tumbling pile of cone-shaped boxes that is Frank Gehry's latest Guggenheim; a performance centre by Zaha Hadid that unfurls vegetatively and swells into pods; a mollusc-shaped Maritime Museum by Tadao Ando; and – after President Chirac charged Abu Dhabi a billion dollars for access to a national cultural brand and the United Arab Emirates further curried favour by spending ten billion dollars on French armaments – a hovering disc designed by Jean Nouvel to exhibit loans from the Louvre. The museums proclaim the advent of an instant, pre-packaged city; what they contain matters less than their fortuitous arrival here, after descending from the sky like Nouvel's flying saucer, poking through the sand like Hadid's serpentine vine, emerging from the sea like Ando's shellfish, or being hastily unloaded from a delivery van like Gehry's crates.

Humanists, wanting to believe that art represented our better nature, used to say it enshrined values that were universal. Now what we ask is that it should be global, instantly convertible like any other currency. The Dubai International Financial Centre therefore stepped in to sponsor John Martin's fair, and in March 2007 the director of the Centre, His Excellency Dr Omar Bin Sulaiman, strolled out of his headquarters into the sultry evening air and offered a casually aloof greeting to a crowd of free, dishevelled spirits whose work is a prolongation of childhood play. The building that houses the Centre resembles Marble Arch as it might look after a course of weight training. Around it, the invited artists had planted a garden of unfunctional whimsies: floor lights that supposedly represented 'multiverse perceptions', a mirrored kaleidoscope containing a tunnel of private reminiscence, a clump of ceramic columns like blue decapitated palms.

'I don't understand what you do,' drawled Bin Sulaiman as his draperies flapped in the wind, 'but welcome anyway.' At that, a long chorus line of grizzled men in traditional Arab dress filed from an office lobby, shuffled into a semicircle, and began a tribal chant, rhythmically jabbing the air with canes that should have been used to discipline their camels (which might perhaps have been stabled by the platoon of valet parkers on hand for the event). Their mesmeric drone went on for ten minutes. They had their hands around each other's waists to form a phalanx, and I noticed that one of them, though pretending to have ridden in from the desert, wore cufflinks encrusted with diamonds.

The next day Bin Sulaiman drove his sports car to a beach hotel to open the fair. John Martin ushered him in, recommending the wares in terms that a specialist in asset management, capital markets and financial flows between East and West would understand. 'There's a hundred million dollars' worth of art in there,' said Martin, 'and it's all for sale.' When art becomes currency, money itself, which is nothing more than a symbol of value, qualifies as art. The exhibit that summed up the fair's agenda, proudly displayed near the entrance, was Andy Warhol's silk-screened dollar sign with its snaky curves, its uprights like the bars of a cell and its pigment as bright as ketchup or blood.

Striding into a booth occupied by a local gallery, Bin Sulaiman ignored the works that scratched at the East's resentment of the invading West: a redesigned American flag with Arab calligraphy in place of the stars and stripes, or Snoopy accessorized with a machine gun. He paused beside a slab of gold with 'NATION OF ISLAM' embossed on it, perhaps unaware that it was a work of art. 'How much is that?' he asked, and was answered by the gallery owner's polite, apprehensive titters. Keeping up a brisk pace, he did not notice Gavin Turk's bronzed bin bags, which joke about art as surplus or expensive trash; he probably also overlooked

Edward Burtynsky's photograph of a Chinese graveyard for rusting ships and Wang Qingsong's photographic triptych of Chinese villagers cravenly welcoming McDonald's, which in its middle panel studies the refuse that festers beneath the golden arches. One of Bin Sulaiman's hands clutched a set of prayer beads: it was sunset, the hour of the muezzin, and while his eyes wandered over trophies he did not covet, his fingers – dispensed from their usual work of calculation – were busy praying. He soon swept off with his entourage, and I forgot about him until two years later, when I read that he had been arrested for embezzlement, corruption and misuse of power. He remained in custody until he repaid roughly twelve million dollars of misappropriated funds, which did not take him long.

John Martin preaches a creed he calls 'art commerce', and at the opening he announced that 'The art world, like finance, is moving east.' In the seventeenth century, what Bishop Berkeley called 'the course of empire' aimed inevitably westwards, crossing Europe and advancing towards America. That course has now reversed, and the Emirates value their closeness to Asiatic metropoli like Moscow, Mumbai and Beijing. At a forum organized by the fair, a functionary from the Gagosian Gallery in New York enthusiastically assessed the Middle East's contribution to 'global art production'. A curator from Barcelona chided museums that mistakenly invested in Latin American painters for 'betting on a different horse' with supposedly 'higher odds', while a Lebanese 'art expert' rallied artists to act as 'creative entrepreneurs' and recommended that Arab societies should 'hedge on art'. The metaphor was not horticultural: in an auditorium next to the fair, hundreds of besuited money-managers had gathered for a conference on hedge funds.

In a tent on the beach, with choppers buzzing overhead to deposit celebrities on the helipad that juts from the spinaker of the Burj Al Arab hotel, I overheard some grumblings from artists who resisted enslavement by the market and rebuffed the new breed of stock-trading curators. Jan Fabre explained why he stopped making saleable objects and instead concentrated on performance. 'You do a theatrical piece and after two hours it has no economic value at all,' he said. 'I find that beautiful.'

Kader Attia, an Algerian brought up in Paris, described an installation in St Germain des Près where he set up a shop called Hallal, which he crammed with Muslim fashion redesigned for the suburban proletariat: tacky sneakers, slickly synthetic T-shirts. Whenever customers took an item to the cashier, they were told, 'Oh no, it's not for sale – it's art!' An entrepreneur who was immune to irony offered Attia a fortune to license the Hallal clothing line for distribution in the Arab world. He refused, thus defining the difference between an artist and a 'galleriste'.

At the fair, Attia showed a recent video documenting the fate of some sugar cubes that melted and fell apart when sprayed with black oil. His audience included a clutch of Dubai matrons swathed in burkahs, jewels glinting in their headdresses and flowers of henna traced on their hands. 'What is your concept?' asked one of them from behind her veil. Attia played the video again, and the sludge once more soiled and corroded the clumps of crystalline sweetness. The woman still did not get the point, or perhaps was reluctant to admit that the confluence of art and petrol might look so mucky. Attia cryptically explained. 'The white cube,' he said, 'is maybe drinking too much oil.' Artists, like holy fools, specialize in dangerous jests: the showiest position at the fair had been commandeered by the London gallery White Cube.

Sarah Strang devised her own wry joke about art commerce in *Marketplace*, which was commissioned by the fair. Signs in Arabic and English explained the protocols of art auctions, and defined the meaning of 'hammer price'. (Christie's had recently held its first sale in Dubai, disposing of most lots to Indian bidders. 'The Emiratis are loaded,' an informant told me, 'but my God they're clueless!') Beneath Strang's placards, artisans recruited in the souk chiselled, filed and hammered thin strips of gold into postcards that boasted 'MADE IN DUBAI'. Is aesthetic value a matter of carats? Are the merchants who sell art the enemies of those who create it, not their allies? In the hand of a craftsman, the hammer is a delicate aesthetic implement. Gripped by an auctioneer impatient to secure his profit, it becomes a bludgeon.

The fair was held in a hotel resembling a fortified sandcastle; on its outer wall, Beth Derbyshire projected a commentary on art, convertibility, translation, and the misunderstandings that vex our supposedly borderless world. Lasers beamed the word 'together' in English and Arabic onto the baked stone. The letters danced, circled, decomposed and reconstituted themselves, then briefly merged in a beautiful, unintelligible muddle. On the terrace below the dancing curlicues of green and purple light, guests ate smoked salmon, pasta, Peking duck and other non-indigenous treats, while drinking wine that Emiratis regard as a heathen abomination. Tirdad Zolghadr, a curator from Zurich who spoke at the forum, explained this culinary Esperanto by remarking that art must nowadays be 'multi-ethnic, widening the choice of flavours on the smorgasbord'. But culture, like food, relies on a rooted idiosyncracy, and dies when it is reduced to gabbling in pidgin.

Home-grown art, unlike that freighted in by curators and auctioneers, struggles to find a footing in Dubai. On an industrial estate, between a cement works and a warehouse stocking fuel-injection parts, I groped through a sandstorm towards a shed marked PROGRESSIVE ART GALLERY, inside which the Palestinian painter Jeffar Khaldi displayed canvases streaked with gore. The gallery did not seem to be a guarantor of progress, and a nearby Ferrari and Maserati showroom had more customers. Further off, on a building site surrounded by piers of reinforced concrete, a banner proclaimed, 'The Most Prestigious Square Kilometer on the Planet'. 'Live the Life' shrieked another billboard, on which happy expats whirled through an existence that consisted of consuming. This is where Burj Khalifa, set to be the tallest building in the world, had begun to twist upwards like a corkscrew puncturing heaven. 'History Rising' yelled a third sign: history here is above not below, ahead not behind, a presumption or prediction not an archive or archaeological deposit.

Burj Khalifa now functions as the city's elasticated totem. But before it could qualify as a centrepiece, like a mercantile minaret, it had to be mythologized. The art fair confirmed that Dubai, despite the efforts of its promoters, remains a bazaar where traders haggle and attempt to outfox each other; Burj Khalifa required the intervention of a high-flying god with a talent for high jinks. In this case, what Dubai needed was a visit from Tom Cruise, who in *Mission: Impossible – Ghost Protocol* removes a window from a suite on the 119th floor of Burj Khalifa, dives into the windy void, then clambers up the glassy spindle towards its pinnacle, attached to the curved surface by nothing more than the suction grip on his gloves.

The film's plot supplies Cruise with a reason for this feat, on which of course the fate of the world depends. He is in Dubai to steal back some misappropriated nuclear codes, with which a crazed physicist intends to instigate a cataclysmic war. To bring off the planned substitution, he has to commute between suites on two different floors of Burj Khalifa. Since he can't use the elevator, slice through impenetrable firewalls or wriggle down ventilation ducts, the only way to manage this is by climbing the outside of the building. Cruise, who refused to use a stuntman, spent several days scampering up, down and around the skyscraper, tethered by a network of rigging cables that were later digitally erased. Nature seemed unimpressed. Almost three thousand feet above the ground, the air was undramatically placid, and a wind machine had to be poked out of an open window to ruffle his hair.

Absurdly gratuitous as it all was, Gregg Smrz, the technician who supervised the acrobatics, had a life-or-death analogy in mind. After a trial run in Prague, using a replicated section of Burj Khalifa, the crew flew to Dubai and promptly launched Cruise through the window. 'Kind of like a military operation,' said Smrz, 'where they're gonna go in and rescue the hostages': he meant that the exploit had to happen without the luxury of rehearsal. In the age of terrorism, American foreign policy becomes ever more like an action movie, which is why George W. Bush chose to land by helicopter on an aircraft carrier anchored off Los Angeles to announce, over-optimistically, that his own mission – the second Iraq war – had been accomplished.

Since then there have been other stunts like Cruise's at Burj Khalifa, which is less a building than a climbing pole or an aquiline perch. A French daredevil spent more than six hours shinning up the tower in 2011, and in 2015 a white-tailed eagle set a record for the highest recorded bird flight from a man-made structure as it set off from the top and filmed the smudged, monotonous vista below with a Sony ActionCam Mini that had been fitted to its tiny head. Dubai has grown so tall so rapidly and so needlessly that it has forgotten why societies are founded and how they are held together. Here art both inflates value and undermines it by hedging preposterous bets, and the purpose of architecture is not to construct a human habitation but to induce a swoony spasm of vertigo.

5 The Human Thing

IN THE DINO GYM

Every human life, during its early stages, recapitulates the history of the species. We start with a wailing protest about our ejection into a hostile world, followed by efforts to crawl and experiments at standing upright. Once we are on our feet, evolution carries us along until, decades later, it goes into reverse and we slide backwards. Childhood, you might think, already contains enough fears – rustling nocturnal alarms, a recurrent panic about being fed, the possibility that we might not get what we want immediately – but recently a new one has been added to its total of terrors: dinosaurs have been brought back from the dead to romp and frolic in our nurseries.

Their presence during those first formative months is evidence that the struggle for survival begins early. Playgro's Dino Gym tucks infants into a Jurassic cradle, where they lie on a padded mat and kick at soft, pastel-coloured Tyrannosaurus rexes and Velociraptors that dangle from an arch. Staring up at this flying circus is supposed to 'encourage visual perception', though who would want those airborne ogres as a primal memory? Supine, the baby would be defenceless if they were to swoop down for a meal. A chewable teething ring is provided for the gurgling morsel on the mat, which does not improve the odds.

Not long ago, toddlers were regaled by the televised antics of Barney, a purple T-rex who sang cheerful ditties about how much he loved little children. His appetites were blander than those of his flesh-tearing forebears: his preferred treat was a peanut butter and jelly sandwich, washed down with a glass of milk. The diets of Barney's colleagues were equally insipid. The Triceratops Baby Bop snacked on macaroni cheese, while her brother B. J. fancied pizza with pickles. Kelloggs saw a marketing opportunity, and advertised its Crunchy Nut cereal in a commercial that showed a vegetarian T-rex foraging for cornflakes. Perhaps dinosaurs appealed to their juvenile constituency because their fangs and claws enabled them to eat whenever and whatever they pleased. Bill Gates said he outgrew his fascination with them when he became tall enough to open the fridge door and prepare his own dinner.

But these relics of the Jurassic era are not so easily dismissed. Graduating to an electronic culture, they now induct older children into the abracadabra of the computer. Barclays Bank has introduced an online game to teach coding to its future customers, whose first lesson involves choreographing the movements of a goofy dino. The animals in Barclays' infantile Eden are even more docile than Barney and the Playgro menagerie, because the child who knows how to tap at a keyboard can shorten or lengthen a giraffe's neck, decide the number of scales on a fish's skin, and teach a dinosaur to dance the moonwalk. 'Help them learn the new language for the new economy,' says the tagline for this promotional scheme. It is the language of a new theology as well as a new economy: coding revises Genesis by equipping children as genetic designers, and at the age of eight they are encouraged to treat those gigantic reptiles as pets and digitally order them to perform tricks.

A decade later, those with driving licences can harness the monsters all over again by acquiring a Hennessey 'muscle truck' called the VelociRaptor. It lacks the sickle-shaped claws of its namesake, but its fender flares, seventeen-inch wheels, thirty-three-inch tyres, off-road bumpers and engine plaques should make up for that.

Fantasies like this can be indulged because dinosaurs have been extinct for sixty-five million years, and are therefore no threat. A century ago, not long after Darwin's account of our simian origins, the prospect of having to cope all over again with this ruthless, rampant species was more alarming. In Conan Doyle's novel *The Lost World* a party of scientists ventures onto a South American plateau where dinosaurs, pterodactyls, outsize fish-lizards and lethal ape-men still thrive in an environment that resembles 'some raw planet in its earliest and wildest state'. Here, while battling the antediluvian ogres, they learn to question their own conceit about their own species. The leader of the group, a professor significantly named Challenger, is dragged back into the company of lowlier creatures by Conan Doyle's metaphors: rampaging through London, this hirsute Edwardian sage is likened to a bulldog, an Assyrian bull and an enraged buffalo. When he finally confronts the king of the ape-men, who is equally squat, choleric and hirsute, he might be meeting his twin.

The journalist Malone volunteers for the South American expedition to impress a young woman, and vows to perform feats of bravery worthy of a superman; Challenger scorns his detractors as 'subhuman'. The boast and the insult, tugging the same term in opposite directions, reveal how unfixed and provisional the condition of humanity is. The apes are finally exterminated or enslaved, which allows the scientists to conclude that henceforth 'man was to be supreme and the man-beast to find forever his allotted place'. Today, it is too late for such biblical decrees to have much credence.

In a less confident moment, Challenger admits that human beings only enjoy supremacy because they had the good luck to arrive in the world after a global catastrophe eliminated the dinosaurs. We evolved from apes, and may be entitled to think that we have improved on the simian prototype; with dinosaurs, we have less reason to be self-satisfied. If a passing asteroid or a volcanic eruption had not wiped them out by altering the ecosystem, then what Darwin called the descent of man – which we think of as our unstoppable ascent – could never have happened. We are the beneficiaries of an accident rather than earth's rightful masters, and a similar disaster could end our eminence – or perhaps we may render ourselves redundant by incautious scientific experimentation. Dinosaurs cannot be relegated to remote, pre-human history; they are waiting to face off with us in the genetically engineered world that lies ahead.

Hence the motto of the zoo stocked with laboratory-designed monsters in the films derived from Michael Crichton's novel *Jurassic Park*. Here a company called InGen, short for International Genetic Technologies, sets up a saurian reserve inside an electrified fence and a concrete moat on an island off Costa Rica. Opening for business, it welcomes visitors by announcing, 'We Make Your Future'.

Crichton's initial idea was to have a graduate student clone a pterodactyl. But where, he asked himself, would a doctoral candidate get the funds for such a project? Sponsorship could only come from the entertainment industry. Crichton therefore decided that the begetters should operate an amusement park, where Disneyland's creaky animatronics would be replaced by live specimens, raptors bred in a laboratory by sequencing genes. Assuming that the resort's primary appeal would be to children, he first told the story about the escape of the dinosaurs 'from a kid point of view'. He then changed his mind again: this Pandora's box had to be opened by a Frankensteinian researcher who aimed to seize godlike power.

In the four *Jurassic Park* films based on Crichton's premise, a squealing childish glee alternates with a sober grown-up conscience that weighs the consequences of rewriting natural law. At the start of the series an obese technocrat called Nedry – an anagram of 'nerdy' – shuts down the park's electrical grid while smuggling dino embryos off the island in cans of shaving foam. A Post-it note is taped to the screen of his computer; on it he has scribbled the credo of the post-war generations that, like Peter Pan, have contrived to spend their entire lives in an affluent, irresponsible childhood. The note says 'Beginning of Baby Boom', and next to it is a diagram of a bomb blast: the boom, a noiseless population explosion, here becomes audible as the soundtrack for a cataclysm. Behind the Post-it notes Nedry has placed a postcard of J. Robert Oppenheimer, the physicist who after the detonation of the first nuclear weapon remorsefully called himself 'the destroyer of worlds'.

Jeff Goldblum plays the equivalent of Oppenheimer, a proponent of chaos theory who spells out the moral and theological risks of the park. 'Genetic power is the most awesome force the planet has ever seen,' he tells the promoter, 'but you wield it like a kid that's found his dad's gun.' Will the children who take those Barclays Bank tutorials rest content with elongating the necks of giraffes? In another suggestive quirk, the specimens with which Jurassic Park is stocked are, like the Kardashians, with the exception of Rob, all female. 'We control their chromosomes,' one of the genetic designers explains; as a safeguard, the beasts are prevented from reproducing by the grubby, grunting time-honoured method. But a hitch that involves the DNA of transgendered West African bullfrogs allows the dinos to overleap this obstacle, and after escaping from the park they dispense with scientific protocols and do their breeding the old-fashioned way. Goldblum summarizes an epochal genealogy, which like all myths curls round into a self-repeating circle: 'God creates dinosaurs, God destroys dinosaurs, God creates man, man destroys God, man creates dinosaurs. ...' Laura Dern, playing a paleobotanist, cuts him off. 'Dinosaurs eat man,' she says with a smile, 'woman inherits the earth.'

The second film in the series, *The Lost World*, borrows Conan Doyle's title but stages the uphill evolutionary battle on a steeper gradient, with no certainty about a human victory. Here the scientists huddle inside a trailer – a house on wheels, with every modern convenience – that two infuriated T-rexes push over a cliff. Anchored only by a cable hitched to a jeep whose wheels try to dig into the mud, the trailer dangles above the ocean while Goldblum and Julianne Moore, as an academic expert on Jurassic family life, grab at the suddenly vertical built-in furniture and try to haul themselves to safety. It is a Sisyphean scramble, not a slow but irrevocable Darwinian advance. 'Increase your rate of climb,' someone urges Moore. Instead she slides back and dislodges her colleagues so that they seem about to tumble into the foaming water, where all life originated. A technician gives them the chance to grapple free by revving up the jeep, only to be torn apart by the dinosaurs. 'The man saved our lives by giving his,' says Goldblum, but Christian sacrifice has no moral force in this murderous, meat-eating parody of Eden: for the big-game hunter played by Pete Postlethwaite, the victim was 'just food'.

Bill Gates may have been right about dinos and dining. A consumerist culture can only adore their voracity, and *Jurassic Park* sees nature as a venomously competitive food chain. The characters eat to cheer themselves up, not to stoke their bodies for combat; with the generators out of action, they have a duty to gobble up all the food in their small world before it spoils. Richard Attenborough, who plays the park's inventor, consoles himself for its ruin with a tub of ice cream that has begun to melt. The children celebrate their escape by pigging out on an un-nutritious banquet of cakes, tarts and jellies. In the kitchen of the hospitality centre, two Velociraptors ransack the shelves of pots, pans and ladles, hoping to fasten on the appetizing humans who cower in the larder. They won't need the cooking equipment that they knock aside: they eat their prey raw, while it is still squirming.

Instead of evolution toiling forever onwards and upwards, the repetitious cycle of consumption and excretion is here speeded up. A gibbering lawyer is bitten in half while he squats on the lavatory in a shoddy outhouse that is demolished by a raging dinosaur. Now he is food; he will soon be faeces. Laura Dern plunges her arm up to the elbow into a heaped mound of dino droppings – for her, a museum preserving botanical evidence. 'That's one big pile of shit,' marvels Goldblum. Is it monuments like this that we will leave behind?

The thrill of watching the accelerated orgy of guzzling and voiding in *Jurassic Park* comes from the feeling that we are at mortal risk; it's like the vicarious alarms of the sublime, which confronted romantic heroes with giddy abysses or stormy elemental uproars. Attenborough predicts that a ride through his park will 'drive kids out of their minds', and this suffices as a business plan. In *The Lost World*, Moore and Goldblum pursue a T-rex that is at large in San Diego. Moore asks how they will keep up, since it has bounded so far ahead; Goldblum replies, 'Follow the screams' – though these might be coming from any cinema in the city. At least they are able to chase the beast by car. In *Jurassic World*, the most recent instalment in the series, Bryce Dallas Howard has to flee from another dinosaur in a muddy jungle while wearing a filmy white dress and high-heeled shoes, an item of footwear invented by men – as feminists point out – to ensure that women cannot outrun them. Given the odds against our hobbled or stilted species, it's remarkable that we escaped extinction. In *Jurassic Park III*, the paleontologist played by Sam Neill wearily listens to an adolescent boy's story about recklessly hang-gliding above some mountains in New Zealand. Neill then sums up our late and laughingly self-destructive phase of evolution: 'Reverse Darwinism – survival of the most idiotic.'

Having reverted so alarmingly to the prehistory of humankind, the films need to reassure us about the moral rectitude of our imperilled species. They do so by reconvening the family and its cosy circle of affection, which raises us above the self-seeking greed of the other animals. In the first instalment, Sam Neill begins by grumpily rejecting fatherhood. Then in the wilderness he cradles Attenborough's grandchildren in a paternal Pietà as they doze off, which signals a change of heart. 'The only thing that matters,' says the remorseful Attenborough as he tucks into his ice cream, 'is the people we love.' In the third film, two divorced parents reunite to search for their son, who has gone missing on InGen's island; when they find him, the father says, 'Let's go home', the music swells like a lump in the throat, and they all scurry back to the safety of Oklahoma. The second film is less encouraging. Julianne Moore wishfully applies the human practice of 'parenting and nurturing' to dinos, which in her view are affectionate homebodies, not vicious megalithic lizards. Her theory is confirmed with a vengeance when the infuriated T-rexes concuss the trailer where the paleontologists hold their injured offspring. 'Mommy's very angry,' says Moore as the slavering matriarch batters the roof: is her rage a paroxysm of mother love, or further evidence of nature's rapacity?

Jurassic Park is a mythopoeic enterprise, a contested zone where man does battle with the deities he envies. In an abandoned hatchery, cloned foetuses slumber in tanks. 'This is how you make dinosaurs?' someone asks Sam Neill. 'No,' he shudders, 'this is how you play God.' Perhaps cloning outrages a biological norm and ruinously disrupts the orderly succession of species – but what about the technological competition with God that enabled Spielberg's technicians to manufacture dinosaurs with articulated skeletons swathed in skins of latex and pressed into motion by a computer-generated walk cycle? In the production of *The Lost World*, robotics and digital wizardry took the place of genetic engineering and the 'thinking machine' that encodes dinosaur DNA in the first film, but with similar results. When electrical power is restored, the light from a desktop monitor left on in a dark office projects lines of computer code onto the body of a prowling Velociraptor. Numbers and letters course across its scales like the circulation of greenish-tinged blood or the twitching of a nervous system that relays terse subcutaneous messages. For a few moments it's unclear whether this phantasmal thing is a contraption or an organism; in either case it is genuinely frightful. We owe our primacy to the fortuitous obliteration of the dinosaurs. In artificially reviving them, we may have outsmarted ourselves.

VAMPING

'Myth,' scoffs Edward the vampire in the first novel of Stephenie Meyer's *Twilight* series. He utters the word to demythologize himself: he is disparaging the mouldy, cobwebbed Transylvanian folklore that obliges vampires to inhabit bat-infested castles, sleep in coffins, and flinch from garlic or the sign of the cross. 'The myths,' he explains in the second novel, are merely 'products of fear and imagination'.

Or the products, more positively, of desire and imagination? Edward's disparagement is evasive. Such stories, like the creatures they describe, are indestructible, deathless. Rather than being forgotten, myth, as Barthes argued, will settle for a 'degraded survival'; it can therefore artificially resuscitate defunct ideas and, as he put it in one of his most haunting phrases, 'turns them into speaking corpses' – vampirish simulations of life. Meyer's hero is no Nosferatu or Count Dracula, dank and sclerotic, with teeth sharpened like ice picks. He and the other members of his coven in the forests north of Seattle are 'inhumanly beautiful', with crystalline skin and gleaming American dental work; they are likened to airbrushed figures in the advertising layouts of a glossy magazine or angels in a Renaissance painting – two sets of superior beings that for Meyer and her teenage readers may be interchangeable.

Aro, a vampire who is visiting from Italy, tells his American counterparts to be grateful for their 'status as mere myth', because the human 'faith in science ... protects us from the weak creatures we hunt'. There is no need for improbable experiments like the extraction of DNA from the bites of mosquitoes preserved in amber, which is how the *Jurassic Park* monsters are brought back to life; vampires never became extinct, and are everywhere among us – especially, perhaps, on catwalks at fashion shows, where they strut along looking pale, implacable, affectless and killingly cool.

Meyer's heroine Bella, infatuated by Edward, does her own research about the legends, and decides that the tales of thirsty female demons and their infantile victims were 'constructs created to explain away the high mortality rates for young children' in benighted unmodern Europe.

But the living dead also ghoulishly thrive in America: in Bella's world they are constructs created to explain away adolescent miseries, or perhaps to rationalize the contradictions of an economy that requires people to be insatiable feeders and even expects them to enjoy their disgust as they lap up emetic images. Pining for Edward, Bella says that unrequited love makes her feel and look like a zombie. To cheer herself up, she goes to a horror movie, but finds it not to her taste because it's so uncannibalistic. 'Why isn't anyone getting eaten?' she indignantly demands as she returns from the concession stand, laden with a fresh tub of popcorn and a supply of carbonated drinks. Her companion shrugs 'Almost everyone is a zombie now', then grabs a handful of the exploded corn. Are the bloodsuckers and flesh-eaters, like Bill Gates's omnivorous dinos, merely advanced versions of our culture's ideal consumer?

Not entirely. After discounting one myth, Edward proposes another that is more eugenic. 'Where did you come from?' he asks Bella, obliging her to consider her own origins. 'Evolution? Creation?' Those questions have an open answer in America, where Darwin is regarded in some quarters as a heretic or a blasphemer; the intelligent designer whose busy first week is described in Genesis has even been given credit for the infinitesimally slow erosion that carved the Grand Canyon. Rather than being a biblical literalist, Edward has in mind his own revised supplement to the Old Testament. The Mormon Church, to which Meyer belongs, allows human beings to join the ranks of the angelic hosts, and Edward with his alabaster physique and his aeronautical skills resembles one of the elect. The question he addresses to Bella also alludes to the Mormon myth that makes America the nation most favoured by God and the site of an alternative, latterday creation – better planned than that described in Genesis, with no need for the Fall and the penalties that follow from it.

The emblem of the *Twilight* novels is a red apple held out in the cupped hands of a young woman. The colour – unlike Jobs' whitewashed apple or the green, unripe Granny Smith favoured by the Beatles – signals sexual initiation. Myth, too, with its enchanting irrationality, might be seen as a forbidden fruit. In Bram Stoker's *Dracula* the heroine Mina teases the vampire-hunter Dr Van Helsing by showing him her shorthand diary, which is unintelligible to him. 'I could not resist the temptation of mystifying him a bit,' she simpers. 'I suppose it is some taste of the original apple that remains still in our mouths.' Bella, however, knows in advance about the apple's perils, which is why Edward adheres to a Mormon edict and gallantly foregoes premarital copulation with her. Eve gave birth and in doing so condemned us to die, but Bella is more like Snow White, who dies only temporarily. When Edward impregnates her after their marriage, she fears that the embryo will gnaw its way out of her womb and kill her in doing so; she saves herself and solves the bothersome problem of mortality that weighs on the rest of us by electing to join her mate's species. 'I took mythology a lot more seriously since I'd become a vampire,' she says in a reflective moment. True, the experience of being biologically rebooted – a transfiguration, or a depraved transgression? – probably would give one pause for thought.

When Bella's friend Jacob refers to superstitions about ghouls, she asks, 'Is anything just a myth anymore?' As it happens, Jacob too is a mythical creature: he is a werewolf, and also – as his Hebraic name indicates – a member of the Quileute tribe which, according to Mormon history, somehow traipsed from Israel to the American continent in the seventh century BC. But like Edward, Jacob is demythologized: his shape-shifting simply acts out the physical and psychological changes that overtake adolescent males.

He and the other members of his pack burst out of their skins, grow fur, and instantaneously bulk up into hormonally overstimulated enlargements of themselves. Bella gapes at the mutation, then remembers that they are 'just four really big half-naked boys'. There is no need to speculate about shamanistic magic; testosterone, a gym membership and a six-pack of beer would have produced the same result.

In spite of the blushing apple's temptation, Mormon morality ensures that Bella remains a prim virgin until after marriage, and Mormon theology converts Edward from a damned soul to an angelic intercessor. His sanguinary appetite remains a problem, but Meyer makes light of that by introducing squeamish qualms and ecological quibbles. Although not exactly a vegan vampire, he has sworn off human blood, despite the fact that it's more invigorating than that of other creatures, and when hunting – his favourite titbit is the carcass of a mountain lion – he takes care not to rip the throats of any endangered species.

The grisly Transylvanian legends are sanitized, or Americanized. Here is Meyer's answer to Marx's claim in *Das Kapital* that 'Capital is dead labour that, vampire-like, only lives by sucking living labour.' When capitalism turned consumerist, greed became good, denying the parasitism on which Marx insists. There is no biting or sucking in *Twilight*; the siphoning of blood from the living to the dead is replaced by a sharing of current, like jump-starting a car that has a run-down battery. Meyer's characters do not need to barter their souls in exchange for this freakish ignition. They already enjoy an augmented life, thanks to the appliances they own and the engines they run. When Bella asks Jacob what he most enjoys about being a werewolf, he replies 'the *speed*', and confirms that it's a more intense rush than riding a motorcycle. Bella's problem is not the wilting languor of Dracula's female victims, who suffer from spiritual distress or sexual repression. Her woes are electronic. 'My modem was sadly outdated, my free service substandard,' she moans. Dialling up the Internet takes her so long that she has time to eat a bowl of cereal while she waits – a symptom, incidentally, of how incorrigibly healthy Meyer's people are. What Bella needs is a comprehensive equipment upgrade. Her Chevy truck 'doesn't get very good gas mileage', her washing machine is a 'stupid piece of junk' that thumps to a halt, her decrepit computer wheezes when she turns it on and groans rather than hums as it thinks.

The human species, Meyer implies, is similarly retrograde. Edward prescribes some mental retuning when he finds that he can't eavesdrop on Bella's mind, as he is accustomed to doing: it's 'like your thoughts are on the AM frequency and I'm only getting FM,' he tells her. Amplitude modulation is good enough for billowy, curvaceous Bella, but Edward – more fixed or fixated and averse to interference – sends out his signals by frequency modulation, which places him in a higher sonic spectrum. Consciousness, on this reckoning, is merely circuitry by other means.

Twilight, which is almost anaemic, replaces blood with another vital fluid, or with the fibrillating current that jazzes America and supplies its sleepless energy. Oil and electricity matter more here than the oozing source that brings a 'red light of triumph' to the eyes of Stoker's Dracula. Meyer, a self-confessed autophile, equates her vampires with their cars, which include a Mercedes S55 AMG and a Porsche 911 Turbo, both with black-tinted windows that turn day into night: Dracula's castle comes with an ample and lavishly stocked garage. When Bella argues with Edward about the propriety of premarital sex, she uses a noun that, among other things, applies to the object whose attributes are borrowed to make a metaphor. 'You wouldn't mind if my vehicle went a little faster,' she says. Her decision to graduate from human being to vampire is treated as an automotive trade-in; she surrenders an outmoded conveyance and is fitted with one that performs better. In the final volume, she speaks of her new body and her new car interchangeably. Her Chevy, she reports, has 'expired of natural causes' after 'a long, full life'. Now she drives a 'glossy, black, sleek' Mercedes Guardian, whose engine snarls 'like a hunting panther'. Moreover, she carries with her a 'shiny black credit card' that feels 'red-hot in [her] pocket'. The instant fulfilment of fantasies no longer requires a diabolical pact. All it takes is that wonder-working piece of plastic, which is set on fire by the desires it instantly actualizes.

Petrol may be Meyer's substitute for blood, but Edward is no gas-guzzler. He has a green conscience, and persuades Bella to travel in his own more fuel-efficient Volvo because 'the wasting of finite resources is everyone's business'. At least he drives scarily fast, so that the headlights as they twist round the curves of a rural road look 'like a video game'. (The analogy is apt, because video gaming often involves genetic mutation and the design of alternative worlds: in the BioShock series, plasmids created with a substance called ADAM do battle against Big Daddies in the underwater city of Rapture.) Bella additionally notes that the Volvo 'growls' on Edward's behalf. His virility is outsourced to the motor, as is his jealous fury, so that when she tells him on the phone that she has kissed Jacob what she hears from his end is 'the sound of an engine accelerating'.

Chastely cuddling Edward in bed during their courtship, Bella refrains from genital contact, but she is pressed so close to him that she reports, 'I felt his phone vibrate in his pocket'. An incipient erection, surely? Despite Mormon vows of abstinence, a man's technological extensions have their little thrills. When consummation with Edward at last occurs, Bella's apparatus tingles. 'Every nerve ending in my body was a live wire,' she gasps. Cardiac rhythms are percussively amped up, as if she had a power tool in her chest: her heart, she says, is 'jackhammering'. Later, giving birth, she achieves metaphorical lift-off. Now her heart is 'beating like helicopter blades' rather than 'thundering like a steam engine', and it distributes heat throughout her body 'to fuel the most scorching blaze yet'. The vehicle spurns the road and takes to the air, though the calorific frenzy of the language is a worry. As in an action movie or a video game, we await the moment when the combustible machine will crash and burn.

The werewolves too have a body temperature that is ten feverish degrees above the human average, which enables Bella to use Jacob as her own shaggy space-heater when she is caught out in a blizzard. But there may be an element of envy in Jacob's inimical description of vampires as 'the cold ones': perhaps, in another leap of scientific evolution, they have advanced beyond the thermodynamism of overheated America and cracked the secret of cold fusion. If so, that's preferable to the catastrophe of nuclear fission. After her transformation into a vampire, Bella is protected by an invisible shield made of an 'elastic fabric' – presumably not nylon or polyester – and is able to project herself through space 'in a bubble of sheer energy, a mushroom cloud of liquid steel'. Can it really be enjoyable to feel like a bomb blast, or to have hot metallic skin? Bella engages in a bout of arm-wrestling to test her new strength, and commemorates the occasion with her most effortfully grandiose automotive metaphor: with her power now serenely under control, she feels 'like a cement truck doing forty miles an hour down a sharp decline'. She has no need to consult an 'inner goddess', that clitoral trickster whose gymnastics are recorded by the satiated Anastasia in *Fifty Shades of Grey*. Bella has her inner juggernaut instead, and keeps a firm grip on its steering wheel.

While she agonizes over her promotion to a new species, Jacob 'phases back' from his vulpine condition to homo sapiens so as not to alarm the other guests at her wedding. But he can't get re-accustomed to being a mere biped: 'I'm out of practice with the whole human thing,' he says apologetically, as if it is like having to go back to a clumsy manual gearshift. In case we resist our advance to the next evolutionary phase, a nativity tableau at the conclusion of *Twilight* hustles us ahead. Bella proudly exhibits her daughter Renesmee, a vampire prodigy who has no use for a Dino Gym: she develops so rapidly that for her first Christmas she is fitted with an MP3 player on which five thousand songs are stored. Here is the future in person, with admiring magi – all of them undead, which is the same as being immortal – clustered around an electronic crib. A new order of the ages, to quote the messianic announcement on the American dollar bill, may be beginning. Or, if you are not quite ready for that, the end of superannuated humanity might be near.

AN ELECTRONIC ODALISQUE

Myth favours geographical extremities: the high, remote plateau in South America or the island off Costa Rica where Arthur Conan Doyle and Michael Crichton corral their dinosaurs, the Tihuta Pass in the Carpathian mountains where Bram Stoker situates Dracula's castle, the Swiss glaciers and Arctic ice floes where Frankenstein's monster appears and disappears – any site in which human habitation has not yet crowded out gods and monsters. The *Twilight* series finds an equivalent in the rainforests of the Olympic Peninsula in Washington State. Here the migratory Quileutes sneak into rationalized America, smuggling their necromantic practices with them; the vampires make their landfall in the same area, because as 'one of the most sunless places in the world' it is kind to their unruddy complexions. Bella, having moved to the Pacific Northwest from furnace-like Arizona, dislikes the constant rain and considers her new home 'too green – an alien planet'.

Less than a hundred miles away from the peninsula is Seattle, the setting of E. L. James's *Fifty Shades of Grey* trilogy, which began as an amateurish homage to Stephenie Meyer's sexually esoteric romance. The city is a frontier of a different kind. Rather than an overgrown route to the tribal past, it is a laboratory where successive futures are designed. Seattle is the home of the Boeing factory and the flying saucer-shaped Space Needle, of Bill Gates and the telecommunications magnate Christian Grey, who in the first *Fifty Shades* novel introduces himself by saying, 'I employ over forty thousand people', which gives him, he adds, 'immense power'.

Christian addresses these pick-up lines to the virginal student Anastasia Steele, whom he entices into a sadomasochistic affair. He is a master of the universe, but more specifically he is Ana's master, enforcing his control with the chains, shackles, cuffs and leather disciplinary aids he keeps in his sequestered 'Red Room of Pain'. Fetishism here replaces the black arts of Meyer's predators: James's Seattle, as the nickname of Christian's annex of implements makes clear, is anything but green. The skyscraper that is 'the headquarters of [his] global enterprise' is made of steel, and Ana's surname suggests that, for all her initial trepidation, she is moulded from the same material. Christian is Grey by name and by nature, wearing 'a fine grey suit' and possessing 'bright grey eyes'; his black tie and white shirt are presumably waiting to merge in that intermediate zone. He imparts his chilly charisma to the first gift he sends to Ana. To woo her, he selects something that is 'sleek and silver', grey but glisteningly so – not jewellery but a MacBook Pro, 'next-generation tech', described as 'the very latest from Apple'. The fruit that is *Twilight*'s emblem has lost its inflamed colour and turned icily metallic. After the Mac, Christian presents Ana with an Audi to replace her rattletrap VW Beetle: a significant gift, because he also thinks of sex as a driving lesson, and says he intends to 'refine her motor skills with the aid of a riding crop'.

Christian's given name triggers associations with the wrong religion, although once, after a shared shower, Ana thinks that the two of them look 'almost biblical, as if from an Old Testament Baroque painting', presumably of Adam and Eve caught in flagrante. She also finds it hard to live down the Bible's manacling together of sex and sin. When Christian inserts a vibrating plug into her from behind while clamping her nipples, her reaction invokes delicious torments available only to those for whom enjoyment is spiced by the proximity of the inferno: '*Holy hell*,' she silently exclaims. Given Christian's prescription of pain, his unexpected admission that he loves her comes, she tearfully says, as 'manna from heaven' – a soppier version of the life-saving bread that God rained down on the famished Israelites.

Otherwise the endearments that the master and his slave exchange are classical, as are her ways of calibrating the excitement she feels. Mount Olympus is visible from Christian's office on the twentieth floor, and he introduces Ana to the polymorphous delights enjoyed by the deities who resided on that peak in classical Greece. She calls him an Adonis or a 'sex god'. He responds, when she compliantly removes her T-shirt, by saying 'You are Aphrodite'. The orgasm he induces sends her hurtling through the air like the seared Icarus: 'I touch the sun and burn,' she gasps before plunging back to earth. At moments of anxiety, snakes extrude from her scalp. Studying herself in the bathroom mirror, she reports that her 'subconscious is furious, Medusa-like in her anger, hair flying'.

Lower down, Ana's 'inner goddess' periodically pops out of her recessive tabernacle to frisk and frolic, translating the mystery of the orgasm into calisthenics. Her goddess twirls and pirouettes like a ballerina, or does backflips like a Russian gymnast and then leaps 'onto the podium expecting her gold medal'. The goddess actually seems more like a nymphet, shrilly adolescent in her enthusiasm, and on one occasion she 'has her pom-poms in hand – she's in cheerleading mode'. Sometimes she resembles a child who has naughtily raided a grown-up's wardrobe: Ana, having discarded her panties, pictures the goddess 'draped in a pink feather boa and diamonds, strutting her stuff in fuck-me shoes'. At one point she is positively infantile, boisterously voicing tastes that are hardly consistent with overheated sexual desire. 'My inner goddess bounces up and down,' Ana reports, 'like a small child waiting for ice cream.' On a side trip to a nightclub in Aspen, the goddess dances to the sound of David Guetta's song 'Sexy Bitch'. But this pelvic grinding is not meant to mime intercourse: she is burning off the calories from Ana's dessert of chocolate mousse.

By the third book in the sequence, the wholesome goddess has become somewhat kinkier, and now possesses a 'gladiatrix outfit' to supplement her girlish tutu and leotards. When Christian lets Ana drive his Audi R8 coupé, James, like Meyer in *Twilight*, turns the body into a revved-up vehicle and wires its sensory zones to the steering wheel and accelerator. 'My inner goddess,' says Ana, 'whips on her leather driving gloves and flat shoes.' Leather adds a fillip, as does the harmlessly flagellating verb, but this is cancelled out by her sensible sacrifice of high heels, whose message she broadcasts when flaunting her feather boa. The perverse metaphors are more athletic than orgiastic. All that's missing is a description of the inner goddess racing her cart down the aisles of a supermarket and grabbing sinful packets of chocolate mousse from the shelves. In his introduction to *Tricks*, a confessional memoir of all-male couplings and treblings by Renaud Camus, Barthes remarks on the savagery of Eros. 'A kind of harpy', he says, usually presides over carnal encounters. But harpies do not twirl batons or perform pirouettes, and when they scream it is not for ice cream.

At least the inner goddess is an energetic extrovert with poetic pretensions. When the whole story is redundantly retold from Christian's point of view in James's fourth novel, his penis is hard put to hold its own. Standing to attention, it behaves like one of Christian's deferential employees. 'My cock twitches in response,' he reports after he has a lewd thought. 'My cock twitches in agreement,' he says elsewhere. 'My cock agrees,' he notes further on. There are elegant variations, such as 'My cock stirs with approval.' What an obsequious yes-man the organ is!

In *Twilight*, Meyer's Mormonism defangs Edward; Christian likewise is less deviant and demonic than expected. His sadism is uncompulsory, not a perversion but – as a soft-soaping therapist puts it – 'a lifestyle choice', and *Fifty Shades* is in fact about his lifestyle and the consumer durables or perishables that go with it. Those trophies include Ana, whom he appraises as gift-wrapped merchandise and calls 'the whole package'. He defines himself appetitively, and when he buys the publishing company where Ana works he says he is asserting his 'democratic right as an American citizen, entrepreneur and consumer to purchase whatever I damn well please'. Ana, in awe of the pleasure he takes in possession and control, calls him 'the ultimate consumer'. But his acquisitive hunger has liberal limits: he invests in farming technologies that will feed the world's poor, because 'we can't eat money'.

The power that enslaves Ana is a reflex of wealth, not whip-wielding bodily dominance. She defines Christian as a win in the state lottery, a cure for cancer, and the three wishes from Aladdin's lamp rolled into one – a trio of metaphors into which the medical miracle has been inserted to offset expectations that are otherwise unabashedly mercenary. Ana's brand-consciousness never deserts her, even while she nervously waits at the hospital to discover whether her adored stepfather will survive a traffic accident. An attendant hands her a paper cup of hot water and a tea bag. 'It's not Twinings,' she winces, 'but some cheap nasty brand.' Cataloguing her baubles, she enthuses over a platinum bracelet Christian bought her in Paris by calling it delicate and exquisite, but reserves high-pitched italics for the price tag: '*It also cost thirty thousand euros.* … I have never worn anything so expensive.'

When he offers to let her see his playroom, she expects to be shown an Xbox and a Playstation, not a flogging bench and a bed to which submissives can be manacled. For her, the machines that afford the keenest pleasure are not vibrators. 'Lying down on the bed,' she says, inviting us to picture her as a lolling odalisque, 'I gaze at my Mac, my iPad, and my BlackBerry', all donated by her besotted tycoon. After 'transferring Christian's playlist from my iPad to the Mac' – a transfusion of consciousness, an electronic marriage of true minds – she uses her finger to rid her new laptop of its frosty sheen by making Google 'fire up'. Who knew that a search engine was capable of arousal? Founding Google, Larry Page and Sergey Brin thought in terms of a gentle massage, not erotic ignition: they called their prototype 'BackRub'. Ana's own on/off button, activated by Christian's tongue, is so electric that she tautologously calls it the 'potent powerhouse' at the junction of her thighs. Christian's penis may be a dull Pavlovian dog, a personal assistant rather than a divining rod, but his body has other more alluring extensions. Holding his hand, Ana stares at 'his long fingers, the creases on his knuckles, his wristwatch – an Omega with three small dials'. The inventory is incremental. If she had been kissing her way up his arm in the way male gallants used to do, she might not have proceeded beyond the covetable Omega. Bit by bit, Christian is fetishized, or perhaps monetized. Ana's metaphors have the Midas touch: his wrist is made of stainless steel and ticks instead of pulsing, and in his mouth he has a set of sharp, bright teeth that must be a tight fit, because when his lips part they expose a wrap-around projection screen – his smile, Ana attests, is 'in full HD IMAX'.

Before erotically initiating her, Christian issues a more primal order. 'Eat,' he repeatedly commands, chiding her if she does not clean her plate. He might be quoting his prototype in *Twilight*, where Edward says 'Just eat, Bella' when he realizes that it is 'breakfast time for humans'; being a vampire, he doesn't bother with such insipid fodder. Christian himself prefers corporate take-overs to gastronomic feasts, and in the contract that formalizes Ana's subjugation he imposes his own asceticism on her by specifying that 'Submissive will not snack between meals, with the exception of fruit'. But sex between them is a kind of bloodless cannibalism, more consumerist than coital, and the alimentary metaphors in Ana's account incline towards the kind of sweet treats favoured by children in the nursery. Her legs turn to wobbly Jell-O when she first sees Christian, and she says that his voice is 'like dark melted chocolate fudge caramel' – too viscous and treacly, surely, to be very articulate. Their first physical encounter is for Christian just 'vanilla sex', but Ana considers it to be 'chocolate hot fudge brownie sex ..., with a cherry on top', which would make it better suited to a soda fountain than to a sadomasochistic dungeon. Her description is almost puritanically off-putting: apart from the cherry, which happens to be urban slang for the ruptured hymen, it has the wrong, repellently cloacal colour. On another occasion they lap up a pint of ice cream while exchanging body fluids, and Ana relishes a probing tongue that tastes 'of Christian and vanilla'. Making her first attempt at fellatio, she licks and sucks what she calls 'my very own Christian Grey-flavoured popsicle'. It's a curiously unaphrodisiac image, because blood-gorged erectile tissue is hot, not refrigerated like an iced lolly – and extreme cold also stuns the taste buds and leaves the tongue insentient.

That may be the point of the food metaphors. They chill sensual ardour rather than stimulating it, because the truly avid desires in *Fifty Shades* are directed elsewhere. In the sequel that he narrates, Christian manfully talks dirty, and pounds a single word into bruised submission. 'I'm going to fuck you,' he tells Ana. As he does so he adds a commentary, which begins with a spelling lesson: '*F.U.C.K.*' he grunts. It's unclear whether the full stops are voiced; if so, he exhibits willed deliberation not lecherous abandon, together with a rhythmic sense better suited to a piston. He then joins the letters up, downgrades the capitals, and gasps '*Fuck*'. Fellated by Ana, he mutters in an aside, '*Ow! Fuck*' as her teeth graze him. At last he post-coitally sums up the experience by panting, 'Fuck. Ana.' Next morning, however, he shrugs, 'It was just sex, for fuck's sake': the precious four-letter word has already dwindled into an expletive, a synonym for insignificance. Christian may have enlarged the range of possible sex acts, but his vocabulary is less expansive. Despite that grunted monosyllable, he is at his lewdest when disbursing cash: thus he gives 'an obscene tip' to the valet who parks Ana's car.

After fifteen hundred pages the pluto-porno reverie ends by recycling the second meeting between the lovers, now narrated by Christian. They bond when he purchases bondage kit in the hardware store where Ana works, and the stages of the transaction – a solemn ritual, after all – are lovingly checked off. She tells him his total is forty-three dollars, to which, as a billionaire, he reacts with italicized shock: '*Is that all?*' She then takes his Amex card, asks whether he would like a bag, packs the rope and masking tape, charges his card and returns it, while James' narrative pays engrossed attention to her every move. Hollywood films used to fade out with squelchy embraces; *Fifty Shades* reaches its climax with the completion of an electronic payment.

The commercial bonanza, however, was only beginning. The sex shop Babeland now invites customers to 'shop the *Fifty Shades* novels' and displays an armoury or battery of vibrators, pacifiers, mouth gags, blindfolds, plugs, floggers, clamps and cuffs, 'toys that inspired the trilogy'. A jocular recipe book entitled *Fifty Shades of Chicken* whips up dishes such as Dripping Thighs or Holy Hell Wings and gives lessons in how to truss a fowl – a parody, but racier than the macaroni cheese or peanut butter and jelly sandwiches eaten by Christian and Ana in the novel. Women who fancy having 'Laters, baby' imprinted on their thighs can buy black tights decorated with Christian's catchphrase. Housewives with laundry to do are offered a consolation prize in 'Flirty Shades of Surf', a range of detergent capsules with fragrances that claim to be 'naughty'. Children too can be turned into branded goods: a hairbow for little girls has a central medallion that loudly whispers, 'Sssh ... Mommy is reading *Fifty Shades* again.' James herself has recently approved an Official Pleasure Collection, which includes a feather tickler, spanking cream, lubricants, and an apparently essential supplementary item called, a little long-windedly, 'the Fifty Shades of Grey Cleansing Sex Toy Cleaner'.

For women who baulk at sadomasochism, a clinic in Kent called The Inner Goddess dispenses 'aesthetic medicine'. Ana might consider signing on for its services when her own frenetic inner goddess grows tired of doing the samba, the tango and the merengue. Recommended procedures here include hyperhidrosis, sclerotherapy, glycolic peels, thread-vein removal and wrinkle-relaxing injections; Tim Box works on the premises as a 'remedial hypnotist'. Cosmetics are supplied by a local company called Fill Your Face, which sounds like an incitement to gluttony. Luckily the filling is not internal: instead it plasters cracks in the facades of its clients.

On the clinic's website a 'transformational therapist' with the radiantly allegorical name of Dawn Forward beams 'big bright blessings' to potential customers. Perhaps in her honour, a room at the establishment pays tribute to Aurora, the goddess of the flushed morning and of fresh beginnings. Other rooms are dedicated to Freia, who in Norse myth grows golden apples that are the diet of the immortals, and to Isis, born of the coition between earth and sky. Even Hecate, the patron of witchcraft, has her own compartment, where she supervises readings of Tarot cards. Goddesses, inner or outer, never grow old, though perhaps they retreat to a sanctuary like this when they decide that the time has come to be aged forever forty-nine.

AN ALIEN FROM MARS

Interrogated by a pesky biographer, Michael Jackson once issued a taunt that might have been a confession: 'Just tell people I'm an alien from Mars,' he said. He was indeed a biological conundrum. Given his tinkering with his body and his migrations between gender and race, how human was he? In his childhood, as the freakily talented leader of The Jackson Five, he was described as a forty-five-year-old dwarf. Aged fifty at the time of his sudden death in 2009, he looked more like a decaying infant, who spoke in a pre-pubescent whisper while concealing the evidence of time's assault behind a palimpsest of surgical masks, coy Islamic veils and Jackie O-sized dark glasses, with a black umbrella to protect his improbably pallid skin from the sun.

For a while it seemed as if Jackson might be what the scientists in Conan Doyle's *Lost World* call the missing link. He counted both an ape and an angel among his close friends. His best buddy during the 1990s was Bubbles, a diapered chimp who travelled with him and slept in a crib in his bedroom, but he also smooched with a mascot who seemed like a harbinger of a time to come. After recording a song for a spin-off from Spielberg's *E.T.*, he cosied up to the gnomic robot: 'I kissed him before I left. Next day I missed him.' One of his stadium concerts in the 1980s concluded with a rocket launch. Fired upwards into the night sky in a burst of pyrotechnics, he was, like E.T., heading home; the moonwalker belongs in outer space, unencumbered by the gravity that tethers the rest of us.

In his *Thriller* video, Jackson regressed to a werewolf, a fiend in a red leather biker jacket. But this ravening wild beast also saw himself, in other moods, as a heaven-sent evangelist. After *Thriller* he appeared in *Captain Eo*, a film that Francis Ford Coppola directed for the custom-built cinemas at Disney's theme parks. Here Jackson commands a spaceship whose crew includes a bicephalous navigator, a pair of cybernauts, and a shipmate with an elephant's trunk; clad in shining white like a Tennysonian knight of the Grail, he has a mission to disseminate peace. How can you play both a vulpine marauder in the urban jungle and an evangelist from the starry heights without puzzling over who or what you really are?

Estranged from his family and its internecine feuds, in reclusive retreat from his grasping, mauling fans, Jackson lived from an early age with a sense of his own peculiarity. He was bewildered by what he called 'normal people'; he said that he preferred the audioanimatronic puppets in his amusement park at Neverland to 'real people' because they didn't grab at his clothes or pester him for autographs. His performance as the scarecrow in Sidney Lumet's film *The Wiz*, released in 1978, touchingly conveyed this separateness. He hangs from a wooden cross like a tatterdemalion Christ, and whimpers as crows peck at him with their beaks. Eased to the ground, he flops around in legless incompetence. Although his dancing is instinctive, he has difficulty learning how to walk. In the witch's sweatshop, he is briskly dismembered, his straw-stuffed limbs hurled around the room. Jackson knew what this might feel like. When he and his brothers arrived in London in 1972 they were set upon at the airport by maenadic teenyboppers, who tore clumps of hair from Jermaine's scalp, robbed Michael of a shoe, and almost choked him by tugging the opposite ends of his scarf. The scarecrow's makeup was a nasty parody: Jackson sports a bulbous plastic nose, a reminder of the feature that his brothers so cruelly teased him about. But this camouflage both concealed and revealed who he was, and he often travelled home from the studio wearing the scarecrow's outsize nose and his bristly wig of steel wool. The scarecrow is pathetic because he feels less than human. Peter Pan, another of Jackson's alter egos, shares this quandary: are immortality and the freedom of the air really preferable to the companionable comforts of mortal life?

Stranded inside a redesigned body, Jackson was never sure what species he belonged to. Hence his affinity with Joseph Merrick, the Elephant Man, whose skeleton he apparently attempted to buy in 1987 from the medical college where it is held. Some doctors attribute Merrick's deformity to Proteus Syndrome, a malfunction in cell growth that causes bones to thicken in grotesque lumps and flesh to sag in spongy polyp-like protrusions: Proteus was the shape-changing god, able to revise his form at will. With his nose jobs and the self-hating diet that left him weighing less than nine stone, Jackson prohibited his own body from rebelling against him as Merrick's did. But he too was a protean character, a specialist in mutation and metamorphosis.

By the end of his life Jackson was a celebrity derisively celebrated for his quirks and crazes, for his health problems, financial crises and legal embarrassments. But the fuss started because he was a great performer, a virtuoso possessing skills that seemed almost supernatural, and at his best he illustrated what the Victorian psychologist Havelock Ellis meant when he said that 'To dance is to imitate the gods'. A filmed memento of the ten year-old boy's Motown audition in 1968 remains astonishing. As he sings James Brown's 'I Got the Feeling', he channels an erotic energy of which he can have had no knowledge; as he dances, he shimmies, swivels and backslides across the floor in a blur of independently operating limbs, triumphantly demonstrating that the human body can be an instrument, not just a dumb appliance.

His performance of 'Billie Jean' at a Motown television reunion in 1983 is a kind of apotheosis. He moves in a blitz of static electricity shaken from the spangles encrusting his socks, his jacket and his single glove. One moment he mimics the plaintive open-handed gesticulation of a warbler in a minstrel show, and the next he jabs the air with high kicks like a martial-arts boxer. The glottal hiccups of his vocal delivery, exploding into high-pitched spasms of delight, exactly match the jerks of his torso. This is less showbiz than a voodoo rite, executed by a demented dervish. He begins 'Billie Jean' with a series of pelvic thrusts, and his right hand spends most of the time clutching his crotch or investigatively groping in his trouser pocket, presumably not looking for spare change. Although the choreography here is blatantly sexual, it's impossible to imagine Jackson dancing with a partner. He and Britney Spears sang 'The Way You Make Me Feel' as a duet in 2001, but while he mimed lust, his hand concentrated on fondling himself; Britney was reduced to petulantly tossing her head as he humped the floor in a vigorous set of press-ups. Jackson was autoerotic, and in 'Billie Jean' the male and female halves of his persona perform a duet. The arrogant sidewalk rowdy who rakes an imaginary comb through his sleek hair bumps up against the glittering, girlish dandy who twirls on tiptoe like a ballerina, and their fusion is announced by the singer's ecstatic throaty gulps.

Fred Astaire remarked with acute insight that Jackson was 'an angry dancer'. Angry at what? Perhaps at the fans who challenged his autonomy by wanting to mate with him: the song repudiates Billie Jean's claim that he has fathered her baby. Its lyrics also vent anger against a world that traduced Jackson and, in his view, made him a martyr. 'Be careful what you do', he warns with the upraised finger of a lecturer or a holier-than-thou preacher, 'because a lie becomes the truth'. In this respect, however, Jackson should have been the object of his own anger, since many of the fictions he so bitterly denounced – for instance the claim that he slept in a hyperbaric chamber because this would help him live to be a hundred and fifty – began as stories he invented or licensed his publicists to spread. Jackson acknowledged that for him truth was slippery and relativistic. A lie told about his image, he once said, 'wasn't a lie, it was public relations'. Where does that leave his denial that he bleached his skin, made during a 1993 interview with Oprah Winfrey, or his indignant assertion of 'complete innocence' in another television broadcast a year later, meant to rebut accusations of child abuse? These were self-mythologizing exercises in public relations, attempts to repair a soiled image.

By then, fame and wealth had turned Jackson into an exorbitant American romantic, a dreamer who, like Gatsby or Citizen Kane, used money to make fantasies materialize before his eyes. J. M. Barrie merely imagined Neverland, the resort where Peter Pan sheltered his lost boys; Jackson actually constructed it, with carousels and rollercoasters, giraffes and pythons, free sweets in the cinema and recessed hospital beds so that terminally-ill tots could watch Disney films while remaining attached to their intravenous tubes.

When he was accused of sexually abusing Jordie Chandler, Jackson was incredulous. 'I can't believe this is happening to me, Michael Jackson,' he said, viewing himself as a third person. Lashings of cash had always bought him love: during his interview with Oprah, Elizabeth Taylor strolled on to sing his praises, and in return for this guest appearance received a diamond necklace costing $250,000. The expenditure of a few million dollars kept vexatious reality at bay and magically silenced the outrage of the Chandler family. Despite this outcome, and despite the victory sign Jackson gave to his fans outside the courthouse at his trial for abusing Gavin Arvizo in 2005, he was effectively destroyed by these scandals. His downfall came when the police, investigating Jordie's reports of genital blotches, photographed his private parts. He called the ordeal 'humiliating' and 'dehumanizing'; in fact the examination humanized him, humbling him by reducing him to parity with the rest of us – odd, imperfect, miserably unmysterious, with mottled testicles, patchily discoloured buttocks, wispy pubic hair, and a peekaboo penis that may or may not (the forensic observers disagreed) have been circumcised. Jackson forfeited his divinity at that moment.

Yet this was when, in a bid for rehabilitation, he began to deify himself all over again. In 'Beat It' he averts war between two street gangs by coaxing them to dance not fight; extending the mission of the video, he assumed he had a duty to pacify and purify the world. 'We're healing LA right now,' he told Oprah, 'we've already done Sarajevo.' Jackson always treated his concerts as a preview of the Second Coming, and on his 1984 tour a sonorous voice from the beyond inaugurated the revels by ordering the resurrection of the dead: 'Arise, all the world, and behold the kingdom.' The kingdom that was to come turned out to be a Disneyfied kindergarten. 'I try to imitate Jesus,' piped the pure-voiced Jackson as Oprah reverently nodded. He added, 'I'm not saying I am Jesus', inserting a brief pause for protests by his apostles. 'But I try to follow his teaching – to be like the children.'

Being like them, as Jackson explained in his interview with Martin Bashir in 2003, involved sharing a chaste bed with them. It also entailed begetting children of his own, bypassing the conventionally messy route: a test tube is the modern version of parthenogenesis, at least for the father. 'I have been blessed beyond comprehension,' said Jackson after taking delivery of his first child, roughly paraphrasing the Virgin Mary's line when the angel announced that the Holy Ghost had rented her womb. Wanting sole credit for the miracle, he spirited Prince Michael out of the hospital five hours after the infant emerged from the body of Debbie Rowe, the dermatological nurse to whom he had entrusted his seed. He was so keen to make off with his newborn daughter Paris that he scampered away with her before the placenta was wiped off.

Once he had been content to imitate Christ; now, as a parent, he felt entitled to behave like God the Father. In 2002 he dangled his third child, Prince Michael II, from a third-floor hotel balcony in Berlin. It looked as if he was about to sacrifice the struggling bundle, offering it as a morsel to be gobbled up by the hungry fans down below. Had he not been treated that way by his own brutal father, sold to venal promoters and to a fickle public? Damaged himself, he could only inflict the same damage on the next generation, while believing that he had a sublimer purpose. In 1987 he wrote a letter to *People* magazine complaining about his mistreatment by the tabloids. Its conclusion could be the unspoken soliloquy of Christ writhing on the Cross: 'I must endure for the power I was sent forth by, for the world, for the children. But have mercy, for I've been bleeding for a long time now.'

At the press conference early in 2009 to promote *This Is It*, a season of one hundred comeback-and-farewell concerts in London, the few words Jackson consented to utter were chosen with care, and they might have been a translation from the Latin Vulgate of St John. 'This is it,' he said, 'this is really it, this is the final curtain call.' Although the theatrical metaphor was Jackson's interpolation, he here paraphrased the last words of Christ, who in the Gospel announces his expiry by gasping, 'Consummatum est'. Yet what kind of consummation were ticket-buyers being promised? An onstage breakdown, or a triumphant resurrection? Would Jackson levitate, leaving only a single glove or a prosthetic nose as a souvenir in the empty shrine? 'They desire our blood,' he said in the self-flagellating testament he sent to *People*. Our society has indeed turned entertainment into a bloodsport, although Jackson, whose timing was a little imprecise, died during rehearsals rather than at a performance.

The extravaganza that was due to follow *This Is It* at the O_2 Arena in London went ahead as planned. It was a staging of *Ben Hur*, with gladiatorial combat, nautical battles, a chariot race, a chorus line in gilded bikinis, and a walk-on by Christ, who later discreetly retired to the sidelines to be crucified. The German producer Franz Abraham, a former racing-car driver who was born again when he converted to Catholicism, wearily summarized his own fund-raising pilgrimage when he said, 'It takes so long time to believe you will find the money in the end.' Inheriting Jackson's mission, he hoped that the noisy, tawdry spectacle would communicate 'my spiritual vision of faith' and propound a 'message of peace and inter-religious and inter-culture dialogue'. This, however, turned out not to be it: the noisy, gaudy, spectacularly violent medium overwhelmed the edifying message. At the O_2, Christ died in vain.

INCREDIBILITY

Pity the poor superhero. What ingrates we are when aerodynamic saviours sew up the gaping San Andreas fault, defuse rogue nuclear bombs, or retrieve our pussycats from trees: intent on destruction, we force our exhausted rescuers to perform their miracles over and over again. In 2004 in Pixar's animated epic *The Incredibles*, a disenchanted intercessor retires from what he calls 'hero work'. 'Why,' he sighs, 'can't the world stay saved?'

Mr Incredible – whose jaw looks as if it was carved from Mount Rushmore, though his lantern-jawed face wears a permanent look of dim-witted bemusement – resigns in disgust after zooming down to catch a man who has hurled himself off a skyscraper. The would-be victim sues him: he wanted to commit suicide, and is enraged by the unwanted interference. Warned off, Mr Incredible retreats to the suburbs and takes a job as a claims adjuster in an insurance office. It marked the ignominious end of a long career.

The superhero was dreamed up by Nietzsche during the 1880s, and has been summoning humanity to transcend itself ever since. Nietzsche – having dispensed with God and belittled the majority of men as miserable fleas – invented the Ultimate Man as his 'prophet of the lightning'. Zarathustra gambolled through mountains and vaulted over crevasses; his feats were mental and metaphorical, though his caped imitator in the comic books defied gravity in physical earnest. The first *Superman* film with Christopher Reeve promised on its posters to make us believe that a man could fly. That indeed was Zarathustra's aim: to launch the uninhibited ego into orbit. Stanley Kubrick famously quoted the brassy sunrise that opens Richard Strauss's tone poem about Zarathustra at the start of *2001: A Space Odyssey*, as the globe is enlightened and electrified by the sun. Now, with the assistance of a rocket, the superman was ready to fire himself into outer space.

Such jet-propelled crusaders, however, have always been a morally dubious bunch. The superman is a man of superior power, which means that from the first his mission was political. Zarathustra soon turned into Wagner's Siegfried, the muscular oaf with the lethal, newly forged sword, who is acclaimed by Brünnhilde in *Die Walküre* as the noblest hero in the world. At the time she pronounces this accolade he is still in his mother's womb, and even after being born he does little to justify it. But his very existence is a rebuke to the inferior species he has outgrown: Siegfried therefore casually slaughters the dwarf Mime, disgusted by the gibbering and twitching of his adoptive parent. The trampling arrogance of the Nietzschean ideology briefly raises its voice in *The Incredibles* when the villain Syndrome jeers about high-school graduation ceremonies, which give semi-literate cretins mortar boards to wear and diplomas to brandish: 'They keep creating new ways to celebrate mediocrity!'

In 1903 George Bernard Shaw appended to his play *Man and Superman* an incendiary handbook to be consulted by revolutionaries. Here he examined 'the political need for the superman', argued that we long for a redeemer because we have mired ourselves in an impotent 'Proletarian Democracy', and instead called for 'a Democracy of Supermen'. Soon enough, just such a political system came into being: it was called the Third Reich. Superheroes are instinctive bullies and braggarts, which is why Arnold Schwarzenegger, who derived a political philosophy from the swaggering tag lines he uttered in his action movies, derided 'girlie men' – meaning limp-wristed liberals – at the Republican convention in 2004.

When *Action Comics* began to chronicle the exploits of Superman in 1938, the character was split in half. He retained the Nietzschean name, but employed his powers only in an emergency, and always for the benefit of others; the rest of the time he lived in modest anonymity. The comic strip removed him from the exalted heights where Zarathustra lives. Forced to ditch the doomed planet Krypton, he plummets down to the American town of Smallville. Nietzsche would have deplored this landing and the small-mindedness that it inevitably implies, but Superman – now disguised as the bashful Clark Kent, a figure of Christ-like altruistic meekness – was billed as 'champion of the oppressed', as if his missions of mercy disseminated the policies of Roosevelt's New Deal. *Superman* comics were stuffed into the knapsacks of GIs sent off to fight the Nazis, although army chaplains feared that the cartoon character might become a substitute for the absentee God they ineffectually extolled in their sermons. Terence Stamp, playing the Mephistophelean Zod in the second of Reeve's *Superman* films, announces that he has finally identified the hero's weak spot, which is his genuine compassion for 'these earth people'.

Despite the oath Superman swears in the first instalment of the comic strip 'to devote his existence to those in need', the rancorous Nietzschean heritage lived on in his rival Batman, who first appeared in *Detective Comics* in 1939. Superman is a humanitarian, but Batman's motives are obsessively and neurotically personal. Traumatized in childhood after witnessing the murder of his parents, he wants to avenge them, and his interventions from on high are the acts of an urban vigilante. His story – in the words of Tim Burton, who directed the first two *Batman* films with Michael Keaton – is '*Death Wish* in a bat suit'. The suit is crucial. Normality is Superman's alias, but Batman chooses a disguise that will terrify his victims and becomes, as the first comic put it, 'a creature of the night, a weird figure of the dark'. The *Batman* films are fashion parades of nocturnal fetish gear. Michelle Pfeiffer as Catwoman in the third film zips herself into vinyl and wields a whip, George Clooney preens in skin-tight rubber through which his nipples protrude, and the camera lingers over the tightly leather-clad buttocks of Chris O'Donnell, who plays Robin. Nicole Kidman, investigating the hero's abnormal psychology in the fourth film, suspiciously prods Val Kilmer and asks why a grown man would dress up as a flying rodent. The perversity is political as much as sartorial: it hints at a private theatre of mastery and submission, an exercise in fascist role-playing. Officially, however, the Nietzschean rantings are assigned to the villains. In *Batman Returns* it is Danny de Vito's lewd, waddling Penguin who sabotages his own campaign to become mayor when he sneers at the electorate as 'the squealing pin-head puppets of Gotham'.

The first *Superman* film with Reeve appeared in 1978, and the *Batman* series began in 1989. In retrospect, we can see that the superheroes limbered up by acting out scenarios of destruction that later passed from fiction to reality. A gang with a bomb seizes the Eiffel Tower in *Superman II*; in its early days, Al-Qaeda planned to fly a hijacked plane into the tower. Stamp and his cronies from Krypton demolish the Boulder Dam outside Las Vegas – nowadays considered such a natural target that new highways are being constructed to bypass it – and then fly on to crash through the roof of the White House. As they topple the flaunting American flag, the president, played by E. G. Marshall, moans, 'I'm afraid there's nothing anybody can do. These people have such powers, nothing can stop them.' 'Where's Superman?' whimpers an aide. In *Batman Forever*, Tommy Lee Jones as the schizoid Two-Face anticipates another atrocity that must have been on the wish list of those George W. Bush called 'the bad guys': he steers a helicopter into the Statue of Liberty's hollow crown, at last lighting up its symbolic torch. Although *The Incredibles* takes place in generic cities named Municiburgh and Metroville, you can see the Chrysler Building, Manhattan's elegant art-deco spire, quivering vulnerably on the skyline.

Batman inevitably returned after 9/11, but in the three films of *The Dark Knight Trilogy* directed by Christopher Nolan between 2005 and 2012 he is preoccupied by private demons, guiltily obsessed with what Christian Bale, who plays the part, called 'that killer within him'. He periodically goes into retreat or exile, reluctant to assume the responsibility that society has wished on him. Nolan was determined not to use Batman as an embodiment of America the war-mongering superpower, and the series accordingly ends with his presumed death, which frees Bruce Wayne to resume his private life and go on holiday to Europe.

Mr Incredible's very name defies us to believe in him, and reminds us that both gods and heroes are insults to the human average. But it is also scary to find ourselves suddenly bereft: just when we most need such a protector, none is forthcoming. *The Incredibles* concludes with the world once more saved, after Mr Incredible wriggles back into his latex tights. Then, in the final seconds, a globular robot called The Underminer rears up to drill through the skyscrapers with its unfeeling calipers. The film abruptly ends before the new menace is defeated. The Marxist epigram has been switched back to front. History, in these harmless escapades with their last-minute rescues, happens first as farce: can we expect it to be repeated as tragedy?

AN ANDROID

Human beings were originally put together from permeable skin, messy blood and brittle bone. Genesis, to make matters even more slapdash, suggests that our progenitor Adam was moulded from a handful of red earth, just as Prometheus in an alternative myth shapes the first ill-formed men from the mud of a riverbed.

Now at last we are being more durably refabricated from top to bottom. In 2004 Sergey Brin, co-founder of Google, described his corporation's projected rewiring of our heads. 'If you had all of the world's information directly attached to your brain, or an artificial brain that was smarter than your brain, you'd be better off,' he said – reasonable enough if you equate thinking with browsing, surfing, or flicking through data. 'Long live the new flesh,' cries the television executive in David Cronenberg's *Videodrome*, a man who has merged so completely with his medium that he has a cavity in his torso into which videocassettes can be inserted; then, a little illogically, he shoots himself in the head where the tapes are unreeling. Brin's cranium with a dataport and Cronenberg's perverse anatomy remain biomedical conjectures. As for our lower extremities, the change is already on view. At birth Oscar Pistorius lacked fibulae in both legs and had distorted feet, but his crippling defect turned out to be an evolutionary challenge, and the athlete's way of overcoming it has given another sign of a mutation in our species.

To the Greeks, Pistorius's handicap would have looked like an inescapable fate or omen. The name Oedipus means 'swollen feet', and it recalls his shaming abandonment at birth, when his parents bound his feet and left him to die in the mountains; it also suggests his lack of metaphysical freedom, as he stumbles along a predetermined path towards disaster. Pistorius's parents, however, insisted on understanding their child's problem, and, as Oscar reports in his autobiography, they asked 'the first in a long series of questions'. Those elementary questions are the stuff of myth, which tries to understand who we are by allegorizing the aptitudes and disabilities of our bodies. If we are made in our creator's image, why did he design us so inefficiently and sentence us to decay?

Or can we congratulate ourselves on having survived by developing quicker-firing brains and swifter legs?

'Fortunately for me,' says Pistorius in his autobiography, 'I have never needed to press those around me for answers.' His parents, however, interrogated the Johannesburg doctors who had somehow overlooked his missing bones; they also did medical research of their own, and in 1987 took the decision to have their child's useless legs amputated below the knee before his first birthday. At the age of seventeen months, Pistorius acquired his first prostheses; they were made of plaster and mesh with a lycra skin, and he declares that he 'loved' them. After his sister was born a year later, he was 'spellbound by her feet and kept kissing them'. But there was no danger of a fetishistic fixation: his own more stalwart limbs had their advantages. As a child he once stopped a runaway go-cart by using his artificial legs as a brace and a brake, which prevented the vehicle from smashing into a brick wall. The incident recalls the moment when the young Superman, still resident in Smallville, single-handedly lifts up a car that has pinioned his father. Here was an augury of the mythical life that lay ahead for little Oscar.

Eventually Pistorius was fitted with blades of carbon fibre – the same material used for the bones of the indigenous humanoids on the planet Pandora in James Cameron's *Avatar*. Just below his knees, skin and bone change to sheets of moulded polymer fixed by a socket, with cushioning foam where his feet should be. A final layer of carbon fibre stores kinetic energy and gives him an aerodynamic boost when he runs; on these blades, he won gold and silver medals in athletic events at the London Paralympics in 2012. He now considers himself better off than those who are held back by what he calls legs 'of the old-fashioned kind'. His shoes and socks do not get smelly, and when he once 'lost a leg' playing rugby it was immediately replaced. While he was away at the Olympics, an acquaintance in South Africa took up with Pistorius's former girlfriend. When he found out, Pistorius swore at the interloper and allegedly threatened to 'break his legs'. It was a boast about his invincibility: his own legs were unbreakable.

Barthes, writing about the Tour de France, observed that the cyclists who took part belonged to 'the epic order' and enjoyed 'knightly imperatives'. Radio commentators relayed their progress to every household in the land; fans gave reverential nicknames to the most popular contestants, and in this act of homage Barthes found 'that mixture of servility, admiration and prerogative which posits the people as the voyeur of its gods'. The same could be said of the sobriquet sometimes awarded to Pistorius: he has been called the Blade Runner, which makes him sound like the Superman of the athletic track – a Zarathustra who does not use the mountains as a trampoline, like Nietzsche's hero, but speeds along the level ground.

His nickname has a complicated provenance. It comes from a film directed by Ridley Scott, released in 1982 but set in 2019; here the blade runner played by Harrison Ford is a detective charged with identifying and executing runaway 'replicants', robotic slaves who escape from servitude in an off-earth labour camp and try to pass as humans. Scott borrowed the title more or less at random from William S. Burroughs' proposed film adaptation of an earlier novel by Alan E. Nourse. For Burroughs and Nourse, bladerunners were smugglers of scalpels, underground healers who outwit the police in a totalitarian state to get banned instruments to doctors; Nourse's hero Billy Gimp has a club foot, which gives him a personal interest in supplying black-market surgeons with the tools of their trade. Scott fancied the phrase but had no use for its medical reference, so it became merely metaphorical. There are no blades, either surgical or athletic, in his film, and the running done by Harrison Ford, which leaves him puffed out, is what we expect from a cop in an action movie. Myths are signs that occasionally signify nothing. But when applied to Pistorius, who literally ran on blades, the phrase got its original meaning back.

Scott's *Blade Runner* is a creation myth for the cybernetic age, and it tells Pistorius's story even though it appeared four years before his birth. It even contains a genetic designer – corresponding to the medical technicians consulted by little Oscar's parents – who manufactures eyes for replicants and amuses himself by playing with animated soldiers. Near the end, a rogue replicant confronts the tycoon who invented him and protests about his limited lifespan and the menial status to which he has been condemned. When the executive ignores his complaints, the replicant kills him. Here we watch the primal scene that Nietzsche was the first to imagine: man, no longer in awe of God, destroys his maker.

Pistorius has an equivalent to that metaphysical murder, a moment of reckoning when he both measures himself against the human norm and challenges the divine organization of nature. He imagines a negotiation with the creator, and admits that 'if God were to ask me if I wanted my legs back, I would really have to think carefully about my answer'. Any God who made such an offer would be a heartless manipulator, deforming his creations for his own amusement. Pistorius implies that he has no need of the meagre benefits doled out to other anthropomorphs; he is his own higher power. For similar reasons, Bella in *Twilight* extols the advantages of being a vampire: you don't have to waste time sleeping or blinking, and for some obscure reason to do with streamlined internal arrangements there is no need for what she coyly calls 'bathroom breaks'.

Long before the cyclist Lance Armstrong was exposed for cheating, Barthes speculated about doping in the Tour de France. He said that the advantage it guaranteed was 'as sacrilegious as trying to imitate God; it is stealing from God the privilege of the spark.' That theft was performed by Prometheus, who in a version of the creation story that contradicts Genesis made off with a spark from the hearth of Zeus and used it to quicken the first men and impart movement to their sluggish bodies. Pistorius had his own version of the stolen spark, which was the spring built into his flexible blades. He always fumed when critics questioned his ethical propriety in competing against runners without this advantage. Did he react so tetchily because his talent was also a robbery from God?

A divine spark jerked the creatures of Prometheus into motion, but the motive force of Pistorius seemed more like a concentrated fury. He ran as if detonated, with spurts of energy that he calls 'explosive'. In 2006, after passing through a security checkpoint at the airport in Amsterdam, he was arrested, handcuffed and escorted away for examination: gunpowder from a shooting range in South Africa had infused the carbon fibre on his legs, and his prostheses registered as deadly weapons.

Acting out the ambiguities of his persona, Pistorius hurtled to and fro between ancient myth and futuristic science fiction. Nike manufactured his spike pads, so he had a professional association with a company named after the Greek goddess of victory. But he also resembled a character from one of H. G. Wells' scientific romances, somewhere between the hybrid specimens grafted together in a private zoo by a fiendish inventor in *The Island of Dr Moreau* and the Martians, literally brains on legs, who make a meal of obsolete humanity in *The War of the Worlds*. Animal or man, superman or inhuman machine? Pistorius admitted his quandary when he likened his childhood relationship with his older brother Carl to the partnership of Buzz and Woody in *Toy Story*. The mischief-maker in the animated film is an astronaut figurine called Buzz Lightyear: that was Carl's role. Oscar saw himself as Woody, an easily manipulated pull-string doll. Carl pushed him, he said, like Buzz leading Woody on. During his athletic career, he did not need Carl as his starting pistol. Both puppeteer and puppet, Oscar willed the insentient part of himself into action.

Pistorius's skills simultaneously promoted him to the sky and tugged him lower, back into wildness. His blades were designed by Flex-Foot, which called its blend of carbon fibre Cheetah, after the fastest of land animals, a hunter with feet like tyre treads; the raptors in *Jurassic Park* run, according to a game warden, at 'cheetah speed'. In the second film of the *Jurassic Park* series, a paleontologist fusses over the fractured leg of an infant Tyrannosaurus rex, which if it can't pivot on its ankle will not be able to outrun other predators. By this logic, physical speed is a skill that humans no longer need: athletic competitions therefore re-run our evolutionary past, when we either hunted or were limping prey.

With their springy lift-off, the Flex-Foot blades also imitated the bounding gait of a kangaroo. As a boy Pistorius had a pit bull, which was removed from the household when it mauled a pet tortoise, and as an adult he kept dogs of the same breed, one of which chewed her way through his house and even gnawed his prosthetic legs.

Which was his spirit animal – the cheetah, the kangaroo or the pit bull? His girlfriend Reeva Steenkamp answered the question when she said, 'I'm scared of you sometimes, the way you snap at me.' In February 2013 he killed Reeva, shooting her through the door of a bathroom in which she was allegedly hiding from him after a quarrel; he claimed to have mistaken her for an intruder in his house. At his trial, Pistorius encountered an attack dog that could not be brought to heel: the abrasive, sarcastic prosecutor Gerrie Nel, nicknamed the Pit Bull.

Pistorius was on his stumps at the time of the shooting, and his lawyers had him hobble through the court without those props to demonstrate how vulnerable he could be – the image of man deprived of the technological stilts that raised him to dizzy heights and enabled him to answer his maker back. In his account of his running technique, Pistorius lays claim to a composure that does sound like the smiling superiority of the Greek gods: in order to judge the instant when the poised body should be thrust forward into the race, 'you need,' he says, 'to be calm and in harmony with yourself'. The trial stripped away this serene equilibrium. Pistorius wailed in anguish during the testimony of witnesses, and even vomited when he saw photographs of Reeva's body, shredded by his bullets. Sceptics suggested that he had been coached to exhibit grief like a Method actor, though not even Marlon Brando could regurgitate on cue. Months earlier, however, Pistorius was more collected. He had no compunction about restaging Reeva's death for the benefit of his defence team: he was filmed without his prostheses, dressed in a Nike T-shirt and brandishing an imaginary gun as he investigated what he took to be a burglary. His sister, playing Reeva, collapsed beside the toilet where she died, and Pistorius screamed on cue as he re-enacted his attempt at rescue by carrying her downstairs.

In Philip K. Dick's novel *Do Androids Dream of Electric Sheep?*, on which *Blade Runner* was loosely based, the detective identifies suspect robots by subjecting them to a lie-detector test that targets their capacity for empathy. Dick's hero believes that this specifically human attribute blurs 'the boundaries between hunter and victim', establishing that we are herd animals, not rapacious loners like the owl or the cobra. 'The humanoid robot,' by contrast, is 'a solitary predator'. How would Pistorius have scored on the empathy test? At home he was never without a gun, and he was charged with firing it from a speeding car or on one occasion in a restaurant, just to release aggression he had not used up on the athletic track. Rage came easily and naturally to him: he often abruptly terminated interviews when a question irritated him. For someone geared to win at whatever cost, compassion, commiseration and remorse had to be learned, perhaps by histrionic mimicry.

Reflecting on the Tour de France, Barthes concludes that heroes are generally brought low when grubby journalism exposes a 'false private life'. That moral collapse gratifies our self-conceit: having created these idols, we reserve the right to destroy them. But the spectacle of Pistorius self-destructively tumbling from the heights was genuinely mythological. The superman with the retooled body extended human capabilities; overcoming limits and handicaps, he performed an act of deicide, like the replicant disposing of his designer in Ridley Scott's film. It is now too late to bring God back from the dead, and when Pistorius sobbed, groaned, retched and threw up into a bucket in court, he proved to be human, all too human.

THE ZOMBIE PLANE

Stories, like journeys, have beginnings and endings, take-offs and landings. Myths are less tidy and less finite. They can begin before the beginning, as Genesis does, and end after the end, like the biblical Apocrypha; they need never finish, and – because variants proliferate so uncontrollably – they are seldom complete.

Just such an obscure, irrational, open-ended happening began to perplex and perturb us in March 2014. At least it had a beginning: soon after midnight on 7 March, Malaysian Airlines flight 370 took off from Kuala Lumpur, carrying two hundred and twenty-seven passengers and twelve crew members to Beijing. It never landed there, but neither did it crash on the way. After a while it simply vanished from the radar. The transponders that relayed information back to the ground were switched off by persons unknown for no known reason; the plane veered away onto a southern arc that took it far out across the Indian Ocean, en route to nowhere. Running out of fuel, it seems to have eventually plunged into the sea off the west coast of Australia. Phantasmal pings were heard, perhaps from its flight recorders, which were never found; more than a year later, barnacled sections of its wing flaps drifted ashore on the volcanic island of Réunion. The rest of the plane presumably remains in an unmapped subaqueous limbo, conserving its secrets. Dredging it up, if that ever happens, will not reveal what happened on board.

Soon after its disappearance, MH370 came to be called 'the zombie plane', a flying version of the corpses reanimated in Haitian voodoo rites. With all on board unconscious, probable victims of a failure in the oxygen supply, the aircraft might have travelled on, steadily driven by its computers for as long as the engines had oil to burn. The fantasy of an undead machine is only too plausible nowadays; it neatly coincides with films made in recent decades that track the ghouls from the superstitious Caribbean to the cities of the West. They overtake a Pittsburgh shopping mall in George Romero's *Dawn of the Dead*, and stumble to north London corner shops in Edgar Wright's grim parody *Shaun of the Dead*. In both places they shuffle along in mobs, rhythmically twitching like marionettes:

these are the ever-greedy automata our economies need. The speculation about MH370 takes the conceit further, reducing those on board to inert passivity, strapped into seats on a machine that for a few hours outlived them. And how different would that have been from an ordinary flight? On most long-haul trips the passengers suspended between time zones stare in a weary stupor at the video monitors in front of them, with the window blinds down to shield their screens from daylight. No one looks at the clouds, the wrinkled ocean or the earth that inches past below; we prefer to be diverted by electronic fictions as the machine does our travelling for us.

But the notion of the zombified plane remains problematic. Without human volition in the driving seat, we cannot tell a story, although for myth, which is accustomed to inexplicable events, that lack is no disadvantage. Barthes said that myth empties reality, disposing of probabilities to leave only 'a perceptible absence' – a cosmic version of the shrug for which the French are famous. Examples of such a vacancy might be the hole in the middle of a cronut or the bite taken out of Apple's apple. In this case, however, the absence was that of the elephantine Boeing 777; more grievously still, the absence is that of the passengers. Myth can perform such vanishing acts with impunity, and because it tells us about a world that was once without form and void, where the elements of earth and water were not yet separate and day merged with night, it cannot be expected to pay much attention to the disappearance of two hundred and thirty-nine human beings.

Such indifference is more than we can tolerate. A story had to be constructed about MH370, with the kind of definitive ending that the therapists call 'closure'; there had to be motives and, if possible, a moral. The first imperative was to identify a villain, and the likeliest candidate seemed to be the man in the driver's seat. Barthes devoted one of his mythological essays to the heroic figure of the jet pilot, so novel in the 1950s, who modelled himself on the machine he commanded. Probably a decommissioned warrior who had previously served in his country's air force, 'the jet man,' Barthes said, 'is defined less by his courage than by his weight, his diet, and his habits (temperance, frugality, continence)'.

That indeed is how airlines used to allegorize their personnel. PanAm said that its pilots possessed 'eyes that see around the world', and assured passengers that 'Uncle Sam's your skipper'. The Malaysian captain, Zaharie Ahmad Shah, may not have been one of PanAm's guardian angels, but he did possess some of the technocratic qualities that Barthes identified in the jet man. At home, he had a flight simulator that mocked up conditions aboard a Boeing 777, so he relaxed by pretending to be at work. He also collected remote-controlled toy planes, and posted videos on YouTube that showed the less adept how to repair air-conditioners and other household gadgets. As a Muslim, he had the ascetic habits Barthes expected, but unlike the 9/11 hijackers he showed no symptoms of Islamic zealotry, and he was so unbigoted that he even admired the briskly scientific atheism of Richard Dawkins.

Should it be taken as a sign of mental instability that Shah was also a fan of the cross-dressing comedian Eddie Izzard? Not really: he was probably contemplating the zany oddity of a human species to which, as a jet man, he no longer wholly belonged. Yet two New Zealanders have written a book on the case that accuses Shah of shutting his co-pilot out of the cockpit, depressurizing the main cabin so the passengers would die of hypoxia, then continuing to fly on in proud solitude until the time came to ditch the plane. They presume that this bland, cheerful, methodical and altruistic man was suffering from 'some personality disorder, depression or emotional breakdown', but they do not know for sure, and never will. The co-pilot who deliberately crashed his Germanwings Airbus into the French Alps in March 2015 did lock the pilot out when he briefly left the cockpit; an investigation of the co-pilot's history also uncovered depressive episodes and periods of medical treatment. Shah, however, had no discernible motive for suicide and mass murder.

Two of the passengers on MH370 were Iranians travelling on stolen passports. Television surveillance cameras showed them passing unchallenged through security checks, where no one thought to question the discrepancy between their faces and the Italian and Austrian names on their documents. Inevitably they were suspected of downing the plane; that putative storyline fell apart when they turned out to be harmless asylum-seekers who had onward reservations from China to Europe. Investigators next rifled through their vague memories of classic Hollywood movies or Broadway plays, in which events were more rigorously plotted. A Malaysian police chief suggested that 'Maybe somebody on the flight has bought a huge sum of insurance, who wants family to gain from it' – a muddled merger of *Double Indemnity*, in which a wife takes out an accident policy on her husband's behalf and then teams up with the insurance salesman to murder him, and *Death of a Salesman*, in which Willy Loman commits suicide by crashing his car so that his wife and son can enjoy a windfall from his insurance policy. But life, in the case of MH370, ignored the consequential logic of art.

With no human culprits identified, a more impersonal scenario was proposed. This too came from a film: in Stanley Kubrick's *2001* a computer with the acronym HAL disconnects the life-support systems of the astronauts on a space ship and attempts to take control of their mission. Barthes could hardly have imagined that his sleek, disciplined jet man would have an even more alien descendant a decade later – a cybernaut who is not a man at all but a bodiless electronic brain. Technology has caught up with the surmises of Kubrick's science fiction. Planes today are flown by computers, and the pilots who make their soothing announcements from behind a locked cockpit door may not, for all we know, be up there at the controls. Was the Malaysian flight hijacked by remote control, directed off course by radio signals sent from a mobile phone on the ground? It is theoretically possible, which means that sooner or later it is bound to happen. An expert who advises the Home Office thinks that hackers could indeed have commandeered the plane's network 'through the in-flight, onboard entertainment system', while the passengers watched action movies about just such a prospect.

For a time, suspicion hovered over twenty employees of Freescale Semiconductor who were on board MH370: the Texas company makes microchips but has also developed a radar-blocking system that allows weapons to speed undetected to their targets, so perhaps the engineers had conducted an experiment to prove just how stealthy their technology really was. Safely translated to some fourth dimension, were they chuckling at the search for a plane they had rendered invisible? A less extravagant scenario proposed that the plane had been diverted to China so that the Freescale technicians could be questioned about American surveillance. In a crackpot tweet, Rupert Murdoch proposed another destination: the plane, he suggested, could have been spirited off to Pakistan, where bin Laden might be planning to use it in some new terrorist outrage. The most dismayingly banal conjecture omitted human agency altogether and blamed the cargo. MH370 carried in its hold a consignment of lithium-ion batteries, used in e-cigarettes, which have a tendency to overheat and catch fire. Simmering unseen in the plane's underbelly, they might have burned through its mainframe – a reminder that we are at the mercy of dumb, inanimate objects, or a further sign that the energy we have stolen from nature is merely biding its time before it casts off its captivity and breaks free.

When the search settled on a turbulent and bafflingly fathomless expanse of the Indian Ocean, assistance was offered by James Cameron, who directed *Titanic* as well as *Avatar*. One of Cameron's toys was a submersible called Deepsea Challenger, in which he had dived to a depth of five miles in the Mariana Trench in the Pacific. He recommended using an unmanned underwater vehicle to travel to and fro making a sonar profile of sunken precipices and sinkholes. Perhaps he was sketching a sequel to another of his films, *The Abyss*, in which a rescue party sent out to recover an American submarine in the Atlantic finds creation happening all over again on the ocean floor. The probe he had in mind would have had to trespass into regions as remote as outer space, though he soon retreated from a mythical confrontation with the unknown to the familiarity of the suburbs: accumulating data from the sonar profile, he said, would be 'kind of like mowing a lawn'. That conveniently demystified the depths, and treated the task as a weekend gardening chore.

Eventually, a global search party was organized, whose members never needed to leave home. Half a million volunteers rallied by the website Tomnod.com inspected satellite images of the ocean's surface on their computer screens, though the only definite sighting, of an oil slick and a plane-shaped blur near the island of Pulau Perak, was made by the endearingly erratic rock singer Courtney Love – not the most trustworthy of scouts, since while shuttling in and out of rehab she sometimes seems not to know where her own head is. Even so, her contribution could not be automatically discounted. A myth is always a compilation, which gathers alternative accounts and is unable to eliminate any of them.

A tabloid sniggered when a shaman came to the airport in Kuala Lumpur to assist the search by smashing coconuts and uttering mumbo-jumbo. But why shouldn't a witch doctor try his luck, since the technical experts had failed? The disappearance of the plane recalled a time when myth had not yet been disparaged and dismissed by science. It re-medievalized the world: just as at Nando's we supposedly tussle with dragons, so in this case we reverted to a dim former state before maps expelled ogres from the unfamiliar corners of the earth, long before radar and satellite surveillance convinced us that we could look down at ourselves with an eye as all-knowing as God's. We were sent back to an age when space was unknowable, a gulf as abysmal and ravenous as time, able to swallow up all things, including the bite-sized morsel of a Boeing 777.

BERGS AND GYRES

Myth is a form of recycling. The stories it tells are often circular, in keeping with natural law. As we grow, we die; as we consume, we excrete or at least discard. The mythological circles or cycles are almost always vicious, penalizing us for our casual vices. Even Judge Judy often warns wrongdoers who escape legal punishment that retribution may occur on an existential carousel where 'what goes around comes around'. This circularity can be exhausting or depressing, because its endless repetitions do not allow for improvement or for any other advance as we are carried from the beginning to the end. Despite Genesis, there was no moment of creation when the world emerged from nothingness. Despite Apocalypse, there is also no such thing as destruction: the things that go round in circles, including our bodies, never entirely disintegrate but are simply remade in another form.

Our economy works in the same way as this cosmic whirligig. Everything has already been created, and originality is replaced by novelty, with obsolescence built in. The mills, factories, foundries and shipyards that used to resound with the noise of making have moved out of sight and earshot. Manufacturing happens far away in China, India and Bangladesh; in the West, we are most productive when churning out waste, and our output of dross is responsible for a new topography. The subterranean passages that drain our cities are now regularly blocked by what sanitation workers call fatbergs, constipated knots composed of cooking oil, congealed grease, uneaten food, condoms and other foreign bodies that have been flushed down toilets, plumped up by stray tennis balls and bits of wood. Sanitary towels, cotton buds and dental floss have to be raked out of the grisly murk. The more conscientiously we clean ourselves, the more we contribute to these agglomerations of stodge and sludge. Wet wipes, meant for use on babies but now in favour with adults, cling to the mess and help it solidify into blocks like concrete.

Similes compete to measure the enormity of something we can't see and would probably rather not imagine. A fatberg dredged up in Melbourne was said to be as big as four footballs, though this was a puny hindrance when compared to the obstruction that clogged pipes beneath the London suburb of Kingston in 2013: workers who struggled back to the surface claimed it was the size of a double-decker bus. A year later the population of Shepherd's Bush produced a fatter berg, said to be as long as a Boeing 747. In 2015 a Chelsea sewer disgorged ten tonnes of waste – less impressive than Kingston's fifteen tonnes, although it acquired an affluent lustre when it was estimated to weigh as much as five Porsche 911s. The employee of Thames Water who supervised the repair of the choked sewer said 'Chelsea has done itself proud here.' Are London's better-off districts engaged in an excremental contest?

But these juggernauts of viscosity are droplets when compared with the expanses of refuse that circulate just under the surface of the Atlantic and Pacific Oceans. Again, language strains to convey their extent. Early appraisals suggested that the so-called garbage patch in the Pacific was the size of Texas, which was a convenient way of declaring it to be unimaginably big. A more recent scientific guess says that it covers an area twice that of the continental United States. As with the discovery of America itself, there was a mythical moment when this new continent of debris – which starts to chug, bob and slurp a few hundred miles off the California coast, extends from there to a point west of Hawaii, and almost reaches Japan – swam into view. Charles Moore, travelling back from Hawaii to Los Angeles in 1997, inadvertently steered his yacht into a soup or stew of rubbish, which gyred or rotated at leisure, held together by the slow eddying of currents and the peaceful ocean's lack of winds, and surrounded his boat for almost a week.

It consisted mostly of bags and bottles made of plastic, the 'magic substance' Barthes celebrated in the mid-1950s, when at an industrial exhibition he watched greenish crystals pass through a machine under the eye of a technician, who like the jet man was 'half-god, half-robot', and emerge as moulded receptacles. Chemistry had taken over the power of the primal creator and produced a flexible, adaptable material that appeared to be immortal. As Barthes recalled, the 'myth of the substantial transmutations of matter' had 'tormented the West from alchemy to atomic physics'. The bomb represented one such eruptive, annihilating transmutation; plastic showed off a more useful domestic alternative, sure to be harmless. Barthes pretended to be amazed by the multifariousness of the synthetic stuff and predicted that 'ultimately, objects will be invented for the sole pleasure of using them'. He may have been joking, but he had come up with a succinct definition of consumerist bliss.

There is a secondary pleasure in throwing those objects away in order to replace them with newer versions of themselves. This, however, is where our invention proves to have been a little too clever. Plastic does not degrade like organic matter. When discarded or consigned to the waves it splits into ever smaller resin pellets or nurdles; on average every square mile of ocean contains forty-six thousand of them, hungrily soaking up chemical spillage like hydrocarbons or pesticides. Being indestructible, plastic is also indigestible. Albatross chicks as large as geese turn up dead on beaches, their insides stuffed with bottle caps, cigarette lighters, tampon applicators, toothbrushes and golf balls – bright, shiny treats that their over-fond parents have scavenged and fed to them. Sea turtles feast on plastic bags distended by water, which they mistake for jellyfish. Evolution has equipped the turtles with retentive throat muscles to cope with the slipperiness of their prey, which proves to be unfortunate when it is a plastic bag they are gobbling down: by the time they realize the taste is wrong, it's too late to regurgitate the strangling morsel.

As well as a wide-open dump, the ocean is a discount warehouse where the flotsam and jetsam are free. The contemporary equivalent of wrecked galleons still shed their loads of treasure in Pacific storms. During a hurricane in 1990 five containers with eighty thousand pairs of Nike sneakers inside were washed off the deck of a ship; much of the soggy but buoyant footwear drifted ashore in Washington or Oregon, where beachcombers held swap meets to reunite matched pairs. In 1992 a crate of bath toys packed in Hong Kong tumbled overboard, releasing twenty-eight thousand rubber ducks, turtles, beavers and frogs, all made of squeaky plastic. Some are still contentedly completing circuits of the gyre, others escaped north to the Bering Sea to make landfalls in

Newfoundland or Scotland, and a few ended their journey icebound in the Arctic. In 1994 two more containers bound for American sports stores were dislodged in mid-Pacific, and thirty-four thousand pieces of hockey kit – chest protectors, shin guards, gloves – spilled out. Footballs have also been found in the gyre, bounced around pointlessly by the currents, along with disparate Lego blocks that will never be slotted together to form robots, ultracopters, *Star Wars* speeders, or cranes for feeding captive T-rexes. Is this what the world will be like when we have vacated it – a litter of equipment for playing games whose rules have been forgotten?

Moore's voyage through the nascent continent of garbage so shocked him that he set up a foundation for marine research, which in 2008 financed the construction of a 'junk raft' made from the fuselage of a downed Cessna, kept afloat on pontoons buoyed up by fifteen thousand plastic bottles. The raft sailed from Los Angeles to Hawaii, dramatizing the problem of ocean debris and demonstrating how future survivors – Robinson Crusoes with a talent for bricolage – might redeploy our leftovers as constructive tools, aids for exploring a newly empty earth.

With fewer financial resources, a Dutch engineering student called Boyan Slat has recently designed a set of booms that will sweep up drifting refuse and suck it into containers until it can be processed back on land. Because no nets are used, fish and plankton can dodge beneath the booms without being trapped. Slat thinks of his invention as a Jurassic mutant with a taste for plastic: the platforms in which the garbage would be stored have wings that are meant to reach out like the fins of a manta ray, catching the mess on the surface and funnelling it into a tank.

Slat himself, now in his early twenties, fits a mythical prototype. Here, apparently, is a reincarnation of the little Dutch boy who sealed a leaky dyke with his finger and spent a lonely night defending the lowlands against inundation by the North Sea. This precocious hero was created in 1865 by Mary Mapes Dodge, an American writer who at the time had never visited the Netherlands: in one of her books for children, the improving tale about the plugged leak – a parable of personal initiative and stalwart endurance – is read aloud to pupils in a schoolroom. The fable so endeared itself to generations of readers that American tourists asked about the non-existent Dutch boy when visiting the Netherlands, and it was for their benefit that statues of him were erected in various coastal towns. In local folklore, he functions as the self-controlled obverse of Manneken Pis, the incontinent cherub who piddles into a fountain in Brussels.

Slat's intentions are noble, but he has a harder task than his imaginary predecessor. Dykes can protect human culture from the incursions of nature; it may be too late for those floating platforms to protect nature from our takeaway, throwaway culture.

ALMOST THERE!

The countdown has begun: we are regularly told that every new year may be humanity's last. Harold Camping, the host of a Christian radio programme in California, began predicting Christ's imminent return in 1994, and as the years anticlimactically came and went he kept expectancy simmering by publishing doom-laden tracts with titles like *Time Has an End* or *We Are Almost There!* In 2011 he set a specific date and, after explaining away a false alarm in May, assured his listeners that the world would definitely end on 21 October. That day Camping remained at home with the curtains drawn, serenely awaiting his reward. When Armageddon was once more delayed, he announced that he was 'flabbergasted', adding that the postponement did not, in his view, oblige him to return financial donations made by his followers as a tribute to his foresight.

Scientists have had nervous qualms of their own, provoked by theoretical physics not biblical prophecy. There were twinges of dread in 2013 when the Hadron Collider, the largest machine on earth, powered up at the European Organization for Nuclear Research in Switzerland. Deep underground, it generated masses of elementary particles to test the disparity between quantum mechanics and general relativity. Tabloid headlines fretted about this recreation of the instigating moment when life on earth began. The Astronomer Royal Martin Rees – who calculates that humanity has begun its final century – worried that the subatomic particles exploding in the collider might set off a chain reaction that in theory was capable of shrinking our planet to 'an inert hyperdense sphere about one hundred metres across'. Luckily we did not implode.

All the same, in a skittish variation of the relativity theory, we feel the future approaching at a faster rate than ever before. When George Orwell published *1984* in 1949, he estimated that it would take half a human lifetime to catch up with his vision of a society regimented by the media – two-way television screens, hidden microphones – and the domineering myths they disseminate. Ridley Scott's *Blade Runner*, released in 1982, was set in a future positioned roughly the same distance ahead: the hunt for replicants happens in 2019, when the inhabitants of a befouled and poisoned earth have begun migrating to colonies in space. Since then, films about the approaching apocalypse have drastically foreshortened the chronology, which suggests that we are impatient for a preview of whatever imminently awaits us. Mimi Leder's *Deep Impact*, about a comet that crashes into the earth, was released in the summer of 1998, which is when the 'extinction-level event' it describes takes place. In 2004, Roland Emmerich's *The Day After Tomorrow* anticipated a calamitous global cooling, with Manhattan suddenly paralyzed by the rigor mortis of ice; the title warned that this could happen later in the week. Emmerich's *2012*, released in 2009, permitted us only a brief interim before the arrival of the year when a Mayan calendar predicts that the world will end. Once the period of grace is used up, Los Angeles splits apart and slithers into the Pacific, while John Cusack accelerates his car and shouts, 'We gotta get to the airport!' If we drive fast enough, can we outrun the clock and evade a predetermined fate?

With evolution stalled, human history reverts to its cowed beginnings, when an angry God regularly hurled maledictions out of the sky. In *2012* a million people selected as survivors are set afloat in arks that launch as a tsunami engulfs the peaks of the Himalayas. One of these vessels is called *Genesis*; Emmerich confided that he 'always wanted to do a biblical flood movie', and digital technology enabled him to wipe out the world, not as a judgement on its wickedness but as money-spinning mass entertainment. With the same eschatological glee, Michael Bay's film *Armageddon* – released like *Deep Impact* in 1998, a year of millenarian foreboding – tracks a meteor shower that torches Shanghai, crushes Paris and, when it reaches Manhattan, knocks gargoyles off the Chrysler Building, shatters Grand Central Station, and decapitates one of the World Trade Center towers. A Japanese tourist, whose taxi veers towards a smouldering crater near the Flatiron Building, peevishly cries, 'I want to go shopping!' Will those be the last words uttered by expiring humanity? In a post-mortem, a scientist from NASA says that the lumps of rock that concussed New York were 'the size of basketballs, Volkswagens'. This commodifies the projectiles and turns doomsday into a high-flying game or a mechanized race, one of our compulsive leisured pursuits.

During the 1950s, the fears that science fiction played upon were geopolitical. Flying saucers were supposed to carry squads of aggressors, determined to take over what Barthes – deploying his most acerbic adjective – called 'our petit-bourgeois earth': this was how the West pictured the menace of the USSR. In the 1960s, after President Kennedy's announcement that the moon was a new American frontier, optimism prevailed. Hence the Odyssean voyaging of the astronauts in *2001*. Kubrick's film begins with the fanfare from Strauss's *Also sprach Zarathustra*, which establishes that these men in spacesuits are pioneers in a mystical realm; the soundtrack then relaxes into a Viennese waltz, whose heady whirling celebrates the weightlessness of life uprooted from down-dragging gravity. Paranoia returned in 1983 when Ronald Reagan announced his plan for orbital missile launchers, which were supposed to shield the United States from incoming weapons. The fantastical scheme took its nickname from *Star Wars*, in which Luke Skywalker and his comrades struggle to disempower an armoured space station with which the hostile Galactic Empire attacks other planets. Addressing evangelical Christians in Ohio, Reagan called the USSR an 'evil empire', prayed that its benighted citizens would 'discover the joy of knowing God', and hailed the arms race as the concluding stage in the perennial 'struggle between … good and evil'. He thus set his own timetable for Armageddon, the final engagement with the Antichrist that in the Bible is meant to take place at the hill of Megiddo, a fortress in northern Israel.

Throughout the Cold War, thinking remained embattled, dualistic. The enemy, whether Martian or Marxist, was always a moral adversary, the devil's representative on earth. Today our fears are more self-reflexive, and the blame for inducing the apocalypse is trickier to transfer. We have exhausted an earth that may soon be unable to tolerate our presence on it; perhaps we brood so obsessively about the dinosaurs because we expect to share their fate. *Armageddon* therefore begins by recapitulating the meteor strike that wiped out these beasts sixty-five million years ago. Then Charlton Heston, the unseen narrator of this prologue, mosaically intones the refrain of myth: 'It happened before, it will happen again.'

Panic online during the summer of 2015 conjured up just such a catastrophe: an asteroid the size of a small town was rumoured to have taken aim at Puerto Rico, and alarmists predicted that when it slammed into the earth the entire continental United States would be wiped out.

In *Armageddon* a new asteroid is sighted that will bring about what the president of the United States – played in the film by Stanley Anderson – calls 'the end of all things' when it crashes into us. But mankind possesses, the president adds, 'the technology to prevent its own extinction'. The collision that upset the balance of nature and exterminated the dinosaurs had, as Heston rumbles in his prologue, 'the force of ten thousand nuclear weapons', and that phrase suggests a retaliatory plan. Declaring war on the solar system, a belligerent general says, 'Why don't we send up a hundred and fifty nuclear warheads and blast that rock apart?' Given the choice, we prefer to destroy the world ourselves, rather than waiting to be wiped out by a stratospheric traffic accident. The actual response in the film is less choleric, but it has its own mythological ingenuity, as it transforms our innate destructiveness into a mode of salvation. NASA recruits a team of specialists from an offshore oil rig, rapidly trains them as astronauts, and lands them on the speeding asteroid. Their task is to drill a hole eight hundred feet deep, plant a bomb in the cavity, and set off a nuclear detonation to split the rock in half and send it careening off course away from the earth. Not unexpectedly, the scenario is diabolical. The asteroid has the same terrain as hell in Gustave Doré's illustrations to *Paradise Lost* – cindery crags, crevasses of perdition, sulphurous lakes, a black, louring sky – and the tactics of the oilmen, with the bonus of the heavy machinery they bring along, closely follow the ingenious digging and delving of Satan's subordinates in Milton's poem: while preparing to fight a war in heaven against Christ's army, the evil legions drill into the ground and set off nitrous explosions, inventing gunpowder, which thus becomes one of the devil's bequests to mankind.

But in *Armageddon* there is a setback: the grandiose product of the science that challenges God proves faulty. 'The bomb is dead,' says a military official at NASA. Its trigger jams after being bashed by a flying rock; a volunteer has to stay behind to detonate the bomb by hand, enlivening it but killing himself. Ben Affleck, chosen by lot as the sacrificial victim, assumes the role with a self-congratulating zeal that could not be less meekly Christian. 'We all gotta die, right?' he grins. 'I'm the one who gets to do it while saving the world.' With seconds to spare, the world is indeed saved, though by Bruce Willis, who knocks Affleck aside and magnanimously takes his place. Our long human history of penetrating or hydraulically fracturing nature to extract fuel or minerals is not quite expunged by his altruism.

We first see Willis practising golf putts on a mat of Astroturf on his oil rig in the South China Sea; it turns out, when the angle of vision widens, that he is lobbing the balls as bullets at ecological protestors in a Greenpeace vessel below the platform. Affleck cheers up his companions as they drill into the asteroid by using the volatile terminology of baseball: 'We can knock this outta the park!' In *Dr. Strangelove*, Kubrick asked how we could learn to stop worrying and love the bomb. Perhaps by recognizing that we loved it all along: our society worships the energy we so greedily consume, and that kinetic force has its loudest, brightest expression in a nuclear blast. In *Armageddon* the most reckless of the mavericks, played by Steve Buscemi, imitates the B-52 bomber pilot in *Dr. Strangelove* when he bestraddles a warhead as if it were a bucking bronco. 'We got front-row tickets to the end of the earth!' he yelps in delight. He is tied up, gagged and eventually killed off, but his kamikaze-like zest infuses the film.

One way of preparing for the end of the world is to buckle up and brace as we careen towards an inevitably combustible conclusion. 'This is a kick-ass ride!' shouts one of the *Armageddon* astronauts during a spasm of jolting turbulence as their rocket launches. A colleague, trying out a laser weapon that he has not been trained to use, yells, 'This is so much fun it's freaky!' The entertainment industry caters to this chiliastic elation by selling tickets to catastrophes: at Disneyland Paris, customers line up to be terrorized by *Armageddon*'s special effects. Crammed into a space station that is bombarded by meteorites, you are warned that 'everything around you either spectacularly blows up, collapses, or gets sucked into deep space'. Lights falter, gas hisses as it escapes from pipes, the ceiling sags, and flaming boulders hurtle past. Finally, as the meteor that threatens to deal a deathblow to the earth zooms nearer, a big bang cues universal darkness and a directorial voice calls 'Cut!', which brings both the show and the world to an end.

In Bay's film, Affleck returns unscathed to be greeted on the Texas tarmac by a NASA spokesman who says, 'Welcome home, cowboy.' The salutation is a reminder that frontiers exist to be tamed, usually by violence, whether the so-called cowboys are laying railway tracks through Indian territory, drilling into the ocean bed or blowing up an asteroid. But the supposed solution only aggravates the problem: there is no point in rallying an army of American heroes to do battle at Megiddo, because our Armageddon will probably be environmental, not a combat with satanic forces or devilish meteorites. In 2010 Stephen Hawking proposed that we should start planning for evacuation of the earth. He believes that 'the long-term future of the human race must be in space', and says that we 'shouldn't have all our eggs in one basket, or on one planet'. His image is cosy, with a twinge of underlying dread: this planet is our nesting place, but eggs are fragile.

When science fiction first speculated about such a migration, it appeared to be no more than an expensive whim. 'I've had my fill of life on the ground,' yawns the tycoon who pays for the research of the astronomers in *Contact*, the film derived from a novel that the cosmologist Carl Sagan published in 1985. This mystical eccentric lives in his private plane, and when he finally takes flight into other galaxies he provides for the cryogenic preservation of his body if he dies en route. In Christopher Nolan's *Interstellar*, released in 2014, that individual initiative has grown into a collective exodus. Matthew McConaughey, a former astronaut now reduced to farming in the Midwestern dust bowl, watches the dessication of an earth that is no longer fertile. Crops fail, killed by blight; when they all wither, nitrogen will deplete the remaining oxygen and leave humanity a choice between starvation and asphyxiation. 'We're not meant to save the world,' says Michael Caine as an all-knowing astrophysicist, 'we're meant to leave it.' Nevertheless, McConaughey is told, 'You're the best pilot we ever had – go out there and save the human race.'

This time there are no capacious arks, like those that set sail from atop the Himalayas in *2012*. A shuttle sets off with five thousand frozen human embryos, to be thawed when a planet conducive to settlement is located.

These stories about the future use science as the cover for an age-old, born-again religious narrative. The NASA official in *Armageddon* predicts that unless the prospect of imminent extermination is kept secret there will be a breakdown of social order, 'rioting, mass religious hysteria – basically the worst parts of the Bible'. The best parts of the Bible are also resuscitated: Christianity, which once saved mankind from sin, is now expected to salvage the earth and its polluting, pullulating inhabitants. Sometimes, simplifying the miracle, a vehicle replaces the saviour. In *Deep Impact* as in *Armageddon*, astronauts are sent to divert the inbound comet by detonating a nuclear weapon. But the characters in Leder's film are not hell-raisers like Willis's gang. Recruited as apostles, they travel in an Orion spacecraft that goes by the name of *Messiah*. McConaughey, the astronaut in *Interstellar*, appears in *Contact* as a theologian and television evangelist. When the astronomer played by Jodie Foster plummets through a wormhole and returns to describe her blessed or blissed-out experience of a 'celestial event', McConaughey takes this as evidence that God is indeed keeping watch from above. As in the Christian afterlife, our lost loved ones await us, open-armed, in some remote corner of the ever-expanding universe. Foster, orphaned in childhood, cries, 'Dad, are you there? Come back!' into a radio that is tuned to receive messages from other planets; her plea is answered, as is that of the daughter McConaughey leaves behind on earth in *Interstellar*. A space-time tunnel – described as a train system, a subway that runs outside the earth rather than beneath it – deposits Foster on a moonlit tropical beach where, fanned by palm fronds and lapped by waves, she encounters an angelic or at least extraterrestrial being who has assumed the body of her dead father.

Foster is bereaved, and the rest of us, stranded on a damaged planet at the margins of an indifferent universe, are metaphysically bereft: that is why we cling to myth and the wishful thinking it encourages. But what kind of welcome can we expect from the other worlds we may be sent out to colonize? Despite the spangled nebulae that glitter above the beach in *Contact*, the gaseous vacuum out there remains inconceivable – an abstraction that is either black or blank. Sandra Bullock, the marooned astronaut in Alfonso Cuarón's *Gravity*, sums it up when she says, 'I hate space.' The refrain at NASA in June 2015, when another rocket taking supplies to the International Space Station blew up after being launched, was only a little less gloomy. 'Space is hard,' said a spokesman.

Gravity is what the limbo in Cuarón's film lacks, and without a sense of grounding there is no possibility of attachment. As Bullock and her colleague George Clooney meander through infinitude in their capsule, he asks her, 'Where's home? ... Where do you pitch your tent?' His phrase is both tender and regretful. Up here, there is no foundation for a tent pole; they lack anchorage, and also a protective covering, even of flimsy canvas. Their plight is confirmed by Bullock's answer, which comes in two stages. 'Lake Zurich,' she says. 'Illinois,' she adds, dissociating the place from its Swiss prototype: the sense of belonging has to be geographically precise. Whirling in the windy void after they leave the capsule, she and Clooney are connected by an umbilical cord, though only to each other, not to a maternal earth. After being wounded by a passing storm of galactic debris, he detaches himself and drifts off to die, arms extended in a cruciform gesture – but where there is no gravity there can be no gravity-defying levitation. Here nothing rises or falls, and even Bullock's tears fly away from her face in a scattered shower rather than running down her cheeks. Alone, unable to communicate with NASA, she has no alternative but to curl up in her uterine pod and aim it at the earth. Luckily she splashes down in an Arizona reservoir – a preserve of tamed water that nurtures human life in a desert – and, wriggling out of her spacesuit, swims ashore. When she takes her first tottering steps on land, she retraces the tentative origins of our species.

Nolan has said that *Interstellar* is about 'what it means to be human', which is something that human beings once had no need to think about. 'I am a man,' says a character in a play written by Terence in the first century BC, 'and nothing human is alien to me.' That may sound axiomatic, but it is a less generous, open-minded sentiment than it sounds: in the original play it is the self-defence of a meddling busybody, who spies on his neighbours, gossips about them, and pretends that his motives are benign. Yet when taken up by Montaigne, who inscribed it on one of his roof beams, the remark became a statement of humanistic faith, and in contemporary usage it stretches to a justification of liberal permissiveness. Can we afford to go on being so complacent?

As long ago as 1973, Rainer Werner Fassbinder's film *World on a Wire*, based on Daniel F. Galouye's novel *Simulacron-3*, conjured up a society peopled by 'identity units' – not human beings but digital wraiths churned out by a supercomputer. In 1982 John Carpenter's *The Thing* told the same story more viscerally. Scientists at an Antarctic outpost are eaten up by a humanoid cannibal from another planet and then regurgitated exactly as before: in their isolated cabin, they eye each other suspiciously, and take blood samples to determine whether any of them are still unmetamorphosed. Having redefined humanity, science fiction goes on to offer new versions of the deity, and even prescribes new ways of imitating or envisaging Christ. *Interstellar* puts its trust in a disembodied cosmic intelligence, emanating from unseen five-dimensional beings who by transmitting signals from on high enable humanity to save itself and go on evolving. This is what Dante called 'the Love which moves the sun and the other stars', except that in Nolan's film it is a force that, like gravity, cuts across space and time. More succinctly, one of Jodie Foster's supporters in *Contact* holds up a placard declaring that 'Jesus is an alien'. In that case, so are all the rest of us.

Far from feeling that nothing is alien, we risk becoming alienated from ourselves, or from whatever makes us human, because we have invented a sequel to that ambiguous, middling condition. Religions traditionally placed us in a lower category than God or the gods, defining us by our limitations and flaws. Hawking, despite his bleak atheism, tugged Galileo and Newton down to the ground by emphasizing the moral cowardice of the one and the petty envy of the other. Technological man is less easy to humanize. In Danny Boyle's biographical film *Steve Jobs*, Michael Fassbender's performance suggests that Jobs was in transition to membership of a steelier, more robotic species. He spurns biology by denying the paternity of his young daughter; his temper tantrums are the misfiring of a cerebral circuit board rather than evidence of our shared fallibility. Although Jobs wants his first boxy Macintosh to say 'Hello' at a product launch, he personally dispenses with such courtesies: the computer is friendlier than he is.

A post-human world lies ahead, shaped by advances in biomedical engineering and artificial intelligence. Digital technology has already redefined reality, altered our sense of identity, mediated communications with others, and changed the balance between mind and body. In a British survey conducted in 2015, one out of four schoolchildren said that playing computer games qualified as physical exercise: so long as our digits get a workout, our limbs are allowed to remain inert, waiting to wither away. Mental effort can also be outsourced to Google, which with its universal index of data claims to perform operations that were impossible for Einstein's laggard brain. According to Larry Page, one of Google's co-founders, 'the ultimate search engine is something as smart as people – or smarter'. The qualification at the end of that sentence is a challenge, perhaps a threat. There may be no need to imagine a bomb or an asteroid finishing us off; it could happen quietly, imperceptibly, without leaving rubble behind. In 2014 the software pioneer Elon Musk tweeted a warning: 'We need to be super careful about AI. Potentially more dangerous than nukes.' The advice perhaps came too late, since in March 2016 a Google AlphaGo programme won a competition against a Go master from Korea, whose brain was corporeal not electronic. In *Star Wars* the hoity-toity robot C-3PO sums up our current situation when his supposed master Luke Skywalker blunders off into a blizzard on an arctic planet. 'He's quite clever, you know,' the android condescendingly remarks, 'for a human.'

We are in the process of being superseded. Mythology first told us where we came from. Now, apprehensively scrutinizing the far distance, it tries to show us where we are going.

6 Wars in Heaven

On a tour of the Greek islands in 1952, Jean Cocteau came to suspect that the eruptive, eroded landscape retained a memory of the chaos that preceded creation, or of the cataclysms over which the irate Olympian gods presided. 'Greece,' he said, 'is a corpse devoured by myths': the obsessive stories had become harpies or hyenas, and after centuries they had abraded the country's terrain and gnawed it to the bone.

The observation was typical of Cocteau's mythomania – not a tendency to tell grandiose lies, which is what the word now usually implies, but a mania for myth, emboldened by a suspicion that the myths themselves were somehow manic, preying like winged Furies on our susceptible minds. After collaborating with Stravinsky on the opera-oratorio *Oedipus Rex*, Cocteau referred excitedly to the 'monstrosity' of the myth, which admitted the irresistibility of incest while conjuring up gruesome penalties to frighten us off; a primitive taboo here recurred as a modern psychosexual ailment.

The gods may have retired or retreated from view, but monsters, instead of being left behind by our evolutionary advance, stalked the land all over again. Among Cocteau's other projects as a librettist was an oratorio about the Apocalypse, for which Paul Hindemith was expected to compose the music. Working on the text in the same year as his Greek trip, Cocteau reminded himself to include the full biblical bestiary: 'angels with swords in their mouths, lion-headed horses, locusts with human faces and crowned with gold, the great whore of Babylon'.

Cocteau's bad dreams became more lurid when he read *Worlds in Collision*, a 1950 mythopoeic treatise in which Immanuel Velikovsky described 'wars in the celestial spheres'. According to Velikovsky, comets – whose extrusions from the planet Jupiter he likened to Athena's birth from the head of Zeus – had once passed close to the earth and briefly stopped its rotation, causing upheavals that were cryptically described in ancient tales about submerged continents like Atlantis or the gushing of lava from Mexican volcanoes and from Mount Sinai. These fables seemed to be rehearsals for a forthcoming annihilation: like Martin Rees brooding about the Hadron Collider, Velikovsky worried that a chain reaction set off by the fission or fusion of atoms might permanently delete our little planet from 'the celestial sphere'.

The catastrophes examined in *Worlds in Collision* occurred, in Velikovsky's calculations, several centuries before Christ. Others feared that modernity had arrived at what D. H. Lawrence called 'the end of the Christian cycle', which meant that the Second Coming was imminent. Lawrence foresaw an earth-shaking battle with a red dragon, a mythical beast possessing 'evil potency'. The primordial omens multiplied. In a radio programme for children broadcast from Berlin in 1931, Walter Benjamin asked his innocent audience, 'Have you ever heard of the Minotaur?' He went on to impart the bad news about the bull-headed miscreant, born from an unlawful intercourse between the species, which prowled in a Theban labyrinth and every year expected to be fed a sacrificial virgin – in retrospect, a prescient warning about the society in which his listeners were to grow up. More skittishly, Salvador Dalí designed a pavilion for a marine Venus at the World's Fair in New York in 1939, stocked it with perverse mermaids, and defended 'man's right to love women with ecstatic fish heads'.

Back in Paris after his Greek trip, Cocteau listened on his car radio to a discussion of an issue that was both ancient and urgently contemporary. The medium contributed a frisson of its own. He might have been hearing voices from the beyond, conveyed by the latest technology: in his film *Orphée*, messages from the underworld are transmitted by short-wave radio. The ethereal debate asked whether we create the gods by naming them, or 'are they named because they make use of men for this purpose?' Thinking the matter over, Cocteau found wisdom in the way that primitive men 'carved a god of fear and sought its protection against fear'; such a carving may have been the first artwork, a weapon brandished at an enemy we ourselves created.

'Our night directs us,' Cocteau concluded, and night is where the gods live. They fade in the sunlight, emerging again whenever reason is overshadowed by fantasy, desire or terror.

*

For Cocteau, myth was a last remnant of religious mystery. What would become of it in an irreligious world?

Cocteau alternated between superstitious reverence for myth and delight in its decorative frivolity. He knew that the once-powerful nocturnal bogeys had declined into amusing neoclassical fictions: he described the Olympian deities as 'the living paintings of a ceiling', frolicking in an artificial sky that actually kept the weather out. Updated to a commercial economy, they could also be the living paintings of a billboard, most at home when posing as mannequins. In Kurt Weill's musical *One Touch of Venus*, a statue of the love goddess comes to life in New York during the 1940s and diverts the lunch-hour crowds on Fifth Avenue by trying on dresses in a shop window.

Marshall McLuhan, who began to analyse American popular culture in the early 1950s, made strenuous efforts to hold together high and low culture, theology and commerce, by identifying icons of his own Catholicism among the shop-soiled wares he examined. McLuhan found scriptural reminiscences even in comic books: he likened Superman to the angels whose errands were described by Aquinas, and he thought of Tarzan as a St Francis of the jungle, given to fraternizing with apes rather than talking to birds. An advertisement for codliver oil, with a mother cooing over her infant, looked to McLuhan like a portrait of the Madonna and child. He was faintly affronted by the travesty, but it pleased him to think that what he called 'the folklore of industrial man' was keeping the candles on the altar alight.

Barthes too used theological tropes, but only when discussing subjects that were entirely worldly, as when he likened the sleek bodywork of the new Citroën to Christ's seamless robe. In his iconographic analysis of the Abbé Pierre, a hero of the French Resistance, he claimed that the priest's aura of saintliness depended on his 'zero degree of haircut', a crop that served as 'the label of Franciscanism'. He regarded the new commercial mythologies of his day as a schismatic cult, a latter-day Reformation. This explains his teasing treatment of the Detergent Congress at which the Anglo-Dutch company Unilever tried to convert France to the cult of cleanliness, freshness and spiritual rebirth by singing the praises of whitening powders like Persil: here was puritanism by other means, unwelcome in the homeland of smelly cheeses and undeodorized armpits. In his essay on agony columns, Barthes remarked that pharmacists who recommended toilet soap for the skin had taken over from the Dominican priests who once ministered to the soul. Unilever's brands included Lux, so called to link its 'de luxe' lather with God's benign 'Lux aeterna'. If you shopped correctly and washed conscientiously, you could shine like one of the elect. Similar miracles supposedly occurred in the kitchen. If soap was divine, fat had to be diabolical, and Barthes pointed out that advertisements for Unilever's Astra margarine aimed to conduct those who stopped buying butter from 'imminent evil' to 'transcendent good'.

After attending a revival meeting led by Billy Graham, who had come to Paris to denounce godless communism, Barthes remarked that the God who used this man as his mouthpiece must surely be very stupid. The evangelist was an entertainer, supported by a Chicago warbler called Beverly, 'an artist of the American radio, who sings the Gospel so marvellously'; Graham was also an undercover politician, whose tirades about faith sanctified the witch-hunting of Senator McCarthy. At the Vélodrome d'Hiver, Barthes noticed that the conversion of the gullible took place among posters for Super Dissolution – a kind of glue that seals holes in tyres, much in demand at the bicycle track when Graham was preaching – and Cognac Polignac. Myth was at best showbiz, at worst electioneering, and salvation had become just another nostrum advertised in the marketplace.

Mythologies appeared at the end of the first Cold War decade, when the available religions were entirely secular: communism on the one hand, consumer capitalism on the other. Barthes inclined towards the Russian option, but he also feared it. 'Revolution,' he said, 'excludes myth', despite official efforts to turn the murderous ogre Stalin into gruff but jovial Uncle Joe; he added – perhaps remembering the French revolutionaries and their disestablishment of the Church – that leftist ideology 'lacks a major faculty, that of fabulizing'. The self-transforming talents possessed by gods and mortals in the age of fable were now available only in the societies Barthes called bourgeois. The Museum of

Modern Art's photographic exhibition *The Family of Man*, which toured the world before being sent to Russia at the end of the 1950s, treated America as the place of origins, the norm for all other societies, rather than a belated historical breakaway. Barthes described the show as an example of American 'Adamism' – a rejigging of human genealogy that aimed to Americanize the rest of mankind.

Based in New York, McLuhan could see how entrenched the new culture was, and he found its demotic glee and slangy wit only too imitable. Hence the puns and parodic tabloid headlines that introduce the essays in *The Mechanical Bride*, his study of advertisements: 'Galluputians' for a commentary on opinion polls, 'Corset Success Curve' for an account of the beauty industry. Such infectious amusement did not come easily to Barthes, for whom sarcasm was 'the condition of truth'. He resented a cultural invasion that was led, as one of his most biting essays suggests, by the Americanized Romans in the Hollywood film of *Julius Caesar*. Here Shakespeare was pressed into making propaganda for the brash new transatlantic empire. The film gave its toga-clad Romans what Barthes slangily called 'Yankee mugs' with haircuts to match; Marlon Brando mumbled and sweated through Mark Antony's soliloquies, demonstrating that Americans had impressive physiques but feeble brains.

Soon afterwards, when Brando became engaged to the French teenager Josiane Berenger, Barthes' tone turned more indignant, and in an essay on society weddings he protested against 'this ravishing of a humble French girl by the Hollywood monster'. Assigning mythological roles to the pair, he claimed that a sultan had carried off a shepherdess (though Josiane was in fact a fisherman's daughter, and the caption to a magazine photograph of Brando out for an evening stroll with his future in-laws said he resembled 'any French petit-bourgeois'). Barthes called Brando 'muscular, Venusian'. He should probably have said that the pumped-up conqueror came from Mars, but the choice of planet and gender may have been deliberate, to ridicule the interloper's overbearing masculinity. In the event, this disapproval was unnecessary, as the marriage never took place.

Another essay in *Mythologies* set wine against milk, French earthiness against the bland pasteurized American diet. Without bothering to produce evidence, Barthes here claimed that milk was the insipid tipple of cowboys and gangsters in American films. True, the thuggish Robert Mitchum improbably downs a glass of milk in a diner in *His Kind of Woman*, and James Cagney asks for the same puerile drink in a speakeasy in *The Roaring Twenties*, which prompts his brassy, gin-drinking female friend to wonder whether he also likes spinach. In *New York Confidential* the crime boss played by Broderick Crawford also sips milk while pining for salami on rye and a kosher pickle. Perhaps the intention was to suggest an innocence that underlies the barbarism of these ruffians – or it may be that they all suffered from stomach ulcers. Whatever the cause, Barthes smiled at the infantile habit because it confounded another myth: American tough guys were exposed as mothers' boys, fastened to a succouring teat.

Once Barthes had brought to light the poetic metaphors hidden in the sales pitches for washing powders and dairy products or for cars and film stars, he expected them to lose their appeal. His aim, he said, was to liberate the coveted object and thereby destroy it. The statement is itself metaphorical. Understood literally, it would have meant sending a communist agitator to harangue shoppers in a supermarket as Jean-Luc Godard does in *Tout va bien*, or blowing up an overstocked refrigerator and watching the contents disintegrate as Michelangelo Antonioni does in *Zabriskie Point*. Barthes was incapable of such aggression, which in any case would have been futile; the commodities he mocked have gone on unstoppably multiplying. Soon after the 1950s, luxuries like Citroëns became necessities. Unilever is still adding to its output of wondrous potions, some of which can now disinfect our insides while others clean our houses: the company's current offerings include Regenerate Enamel Science for whiter teeth and Flora ProActiv margarine, said to be 'on a mission to lower the nation's cholesterol'. As they spread through a global market, consumerist trophies have sponsored their own revolution by levelling social inequalities and political divisions. The products themselves veto a return to the Cold War, when people on the wrong side of the Iron Curtain had to go without Western novelties. At the end of October 2014 the Lugansk separatists in Ukraine resolved to synchronize their watches with Moscow, and announced that their territory would ignore the seasonal change to daylight-saving time. But iPhones throughout the country switched back an hour regardless: the gadgets cast their vote with Western Europe and ultimately with California.

What Barthes called the fabulizing faculty is established as an indispensable marketing tool. A London department store has the motto 'Make life fabulous' printed on the carrier bags into which customers stuff their purchases. A line of sporty female outfits bears the brand name Fabletics, suggesting that an athletic workout is the quick way to attain that state. The television therapist Dr Phil, who soothes anxieties for an hour every afternoon on CBS before Judge Judy takes over to prescribe penalties, encourages his viewers to participate in an online campaign entitled 'The Reasons I'm Fabulous', while an American 'life rescripting' psychologist at Makeyourlifefabulous.com offers her clients – weary wives and harassed mothers who want to release their 'inner intellectual-hipster-sex-kitten' – the chance to 'get excited about you' by refilling what she calls 'your own gas tank'. As consumers, we live in the hope of imminent transfiguration, and we rely on myth, as Icarus did on his waxen wings, to lift us aloft.

*

Barthes introduced the final section of *Mythologies* by asking, 'What is a myth, today?' Having put himself on the defensive, he gave a simple and perhaps reductive answer. '*Myth*,' he declared, '*is a type of speech*', and he went on to explain that it is 'a system of communication … a message', or, in the more portentous case of Billy Graham, 'the *Message*'. The message or missive was the medium; it hardly mattered whether it was an advertisement, a Hollywood film, a sermon or a report on a murder trial. Again Barthes' purpose was to dispense with mystery and mystagoguery. If myth is merely speech, its pretensions are easily disposed of, because words – according to the semiotic theory that was Barthes' own message to the world – are signs that do not correspond to the things they name, like the promises of politicians or the attributes of a non-existent God.

In another italicized dogma Barthes claimed that '*myth is depoliticized speech*'. Taking pride in the negation, he emphasized the 'active value' of 'the prefix *de-*', which 'permanently embodies a defaulting'. Simplified, this means that the political import of a story or an image is concealed: myth pretends to innocent neutrality, as in a *Paris Match* portrait of a black soldier in French uniform saluting the tricolour – an image that, as Barthes pointed out, served to justify the colonization of Algeria.

Today it might be more accurate to say that politics is remythologized speech. The canniest politicians now have image consultants on their staff, and are as much concerned with publicity as with policy, so their conduct on the campaign trail or in office is a mythopoeic exercise. More than a type of speech, myth for them is a form of storytelling – an anthology of tales that are endlessly recycled, a dressing-up kit stocked with adaptable personae. Ronald Reagan, more avuncular than Uncle Sam, regaled Americans with folksy reminiscences that often touched on his military service during World War II, when in fact he never left Hollywood: he was describing the war movies he had made, not actual battles. Margaret Thatcher likewise played at being the warrior queen Boadicea, and referred to herself as the adamantine 'Iron Lady of the Western World', a metallic monster like the false Maria in Fritz Lang's *Metropolis*. After her removal from office, she assumed an even more ominous identity. During an address at an election rally in Plymouth in 2001, she remarked that while being driven to the hall she had passed a cinema billboard that might have been proclaiming her arrival: the film it advertised was *The Mummy Returns*. Did she mean to portray herself as a comforting granny or a menacing ghoul?

Although Barack Obama once derided Reagan's garrulous way of making 'policy by anecdote', the techniques he employed for self-projection and self-imposition in his early career were much the same. Authority for him was a matter of authorship. Obama attempted, as he says in his autobiography, to 'bind my world together' by collecting and collating information about his absent Kenyan father and the unknown Africa he came from, and when he moved to Chicago as a young community organizer, he immersed himself in the city by appropriating stories from the novels he had read about the place, 'borrowing other people's memories'. In the slums, his task was 'building up a culture', which meant 'building up stories', and by this act of validation he encouraged the teenage mothers and impoverished elders he met to see 'how people in the neighbourhood can be heroes'. Obama hoped that the outcome of his efforts might be a 'collective redemption' for his disadvantaged fellow citizens. That phrase is not as devout as it sounds. The sociologist Émile Durkheim described religion as a kind of 'mystic mechanics', which energizes bodies and gives people the sense of being infused by a supernatural force – enrolling them in a movement, as Obama did when he rallied the tenants of Altgeld Gardens, an unpastoral housing estate adjacent to a poisoned river and a sewage treatment plant, and led them downtown to confront the city's housing bureaucrats. His rhetoric may have been messianic, but the intellectual self-awareness with which he used it makes him an agnostic Messiah.

In an early speech, Obama said that people 'want a narrative arc to their lives' – a curve that, like the span of a rainbow, can be relied on to return home to earth, perhaps with a pot of gold to mark the spot. This concern with narratology replaces truth with the artful management of an essentially fictional game plan. When the television talk-show host Charlie Rose probed him about the disappointments of his first term as president, Obama admitted that he might have literally lost the plot. Referring to himself in the third person, he conceded that voters were asking, 'Where's the story that tells us where he's going?' He understood, he said, that 'the nature of this office is to tell a story to the American people that gives them a sense of unity and purpose and optimism, especially during tough times'. That could be the credo of a Hollywood scriptwriter, contractually obliged to engineer a happy ending.

To complicate the problem, there is no longer just one story. The media that relay such tales are fractional, fractured, and there has to be a different version for every outlet. Obama understood that the mythical hero must have a thousand faces – or at least a dozen of them, adapted to whichever group he is currently addressing. Whenever he bounced down the stairs at the front door of Air Force One, he was a symbol of

American confidence and energy; when he made the return journey up those stairs and waved on the top step before the door closed, he retreated into an impregnable American fortress. But Obama could also discard pomp and present himself as a dogged political scrapper, as he did in 2012 when he allowed a Virginia rainstorm to soak him to the skin as he delivered a speech – although right-wing commentators on Fox News bemoaned the indignity of the scene and said that the president looked like a union agitator hectoring a mob. A few days later, his role was that of a sitcom husband. At a basketball game between the United States and Brazil, he smooched with his wife and coaxed her to kiss him, aware that a camera was projecting their embrace onto a giant screen. At the end of the same week, after the mass murder at the screening of Christopher Nolan's *The Dark Knight Rises* in Colorado, he switched to being the sober, grizzled father of the nation and reminded Americans that life is short. In 2015 another calamity, the shooting at a Charleston church, turned him into a shock jock: in a radio interview, after a subtly histrionic hesitation, he uttered the infamous 'N word', and in doing so compelled his listeners to acknowledge the racism that did not disappear when its vocabulary of taunts and insults was banned.

Obama negotiated these register shifts with such finesse because he was the first president to have a nodding acquaintance – acquired in the courses he took as a graduate student at Columbia University – with structuralism and cultural theory. His mother was an anthropologist, aware that ancestral folkways are patterns of learned behaviour, intricately structured conventions not nature's ineradicable decree. In *Dreams from My Father* he describes how as a teenager he learned to 'slip back and forth between my black and white worlds, understanding that each possessed its own language and customs and structures of meaning'. Everything, this implies, is reducible to language – but language is air and artifice, while the slippery self, so adept at changing colour, is a fictional character.

Myth, Barthes said, relies on a 'metalanguage' to cover a sneaky transition 'from history to nature'. This was exactly the change Hillary Clinton made in the eight years between her two filmed declarations that she was running for the presidency.

In 2007, when she announced that she was forming an 'exploratory committee' to prepare for her candidacy, she sat ensconced, even enthroned, in history. She delivered her speech from a couch in her living room, between a table with a lamp whose base was a pile of unreadable but presumably sober and weighty tomes made of metal and another table displaying the family photographs that silently demonstrated her connections and her sense of entitlement; her hands were clasped with a composure modelled on the deportment of the Queen during her Christmas broadcasts – though she did later gesticulate with those supposedly unmanipulative hands, reaching out to America or holding it protectively between her palms, and when she aimed a blow at George W. Bush's administration she settled back into the relaxed manner of a confidential truth-teller, elbow raised on the back of the couch, once even clenching her fist to signal the pugilism of a political careerist.

For the 2015 announcement, she stood in nature, or at least beside a trimmed hedge of evergreen plants outside her white-painted house. This time there was no history: no warming and luminous table lamp, no learned volumes, no snapshots of the other members of the once and future First Family, no precedents and no pedigree. A garden, however, is also a mythological setting, and an out-of-focus pergola over her shoulder admitted the presence of culture, control and grooming. Because the house obviously belonged to a privileged and extremely wealthy woman, before she appeared outside it Hillary – seen at first from behind, not out of modesty but because she is recognizable even if her face is not seen – was glimpsed standing at the deli counter in a supermarket or drinking coffee from a plastic cup in a diner. Instead of talking about herself, as she did in 2007, she now relied on a choral overture contributed by a folksy smattering of everyday Americans – ethnically diverse, young and old, gay and straight, feline, canine and human. This supporting cast included a tomato-planting woman with green fingers and muddy hands: her dabbling in the soil was intended to make Hillary, whose garden is surely tended by unseen menials, look a little more earthy. For two minutes these good-humoured, effusive characters talked about their own dreams, which by implication they would be relying on the next president to help them realize. By the time the camera caught up with the candidate herself in the last thirty seconds, she had grown into a compound being, the 'champion', as she put it, of her hopeful compatriots. But words remain tricky, and the deftly chosen word bifurcated: a champion meaning one who supports a cause, or a champ with a doggedly self-willed determination to win?

The little commercial ended as Hillary – travel-ready, unlike the poised hostess of 2007 – restated the eternal American creed of perpetual motion and upward mobility. 'I'm hitting the road,' she said, sounding more energetic than the woman who in her previous announcement expected others to do the exploring, 'and I hope you'll join me on this journey.' Immediately she morphed into a sign, a logo, a propulsive symbol – an arrow that sped directly towards success as it shot into place to form the crossbar of the initial H in 'Hillary for America', her campaign slogan. But despite invoking road trips, personal quests, and a communal journey in some updated, all-accommodating wagon train, she delivered her message while standing still. She was speaking a metalanguage, and her metaphors did the walking.

*

The 'unveiling' Barthes carried out in his essays was, he claimed, 'a political act', but in this combat he felt relegated to the sidelines. He regretted that the mythographer had to make do with a 'theoretical sociality', and could 'live revolutionary action only vicariously'.

Today that action would be virtual not vicarious. The revolution has been indefinitely postponed while we await the launch of the next iPhone or the latest happy addition to what Microsoft calls 'the Windows NT family of operating systems'; meanwhile everyone with Facebook friends and Twitter followers enjoys a social life that is theoretical or notional. The mythical mask or alias is available to all, and in chatrooms or on dating sites our technoselves lead alternate lives. Glyphs and icons assure us that we are invisibly connected to everyone and everywhere: the props we grip are our wands or divining rods, and a triangular wedge of curved stripes mimics the bands of radiant energy that bounce our words or voices around the curvature of the earth. We assume that we are communicating or even communing, though maybe we are simply enjoying our ownership of those crafty devices and spending money as we do so. David Fincher's film *The Social Network* sums up our long trek from nature to culture and our rapid advance into cyberculture when Sean Parker – the entrepreneur who founded Napster, here played by Justin Timberlake – predicts that Facebook will bring about 'the digitalization of real life'. 'We lived on farms and then we lived in cities,' he says, 'and now we're going to live on the Internet.'

If so, is the world we are supposed to share with each other turning into a simulacrum? That was the far-sighted suggestion of Philip K. Dick's *Do Androids Dream of Electric Sheep?*, published in 1968. Adapting the novel in *Blade Runner*, Ridley Scott eliminated a subplot about the cult of Mercerism, which gives Dick's latter-day human beings an education in fellow-feeling. In their homes, citizens grasp a device called an empathy box, which connects them to a video representation of a Man of Sorrows who toils forever uphill in a stony desert, assailed by the jeers of invisible disbelievers. This Sisyphean trek or stumbling progress towards Calvary appeals to an altruism that remains notional, purposeless. No action or intervention is required, since the aim is to make the empathizers feel better about themselves. But subversive androids reveal that the landscape is painted, with brushstrokes visible on the backdrop; the pebbles hurled at the oppressed hero are probably soft, harmless plastic. Mercer, a wizard of Oz, admits the imposture and says that his real name is Al Jarry. His homonym was the inventor of Ubu Roi, the foul, savage oaf in the surrealist play who imagines himself to be a hero. Deckard the detective is affronted – 'Mercer isn't a fake. Unless reality is a fake,' he says to himself – but his afterthought leaves the matter dangling.

Myth here is a spell, an enchantment, designing a neural facsimile of our environment: rather than a fire, a video screen flickers in the depths of Plato's cave, in which – as described by one of the oldest and most pertinently modern myths – we are currently living, our backs turned to the sunlight outside. A series of films, symptoms of the malady they diagnose, shows how this illusory society came into being.

In David Cronenberg's *Videodrome*, a McLuhanesque guru called Professor O'Blivion foresees a future in which television will replace daily life, and projects himself into it by recording videos that enable him to be beamed back into the world after his death. In Josef Rusnak's *The Thirteenth Floor* an expert in virtual reality plugs his brain into a computer and dreams up a simulation of Los Angeles in 1937, populated by Angelenos who don't know that they are chimeras. 'What did you do to the world?' asks someone who still believes in the old-fashioned notion of reality. 'Turned it off,' says the wizard. Christopher Nolan's *Inception* is about espionage conducted inside the heads of sleepers, whose business secrets are extracted from them as they dream. To demonstrate how the subliminal thefts occur, a street in Paris uproots itself, distends, pitches forward, and then – after a hail of flustered pixels subsides – folds round the characters before being neatly compressed into a cube, a capsule that is a container for images. In *Interstellar*, Nolan recreates the world inside a habitat cylinder, one of the rotating spheres designed by the physicist Gerard K. O'Neill to house off-earth colonies: cinematic murals on its curved walls allow the colonists to believe that they have not left placid small-town America.

In *The Matrix*, devised and directed by Larry and Andy Wachowski, nature is a dessicated waste, ruled by predatory machines that like H. G. Wells' Martians imbibe sustenance from human beings. The people being cannibalized do not complain. Wired to a mainframe of tawdry fantasy, they are pacified by scenarios of sex and shopping, less emotionally demanding than the empathy Mercerism elicits. God the Father – known here as Morpheus, leader of the Oneiroi, who were the Greek spirits that populated dreams – begets a Messiah called Neo whose purpose is to smash this cybernetic womb, a uterine version of Plato's cave. 'We're inside a computer programme?' asks Neo incredulously when his task is explained to him.

That may be better than life inside a television studio, which is the fate of the hero in Peter Weir's *The Truman Show*. Truman potters through his life in a cheery, sunny suburb, unaware that he is performing in a reality show directed by a 'conceiver and creator' called Christof who, with the aid of five thousand cameras, oversees events from inside a moon that is actually his control room. Truman's domed Eden – an actual seaside resort in Florida, which demonstrates how nearly the fantasy approximates to life – is a consumerist idyll, and his wife's chirpy small talk recites commercials for the products she advertises to the unseen television audience. Alienation effects alert Truman to the truth: an arc lamp crashes down from a gantry in the clear blue sky like a burned-out asteroid, and the predictable succession of passers-by outside his house makes him suspect that he is watching looped footage. He decides to escape from this insular panopticon, and sets sail for what he takes to be the mainland. He does not get far: the prow of his vessel merely jabs a hole in the painted cyclorama that encloses him. A myth, or a map of our current condition? Kanye West considers the scenario to be a description of his own existential predicament, and he recently announced, 'I've reached a point in my life where my *Truman Show* boat has hit the painting.' That, surely, is as far as Kanye wants to go, because if he escaped through the wall he would no longer be on camera.

'Anything is possible,' says Hayden Christensen as Anakin Skywalker in one of the later *Star Wars* films. He is wooing Natalie Portman, cast as a gravely liberal senator from the planet of Naboo, but his plea makes better sense as a manifesto in praise of digitization. Padmé, preoccupied by her need to vote against a military build-up, is unpersuaded. 'We live in a real world,' she replies, 'come back to it.' Her objection is not heeded, and why should it be? She too is composed of pixels not molecules and corpuscles, and she exists in an alternative universe that has been conjured up on a green screen.

The illusion we collectively inhabit is so accommodating and so resilient that it can instantly assimilate death and disaster. Terrorists mimic cinematic scenarios, and the victims or those who come to their aid cast themselves as unwitting extras in the apocalyptic spectacle. Before 9/11 the Taliban in Afghanistan studied pirated videotapes of *Godzilla* and set themselves to outdo the lizard's demolition of the Brooklyn Bridge. In March 2015 a witness at the trial of Dzhokhar Tsarnaev, who with his brother set off bombs at the Boston Marathon, described the carnage on the street – mutilated or eviscerated bodies that were smoking or on fire, people staring in disbelief at their disjected feet or hands, puddles of blood – by likening it to a scene from Spielberg's *Saving Private Ryan* or Oliver Stone's *Platoon*. Screens are everywhere; the cave may be inescapable.

Lévi-Strauss warned that myth was 'the most fundamental form of inauthenticity'. He meant that it overrules our concrete knowledge, which is replaced – as in advertisements that show the faithful enjoying a well-nigh heavenly happiness if they buy the correct product – by an abstract exercise in what he called 'symbolic logic'. We know better than to trust such delusions, but still we long to be duped.

Dan Brown's epidemically popular novels batten on this susceptibility: they destroy a myth that for centuries claimed a monopoly of truth, then fabricate another which is just as insidious. The Catholic Church, as Brown points out in *The Da Vinci Code*, owes its power to a specious conflation of myths, which are picked apart by his hero Robert Langdon, a Harvard professor whose non-existent academic discipline is called not semiotics but 'symbology'. The novel unseats the militaristic God of Hosts and instead promotes a milder goddess, 'the lost sacred feminine' with her enticing Mona Lisa smile; the Vatican, aware that Brown was employing the same techniques as its own theologians, appointed a doctrinal enforcer to combat his insinuations about Christ's dalliance with Mary Magdalene. None too soon, perhaps: in *Angels & Demons* Brown had already had the Illuminati murder the Pope and threaten to destroy St Peter's Basilica during the conclave to elect his successor. The weapon deployed by the enlightened terrorists is a canister of anti-matter stolen from the accelerator at CERN in Switzerland. Although the energetic Langdon intervenes, the so-called 'God particle' is primed to blow up God's palatial earthly dwelling place.

Having demythologized Catholicism, Brown turned aside to deal with the rabid religiosity that has overtaken the United States. In *The Lost Symbol* he alleges that Washington DC is run by a coven of Freemasons who practise rites so secret that Brown likens them to 'the recipe for classic Coke': what could be more darkly arcane than that formula, kept under close guard in an Atlanta vault? More recently, Brown's *Inferno* deals with bioterrorism, menacing the over-fertile human race with a return of the Black Death. His outrageously convoluted plots defy belief, but events have a way of catching up with them. His first novel, *Digital Fortress*, published in 1998, was about a code-breaker who invaded the National Security Agency's computer – a protest against the government's god-like capacity to snoop electronically, penetrating our dreams and eavesdropping on our fantasies. The prospect remained remote until 2013, when Edward Snowden followed the lead of Brown's seditious hacker.

Brown rationalizes the appeal of his books in one of Langdon's reflections, considered to be of such significance that it is electrified by italics. '*Everyone*,' says the Professor of Symbology, '*loves a conspiracy*.' Whether or not we love them, conspiracy theories do simplify history and concentrate blame; they rule out randomness and invest events with a purpose, even if it is malevolent. Hence the teleological retelling of episodes like President Kennedy's assassination, or the traffic accident that killed Princess Diana – and *The Da Vinci Code* purports to identify Diana's executioners and explain their motives. A fantastical rumour expounded on the Internet traces her ancestry to the Merovingian dynasty, the French royal line that supposedly descended from the offspring of Christ and the Magdalene; the Pont de l'Alma tunnel, where the fatal crash occurred, is on the site of the earliest Merovingian tombs. Was Diana sent to join her remote predecessors because she had revived the gynocratic cult suppressed by the Church? During an interpolated lecture on Masonic symbolism and the keystone arch, Langdon says, 'it was all interconnected'. Conspiracy is the equivalent on earth to the Unified Theory that scientists like Hawking have projected into the sky.

Langdon views 'the world as a web of profoundly intertwined histories and events'. In effect he equates the world with the World Wide Web, where happenings are linked adventitiously, whether or not they are intertwined or causally related. But the adverb he uses is bogus. Algorithms spot superficial analogies, and don't bother with profundity: all nets are full of holes. Could the web Langdon refers to be a sticky trap, woven by some mischievous cosmic spider? In *Avatar*, James Cameron replaces this adhesive, enmeshing myth with something sturdier and more sheltering – a Hometree. This is what the blue-skinned forest people call their equivalent of Yggdrasil, the world ash in Teutonic folklore; its long-limbed, fingery branches and prehensile roots make up a network with 'more connections than the human brain' and, as the botanist played by Sigourney Weaver guesses, 'some kind of electrochemical communication' courses through the wood like sap and mimics the firing of synapses in our heads. Worshipped by the Na'vi, the Hometree is an arboreal Internet: after all, long-distance phone conversations were once known as trunk calls, and Langdon's collaborator Sophie explains Leonardo's cryptex, which helps to decipher the Mona Lisa's mystery, as the painter's way of sending messages securely 'in an era without telephones or email'. Readers of Brown's book, however, end as flies transfixed in the spider's larder. The cryptex is said to be stored in the Depository Bank of Zurich – a fictitious institution, though Brown invented an online site for it and supplied it with a motto, 'Votre confiance est notre plus grand trésor', which jokes about our readiness to fall for such confidence trickery and to top up Brown's personal treasury. This version of the Internet is a vast, voluminous cloud of unknowing, or a fog of half-truths.

Dan Burstein, the editor of a book of essays on the *Da Vinci Code* phenomenon, suggests that the novel is about the other 'Holy Grail quests' that engross us: the endeavour 'to unlock the secrets of the human genome, to go to Mars, understand the Big Bang' – the frontier of speculation explored by Hawking and his colleagues, and cheekily invoked by Nando's with its High Five Card. Brown's denouement, however, does not unriddle the cosmos or even win us a year's worth of free meals: Langdon cautions Sophie that every faith is a fabrication, and says that problems only arise 'when we begin to believe literally in our own metaphors'. But despite his own warning, he goes on to track a mystical meridian through the streets of Paris, and is led to the inverse pyramid that aims its glassy apex at the floor in the Carrousel du Louvre, a commercial mall beneath the museum. Here, we gather, the Grail is interred. The destination is not a surprise. Throughout his narrative, Brown conscientiously notices that his characters carry iPhones and

Blackberries, or that they wear suits of Harris Tweed and flashier clothes designed by Brioni. They conduct their high-speed chases while travelling in a 'white Volvo' or perhaps 'a Falcon 2000EX corporate jet' with 'dual Pratt & Whitney engines', and when relaxing they drink Bombay Sapphire gin and Gaja Nebbiolo wines. Since gemstones cannot be distilled and gin is not blue, the sapphire is presumably mythical, and the vineyard owner Angelo Gaja explains the name of his Nebbiolo brand – 'nebbia' means mist in Italian – by likening the wine to Marcello Mastroianni, often cast as a silent brooder who lurks in a corner guarding his mystery. As if imbibing Christ's blood at communion, we are, thanks to Brown's commercial endorsements, sipping symbols. It is therefore apt that a mystical quest should dwindle into a shopping expedition; the modern-day Grail belongs in a mercantile cathedral that has side chapels for Lacoste, L'Occitane, Brin de Fantasie, and the glazed, gleaming Apple Store.

'The greatest story ever told is the greatest story ever sold,' snarls Sir Leigh Teabing, Brown's villain. Although he is deriding the chastened version of Christ's life upheld by the Catholic hierarchy, he might be describing *The Da Vinci Code* itself. There is no need to excavate the Parisian mall to dig up the Grail because Brown's book is the Grail – not a vessel filled with holy blood or Eucharistic wine but a paper bag containing an elixir that purports to resolve our spiritual malaise and to clarify the meaning of the universe.

*

The rationalizing march of mind that began in the Enlightenment got only so far, and some time ago it halted. 'What,' Jung asked his followers in 1963, 'is the myth by which you live?' No one, he assumed, could live without this psychic prop. In 1970 McLuhan suggested that our age was 'probably the most religious that has ever existed'. Or, since he added that he used the word religious 'in the vulgar sense', the most religiose: the vogue for extrasensory perception and the occult struck McLuhan as a response to the all-enveloping 'electric consciousness of the time'. Barthes, who reduced myth to rhetoric or verbiage and mocked the commercial trickery of mystification, would have been appalled. But so long as you equate religion with myth and accept that electronic gadgetry is somehow supernatural, the intervening decades have confirmed McLuhan's claim.

Steve Jobs, a latter-day evangelist as well as the chief executive officer of the world's most valuable company, brought about an awakening more permanent and widespread than Billy Graham's soul-saving campaign. The appliances engineered by Jobs were not merely tools or toys. They conferred on their users powers that seemed more than human, and this entitled Jobs to play the role of an emissary from elsewhere, a galactic travelling salesman who had alighted in our muddled, meaty world. He staged Apple's product launches as space invasions, showing off inventions that looked, as he said about the 1988 Macintosh computer, like imports 'from another planet. A good planet. A planet with better designers.' Gaining confidence, he cast himself as an electronic saviour: he attended Apple's first Halloween party dressed as Christ, so it was logical enough for the iPhone to be nicknamed 'the Jesus phone'. Jobs managed to combine his New Testament role with the powers of an Old Testament prophet; in both capacities he seemed to have an open line to the demiurge. When he turned up at an Apple store as the first iPhones went on sale he was greeted, according to his biographer Walter Isaacson, as Moses might have been 'if he had walked in to buy the Bible'. The arrival of the iPad prompted a journalist to remark that 'The last time there was this much excitement about a tablet, it had some commandments written on it.' In the days after Jobs died in October 2011, the windows of Apple stores in cities around the world were plastered with Post-it notes on which customers scribbled tributes and rawly personal expressions of grief. The faithful commiserated with each other as they studied the display, gripping iPhones that glowed like unsnuffable candles.

George Lucas, who wrote and directed *Star Wars*, has justified the grab-bag of Christian, Greek, Teutonic and Asiatic myths in his films by arguing that 'All the religions are true.' In any case, as he added during an interview with Bill Moyers in 1999, 'religion is just a container for faith'. Although this sounds like a back-to-front version of Barthes' claim that a myth's form matters more than its content, it amounts to the same thing. If all religions are true, then none of them are; faith that is an end in itself – a feeling rather than belief in a doctrine – is mere credulity. Defined like this, religions hardly need gods as sponsors. Hence the cult of Jediism, a spin-off from *Star Wars*. In Lucas's film, the Jedi are latter-day monks, shadily hooded and equipped with lightsabres rather than the more traditional staff; they believe in a 'Force' that, according to the American Temple of the Jedi Order, empowers those who are infused by it 'to better themselves and overcome any obstacle' – an aim with which all right-thinking citizens of the United States are honour-bound to agree. The sage Obi-Wan Kenobi promises no such boost to believers when he initiates Lucas's namesake Luke. More concerned with astrophysics than with careerism, Obi-Wan defines the Force as 'an energy field created by all living things' and specifies that 'it binds the galaxy together'. His phrase anticipates Dan Brown's collusive web; it also sums up the connective work of myth.

On the 2001 census almost four hundred thousand residents of the United Kingdom declared themselves to be Jedi when asked about their religious affiliations. No doubt most gave this answer because they considered religion to be myth and myth to be fiction or falsehood, but even without such atheistic jokers the Church of Jediism claims two hundred thousand members around the world. In 2009, Daniel Jones, who founded the Church, was asked to leave a branch of Tesco in Wales because his headgear looked sinister to other shoppers. In retaliation he accused the supermarket of religious bigotry, only to be outwitted when a Tesco spokesman explained that he had been asked to lower his hood so that he could better see the items on special offer. The company has since made its peace with the metaphorical religion: it now sells children's hooded Jedi robes made of polyester, 'ideal for parties & pretend play', which can be accessorized with lightsabres that are actually stubby battery-operated torches.

Isis, or the Islamic State of Iraq and the Levant – with its garbled history, its incoherent warping of theology, its fantastical goal of a revived caliphate, and its balefully black flags and battle dress – is a similarly fictitious or mythopoeic enterprise: the terrain of the would-be state is notional, just as the churches and temples in which American and British Jedis worship are unbuilt, existing only in cyberspace. While catering to the fervour of radicals, Isis also attracts Western malcontents for whom a holy war is another kind of 'pretend play'. Of course when Isis fighters execute their captives on video, they revert from pretence to reality, although they may no longer recognize the difference, given the time that young recruits have probably spent killing digital opponents in video games. Other would-be terrorists ignore the gore and think of jihad aspirationally. In 2015, Tairod Nathan Webster Pugh was arrested in New Jersey while attempting to join the army of Isis in Syria. Pugh, a veteran of the US Air Force and a former American Airlines maintenance mechanic, had gained his wife's consent to this plan by assuring her that 'if I am made a martyr, we will have a mansion of indescribable beauty on a magnificent plot of land'. Death, in his view, was the fast track to a heaven of posthumous luxury.

A degraded mythology attracts such credulous neophytes, along with the false prophets who minister to them. After being given asylum in Australia, the Iranian refugee Man Haron Monis awarded himself the titles of sheik and ayatollah in order to set up a 'spiritual consultation business' in the deprived western suburbs of Sydney, where he practised black magic and deployed astrological and numerological abracadabra to predict the future for paying customers, more than forty of whom charged that his healing therapy involved sexual assault. Then one morning in December 2014, Monis entered the Lindt Chocolate Café in the centre of the city, tied on a headband that announced his willingness to surrender his life for Mohammad, produced a gun, and held all those on the premises hostage until he was shot dead by the police early the following day. Was the café an appropriate place for a showdown between civilizations and religions? Hardly, even though Lindt's official history calls cocoa 'the food of the Gods', remembers that it was offered sacrificially on Aztec altars, and declares that Rodolphe Lindt's accidental discovery of chocolate fondant in 1897 transported him to 'seventh heaven'. Monis may have chosen the café at random, but the symbolism of the siege mattered to him, and he made his captives hold up against the window a Shahada banner proclaiming that Allah is the only god and Mohammad his prophet. As it turned out, the flag he brought with him had no political affiliations. When he realized his error, he demanded one that propounded the mission of Isis. The police found it for him – a worrying detail, given the short notice – but never passed it on.

After Monis's death, the authorities decided that he was not a terrorist, classifying him as a zealot whose personal grievances were aggravated by psychological problems. It was a nice distinction. Here, as in other similar cases, mythomania turned truly maniacal. Monis was engaged in what might be called mythomachia – a battle incited by myth, fought with real weapons not laser-lighted wands. Walter Benjamin called fascism 'politics aestheticized', power made manifest by spectacle and scenography. Isis – whose strategists argue that Islam has for centuries been forcibly 'submitted to Caesar', and as a remedy call for a fire-breathing march on 'Rome', meaning any Western citadel – is politics mythologized. In 1996 Osama bin Laden railed against what he called 'the myth of the super-power', meaning puffed-up America. But the subversive power of Al-Qaeda was equally mythological, and like so many myths it rested on the infirm ground of etymology: although 'qaeda' means 'base', the exiled, elusive Osama was based nowhere and everywhere, and exercised power linguistically by circulating tapes on which he exhorted his followers to 'Go forth!'

In January 2015, Chérif and Saïd Kouachi, who claimed to be vindicating the one true god and his defamed prophet when they invaded the offices of *Charlie Hebdo*, came forth from their hiding place in a factory on the outskirts of Paris, fired at the police and were gunned down. Did they experience a sudden gust of transcendence as they attained martyrdom? Perhaps they had chemical help: the jihadists in the Paris attacks of November 2015 had apparently taken the amphetamine Captagon, which induces a dangerously fearless rush and must be especially heady if you are carrying a Kalashnikov. Or were the Kouachis copying the reckless flair of cornered cinematic bandits like Butch Cassidy and the Sundance Kid? Theology and fantasy probably colluded in their blazing heads. In extremity, individuals slip back into a story that eternally returns from the remote past to the here and now.

Mythical events do not happen once only; like natural disasters they go on recurring, whether we want them to or not. Monis, the Tsarnaevs, the Kouachis, or their ally Amedy Coulibaly who took hostages in the Jewish supermarket – all of them were participating in the same rite. So were Michael Adebolajo and Michael Adebowale, who in 2013 killed a British soldier, Lee Rigby, in the street near his London barracks and then tried to hack his head off with a cleaver; and so too was Zack Davies, who achieved the dialectical feat of being simultaneously a neo-Nazi and an admirer of Isis, and as a madly illogical revenge on Adebolajo and Adebowale battered a dentist with a hammer in a branch of Tesco and then tried to behead him with a machete. For them all, conversion and purification came first, probably accompanied by paramilitary training (which in Davies' case involved posturing on camera in front of the Third Reich memorabilia in his bedroom). Finally the time arrived for a self-glorifying act of faith, the public execution of infidels. In 2015 in Charleston, South Carolina, Dylann Roof inventively varied the preordained plot by staging its climax on consecrated ground. He invited himself to a Bible study class at the Emanuel African Methodist Episcopal Church, listened quietly for a while, then pulled out his handgun and killed the pastor and eight members of his congregation. 'Someone,' Roof had previously written in a mission statement about racial war, 'had to have the bravery to take it to the real world.' But for him, the real world was a murky theatre of paranoid delusion – Plato's cave with a private arsenal stowed in its depths.

'A myth,' as Karen Armstrong has said, 'demands action.' Although recent events prove her point, they distort what myth originally meant: A. S. Byatt points out that in Greek it refers to something said, not something done. Battle lines have now been drawn between the two definitions. After the *Charlie Hebdo* attacks, a pro-Palestinian group of hackers or cyber-jihadists began a campaign of Internet sabotage in France, taking down websites of which it disapproved or replacing their pages with images of a gloating skull and messages defaming those killed at what it called *Charlie Pedo*. 'Your freedom of speech,' the attackers from AnonGhost warned, 'meant that it was only a matter of time before someone else displayed their freedom of action against you.' Speech, unless it solemnly quotes scripture, is from this point of view merely a futile expenditure of breath; action overrules it, because death ends all verbose arguments.

Barthes respected the Greek etymology and treated myth as a more or less frivolous linguistic game. He therefore sought to cast out devils with ridicule rather than sacred incantations. He knew he had not succeeded, because society in the mid-1950s was still 'terrorized', as he put it, by the kind of magical thinking he found in the advertisements that browbeat customers into making purchases. The verb he chose, a favourite of his, now sounds a little high-pitched: we have learned to use it more cautiously. Later in his life, as Barthes looked back and forth between the allure of fiction and the terrifying prospect of extinction, his tone became less flippant. 'As long as there is death,' he said in an interview in 1970, 'there will be myth.'

Yes, as long as we have war, slaughter and ideological fulmination, these stories will go on being told. The myths that confront us today are lethal, malign and – since irony is no match for fanaticism – immune to sophisticated joking. We are now bedevilled all over again by taboos and curses, by genocidal purges and enraptured visions of a universal end, as myth challenges reason for control of our newly mystified and maddened world.

*

And then, as if it were not bad enough to have ideologues glorifying Allah as they blow themselves up in airports and dance halls or steer cargo trucks into crowds of revellers and holiday shoppers, our age of unreason performed its own suicidal rite when it installed a mythomaniac in the house whose whiteness once vouched for the dream of a bleached, purged world, from which the stains of history had been wiped away.

Trump, accustomed to a gilded penthouse with a jaggedly diamond-studded front door, looked sulky on his first visit to the White House in November 2016. Did he find the decor of the Oval Office drably unpalatial? Perhaps he was dismayed to discover that he had tumbled from his opulent eyrie into a reality that consists of exhausting effort and frustrated compromise rather than boasts, threats, and the boosterism of an ego that has expanded to fill up all the space available.

Atop his tower on Fifth Avenue, Trump inhabits Olympus. On one of his ceilings, Apollo's chariot is drawn across the sky by Aurora: an allegory representing the owner's claim to celestial dominion. It is the task of the lucid god to enlighten the world during his daily transit across the sky, though in Trump's living room Apollo has the help of several crystal chandeliers. On a side table stands a coy bronze statue of Cupid amorously clasping Psyche and sealing her lips: possibly a hint that the god's wives and girlfriends, along with assorted contestants in beauty pageants, could be privy to the secrets of his supernatural realm. But our culture has outgrown puritanical guilt and replaced shame with confessional blabbing; in such a world it is hard to imagine what further revelations there could be about life in an amoral heaven where, as Trump bragged to a cousin of Presidents George H. W. and George W. Bush during a discussion of his licentious forays, fame means that 'you can do anything'.

Having studied that Apollonian ceiling, Trump planned his presidential campaign as the enactment of a myth. To announce his candidacy, he descended triumphally to earth, gliding down into the lobby of his tower on a golden escalator. He then travelled around the country on a Trump-branded 757, and when he deplaned was frequently greeted with a blaring excerpt from Jerry Goldsmith's rousingly brassy score for *Air Force One*, the film in which Harrison Ford's bouts of fisticuffs with hijackers made him, in Trump's view, an ideal commander-in-chief. Trump hardly needed to bother with the dreary business of running for office or explaining what he would do when elected: his personal jet – with its ultrasuede ceiling panels, silk-clad walls, mahogany cabinets, headrests embroidered with his spurious family crest and seat belts plated in 24-carat gold – was already more luxurious than the actual presidential aircraft, and his unlicensed borrowing of Goldsmith's fanfares implied that he had made America great again simply by personifying it.

G. K. Chesterton argued a century ago that the American presidency was incompatible with the republic designed at the Constitutional Convention in 1787; the office, Chesterton claimed, was in fact 'the last medieval monarchy', and indeed Trump's most fervent admirers invoked a divine right akin to that which placed medieval kings on their thrones. As votes were counted on the evening of 8 November, the evangelizing cheerleader Michele Bachmann rallied Trump's Texan supporters in a televised 'corporate prayer', which in her view immediately caused Clinton's results to falter. Trump's win, she later declared, exhibited 'the strong right arm of a merciful God'.

It is doubtful that Trump shares Bachmann's respect for the deity with a big and probably tattooed bicep. 'I love God,' he asserted at a Family Leadership Summit in Iowa in 2015, though the statement might have been a reflex of his notorious narcissism. God in Genesis repeatedly surveys his work and reflects that it is good; Trump must think the same when he peers down at Fifth Avenue from his skyscraper or adjusts his hairdo in the bathroom mirror. The breathlessly devout Omarosa Manigault – fired by Trump in his reality show *The Apprentice* and now rehired as a White House aide – considers her boss a demiurge: as she told a television interviewer, 'He has a way of drawing you into his universe, and he controls that universe'. When Trump elaborated on his religious credentials at the revivalist meeting in Iowa, faint misgivings could be heard in his phrasing. 'I go to church, and I drink my little wine – which is the only wine I ever drink – and I eat my little cracker,' he said. Did he wince at the littleness of the symbolic transactions, which his repetition underlined? Then, asked whether he ever prayed for forgiveness, he admitted that he was not in the habit of abasing himself: 'I don't bring God into that picture.'

At his press conference in early January 2017, Trump promised that he would be 'the greatest job producer God ever created', which implied a certain rivalry between creator and producer. God made men and women, but it is Trump who will find work for them. No, not by devising the kind of gardening chores prescribed in Eden: he will re-open defunct coalmines, reanimate derelict factories, and enlist more scullions for his hotels and caddies for his golf courses. Would that not make him, at the very least, God's most exemplary specimen? Could an only-begotten son claim to be greater? It is useless to expect piety, penitence or any other moral sentiment from Trump. Like the Kardashian nymphets or the sadistic tycoon in *Fifty Shades of Grey*, he is an unabashed pagan.

In 1788, in a lyrical rhapsody about the gods of Greece, Friedrich Schiller described them as figures aglow with 'truth's youthful beauty'. He called them 'the happy ones', disdaining Christian misery and self-denial: on Olympus, shrines were palaces and 'the beautiful alone were holy'. Keats said the same in a poem about Apollo's ascent to power, which – in an unfortunate anticipation of Benjamin's 'politics aestheticized' – decrees that 'first in beauty shall be first in might'.

This smug, scornful aestheticism survives in Trump, who prefers form to content, skin to soul. He once thought he had refuted a biographer's compromising tales about him by calling the man who wrote the book 'unattractive', and he said the same about the women who accused him of sexual harassment. Although for many he fits the profile of the ugly American – the ogre dreamed up in the 1950s to characterize the venality and crassness of the newly imperial United States – Trump's favourite adjective is 'beautiful'. He has applied to it to the brutish wall he proposes constructing along the Mexican border, and to the Twitter account he uses to fire sub-Jovian thunderbolts at opponents. Schiller's gods grace nature with their own divinity. Trump, even more lavishly, beautifies bureaucracy: at the press conference before his inauguration, he predicted that his appointee would transform the Department of Veterans' Affairs into 'a beautiful thing'. On the campaign trail, during an elliptical spat about penis size and ways of gauging it, he modestly insisted 'I have the most beautiful hands', after which he flapped them about to prove his point. LBJ was less bashful when airing 'Jumbo'.

Despite his bankruptcies and the $916 million loss he recorded to earn a tax rebate in 1995, Trump likes to think that he possesses the Midas touch. His name in gold capitals surmounts the entrance to his tower; in the penthouse, furniture, fittings and kitchen equipment are laced, trimmed or rimmed with gold, and the same aureate shade distinguishes his precariously cantilevered hair. The metal inevitably does duty as a metaphor: 'I never miss a golden opportunity,' Trump gloats in an advertisement for a version of his eponymous tower that has sprouted in Mumbai. But he may not have pondered the meaning of the myth. Midas mortified whatever he touched, just as Ian Fleming's Goldfinger suffocated a disloyal girl by coating her with gold paint. Trump similarly devalues everything he brands: people, principles and institutions are left at best with a tincture of glitz or meretricious glitter adhering to them. As for his notional bullion, no one can be sure, given his refusal to release his latest tax return, how much he is actually worth.

The later life of Midas spells out another warning. Disillusioned with wealth, he is said to have started worshipping the rustic pipe-player Pan, whom he even supported in an ill-advised musical contest with Apollo. The insult enraged the god, source of the harmony that tuned the spheres; he called Midas an ass and punished him by extending his ears until they resembled those of a donkey. Midas hid his disgrace under a turban, although, as Bulfinch points out in *The Age of Fable*, 'his hairdresser of course knew the secret'. Trump's own trichological mystery is closely guarded: the stylist who titivated him for *The Apprentice* has suggested that his hair is cut by someone in the family – his wife or a daughter – to conceal the traces of scalp reduction surgery that allegedly underlie his comb-over and the bizarre fringe that covers his forehead like the pelmet of a curtain.

Everything about the man, from his coiffure on down, is fabulous in Bulfinch's sense, which is to say that it is inauthentic, unverifiable. Trump functions by attributing that bad faith to others, as he sketches insidiously elaborate plots that belong in paperback fiction. Have the Chinese perpetrated the hoax of global warming to gain an economic advantage over the United States? Did the 'Arab population' of Jersey City rejoice in the streets when the World Trade Center was toppled? Was Obama a Kenyan Muslim and therefore an illegitimate president? Does Hillary Clinton suffer from some debilitating ailment, soon to be fatal? Was Supreme Court Justice Scalia murdered, and if so, who placed the pillow on his face? Is autism a by-product of the inoculations prescribed by paediatricians, at least those belonging to liberal metropolitan elites? These crazed conspiracy theories flashed through the air electronically on social media and rabidly partisan websites, and were repeated so often that they earned the benefit of the doubt. During the battle for the Republican nomination, Ted Cruz deflected Trump's insinuations about his Cuban father by jokily anthologizing urban legends. 'Yes,' Cruz said, 'my dad killed JFK, he is secretly Elvis, and Jimmy Hoffa is buried in his backyard.' Immune to irony, Trumpists on Twitter and Facebook took that to be a triple confession.

As a font of fake news, Trump is a prolific mythmaker. Corrections or retractions should not be expected. Omarosa Manigault, questioned about the way the competitors in *The Apprentice* played to the cameras when Trump inflamed the conflicts between them, sighed at such old-fashioned simplicity: 'Does it have to be real? I mean, come on.' True, the quaint concept of the real is unlikely to survive the advent of reality TV. We are now in a mental and moral zone known as 'post-truth', where tales as fictitious as those about albino alligators enjoy credence and, even after being disproved, weigh on our decision-making. Ours is a mythopoeic era, and it is technology – the shiny product of science and engineering, supposedly serving rational ends – that disseminates the falsehoods. Cocteau thought that the Greek landscape had been eaten away by myths. If we are not careful, the same thing may happen to our heads.

Index

INDEX

INDEX